ROBERT LOUIS STEVENSON AND

'THE BEACH OF FALESÁ'

BARRY MENIKOFF

Robert Louis Stevenson and 'The Beach of Falesá'

A STUDY IN VICTORIAN PUBLISHING

With the Original Text

STANFORD UNIVERSITY PRESS
Stanford, California 1984

STANFORD UNIVERSITY PRESS, STANFORD, CALIFORNIA
© 1984 by the Board of Trustees of the Leland Stanford Junior University

Printed in the United States of America

ISBN 0-8047-1162-3   LC 82-61072

Published with the assistance of the Andrew W. Mellon Foundation

To my children
Carrie   Alec   Aaron

PREFACE

"He lighted up one whole side of the globe," wrote Henry James shortly after learning of Stevenson's death in Samoa, "and was in himself a whole province of the imagination." This is not a biography—there are enough of those. But it is not possible to write of Stevenson without thinking of biography. Wherever he went—and he traveled far even by modern standards—he left behind legends and myths such as he himself was fond of collecting. He may even have known this, or sensed that in some odd way people could not fail to be touched by the lean, almost wraith-like figure with lank hair, a cigarette perpetually between his long fingers, and eyes that were nearly mesmeric. Yet Stevenson may well have been hurt by the very qualities that kept his name before a reading public for more than a century. Where the popular audience continued to revere or reflect nostalgically upon *A Child's Garden of Verses*, or *Treasure Island*, or even an animated version of *Kidnapped*, the serious critics disregarded Stevenson altogether. In time, the academics could not be depended upon to have read the work themselves. Stevenson, living in the shadow of James and Hardy, has long been consigned to a literary never-never land. It is time that he was read again by adults—not as a bohemian or Victorian rebel, a suffering tubercular writer trying to find health, or a commercial hack who provided fantasies for boys in their early adolescence, but as a man who by talent and training was probably the best prepared of his generation to exploit the art of fiction and explore the meaning of his times.

Permission to publish the manuscript of *The Beach of Falesá*, as well as Stevenson's correspondence cited within the text, has been kindly granted by Alan Osbourne, executor of the Stevenson estate. I also wish to thank individual libraries for permission to reproduce primary materials from their collections: the Huntington Library, San Marino, California; the Beinecke Rare Book and Manuscript Library, Yale University; the Houghton Library, Harvard University; and the Princeton University Library and Charles Scribner's Sons, for correspondence in the Scribner's Archive. For support during the writing of this book I thank the American Philosophical Society, the Newberry Library, and the Huntington Library.

Barry Menikoff
Honolulu, 1984

CONTENTS

Part One
A STUDY IN VICTORIAN PUBLISHING

Part Two
THE BEACH OF FALESÁ

Ten pages of illustrations follow p. 98

A Study in Victorian Publishing

I

Introduction

On 2 January 1892 Robert Louis Stevenson wrote to E. L. Burlingame, editor of *Scribner's Magazine* and the chief intermediary between the novelist and the New York publishing house of Charles Scribner's Sons: "McClure is publishing a short story of mine, some 50,000 words, I think, the *Beach of Falesá*; when he's done with it, I want you and Cassell to bring it out in a little volume; I shall send you a dedication for it: I believe it good, indeed, to be honest, very good. Good gear that pleases the merchant."[1] Stevenson had sound reason for thinking well of his story. By this time his mastery of fictional technique was unsurpassed. His cruises through the South Seas had restored him to health and vitality. More than that, they had furnished his imagination with material beyond anything he might have invented. Coral reefs, tropical mountains, endless seas, and cobalt skies. And always the people—Marquesans, Hawaiians, Gilbertese, Tahitians—all different, all polyglots, with their private myths of creation and their common history of destruction. Stevenson recognized both the immediacy and the value of his subject: the irrevocable advance of European whites throughout the Pacific, and the

1. Virtually all the correspondence quoted in this study may be found in three research libraries: the Princeton University Library, the Houghton Library at Harvard, and the Beinecke Library at Yale. Unless otherwise noted, Stevenson's letters to E. L. Burlingame and the in-house correspondence between Charles Scribner and L. W. Bangs are all part of the massive Scribner's Archive, housed at the Princeton University Library, and Stevenson's letters to Sidney Colvin are all in the Houghton Library. Stevenson's letters to Charles Baxter are taken from the carefully edited versions included by DeLancey Ferguson and Marshall Waingrow in their *R. L. S: Stevenson's Letters to Charles Baxter* (New Haven, Conn., 1956); the originals are in the Beinecke Library. The main printed editions of Stevenson's letters were edited by Sidney Colvin and are unreliable because of Colvin's systematic alteration of the texts. Thus, with the exception of the letters edited by Ferguson and Waingrow, I have quoted wherever possible from the holograph letters themselves.

consequent decline of Polynesian culture. He was determined to appropriate this subject for his writing, and perhaps immortalize it through his
art.

The Beach of Falesá was born of that effort. Although Stevenson was
a hard and severe critic of his own work, prone to find technical weak-
nesses hidden from the casual reader, he never wavered in his regard for
this short novel, placing it at the very top of his artistic achievement.
"These labours of the last year—I mean Falesá and D.B, not Samoa of
course—seem to me to be nearer what I mean than anything I have ever
done—nearer what I mean by fiction; the nearest thing before was Kidnapped."[2] Stevenson was not alone in his judgment. He heard from his
good friend Henry James in the summer of 1893: "The art of The Beach
of falesà seems to me an art brought to a perfection & I delight in the
observed truth, the modesty of nature, of the narrator." James had never
succumbed to the common delusion that the author of Kidnapped com-
posed for children; he considered Stevenson a superb prose stylist and an
astute theorist on the nature and practice of fiction. His recognition of
what Stevenson had accomplished in The Beach of Falesá is especially
telling because of his own admitted indifference to its subject. "Primitive
man doesn't interest me, I confess, as much as civilized—and yet he does,
when you write about him."[3] This remarkable tribute is an unwitting
reminder of the bur that stuck to Stevenson's work these last years in
Samoa. As long as Scotland served as subject, historic yet comfortable
Scotland, the fiction was eulogized. The moment Stevenson turned to
the modern world, to a Pacific of shipwrecks, derelict whites, and natives
speaking broken English, the novels were received with suspicion and
distaste.

Stevenson was well aware of the hostility toward his new material—
particularly since one of the most vociferous detractors was Sidney Colvin, his close friend and de facto literary counselor. But there was little
he could do about it. The Beach of Falesá, among the novels, bore the
whip's lash of an antagonism that was directed at all his exotic writing.
The book ran counter to some of the most deeply held political, sexual,
and religious convictions of those responsible for its publication. Set in
the Western Pacific, using the pidgin and rough slang of the region, and
told by a white trader who sleeps with and later marries a stunning native

2. RLS to Sidney Colvin, 30 September 1892.
3. Janet Adam Smith, ed., Henry James and Robert Louis Stevenson (London, 1948),
p. 230.

girl, *Falesá* undermined the ethos of imperial England. It took for its subjects miscegenation, colonialism, the exploitation of brown people, and, indeed, the very idea of the white man's presence in the Pacific. *Falesá* never appeared in print as Stevenson wrote it. Of all his texts, this was the most mutilated and corrupted. Punctuation was systematically altered; language was revised, distorted, or deleted; entire passages were garbled or bowdlerized. How this came to be is the subject of this study: a story of what happens to a work of art when it is converted into a commodity to satisfy the taste and prejudices of the period—a story of stylistic abuse by printers and proofreaders, of literary abuse by publishers, editors, and friends, and finally of the abuse of art by Stevenson himself in sanctioning the publication of a corrupt text. For despite his stature and authority, Stevenson was daunted by distance, by domestic responsibilities, by the evasive and hesitant practices of publishers, by the squeamishness of periodical editors, and above all by his trusting relationship with Sidney Colvin, a man who had Stevenson's authority to make manuscript decisions, yet a man who by temperament was unlikely to understand or to tolerate Stevenson's artistic aims.

The genesis of *Falesá*, from its inception in Stevenson's mind—he referred to it as early as November 1890—to its first publication in the *Illustrated London News* in July and August 1892, and to its first book publication in 1893 (under the title *Island Nights' Entertainments*), can be traced in some sixty letters. This correspondence, postmarked Samoa, Edinburgh, London, and New York, forms the documentary history of the novel. We witness the evolution of the story, the roles played by Colvin and Charles Baxter, and the debate over the book within the editorial offices of Scribner's. What these letters show, above all, is the frenetic and continuous correspondence that characterized the publication of *The Beach of Falesá*. At the same time, these letters are part of a larger correspondence. Stevenson was enormously productive during the last years—"the Samoan years," as Graham Greene called them—writing history, poetry, sociology, and fiction, and projecting books for the future at a dizzying speed.[4] Indeed, one of Charles Scribner's complaints was that Stevenson was overproducing and thereby glutting the market for his work. Thus *Falesá* is only a component in a larger drama of Stevenson's works and the problems of their publication. What got printed was a compromise at best and a mutilation at worst. The causes for this

---

4. Graham Greene, *The Lost Childhood and Other Essays* (London, 1951), p. 66.

were various—not the least being Stevenson's insistence on higher and higher prices for his writing, coupled with a conscience that compelled him to produce in order to satisfy the demand he had himself created.

Some central issues emerge from this sheaf of correspondence. Stevenson was either incapable of or perhaps unsuited to dealing with his business affairs on a steady, diligent basis. He was involved in a surfeit of literary projects, and he tended to fluctuate in his dealings with publishers and syndicators from geniality to peremptoriness. Stevenson's impulsiveness was thus in the largest sense responsible for the bowdlerization of *Falesá* and for the liberties that were taken with his work throughout these last years. Stevenson was constantly beset by worries—financial fears, domestic crises, and artistic problems. Perhaps his only calm came when he was working "at ½ past five in the morning by lamplight,"[5] when the rest of the household was not yet awake. When he negotiated, he could hardly be expected to recall what he had written to whom: he kept no files and no copies of his letters. Stevenson's single fortunate act was to retain Baxter as his financial agent. By the end of 1892, and as a result of his experience with *Falesá* in particular, Stevenson turned all his business affairs over to Baxter: he was clearly tired, as he said, of giving with one hand and taking with the other.

Another theme that emerges from these letters is the deference exhibited by Stevenson's publishers, a deference unquestionably based on an admiration for Stevenson and for his work. Burlingame, Charles Scribner, Wemyss Reid at Cassell and Company—all showed toward the self-styled "exile of Samoa" a regard that is almost reverential. The significance of this attitude cannot be overemphasized, for it clearly bears on the immediate issue of *Falesá* and its bowdlerization. Scribner and Reid would not have tampered with Stevenson's text in nearly the way it was tampered with. This is not to say that they were averse to having alterations made: quite the contrary. But on the whole they would only have had them made by Stevenson himself. There was, of course, a subtle interlacing of motives and acts here: the publishers would not print *Falesá* as Stevenson wrote it, but they would not themselves make substantive alterations. And Stevenson, for personal and domestic reasons, acquiesced in the demands made by the powers that be.

This brings us to the third theme in the correspondence, the role of Sidney Colvin. Although the relationship between Stevenson and Col-

5. Joseph Strong, Stevenson's stepson-in-law, to Charles Warren Stoddard, 15 June 1892; Huntington Library.

vin was complex and in some respects obscure, there is no doubt that Colvin had few scruples about Stevenson's texts, and indeed he probably felt he was improving them. Colvin's intimacy with Stevenson, well known by people at Cassell and at Scribner's, conferred on him special though largely tacit privileges. What this meant in practice was that Colvin acted on Stevenson's behalf with the publishers: if he suggested that *Falesá* come out with "The Bottle Imp," then nobody thought to ask Stevenson for his approval. Cassell acted with strict instructions from Baxter. What their instructions were with respect to Colvin is unknown—but they had the effect of conferring editorial status on him. Colvin exhibited the curious attitude of the man whose best friend is virtually his sinecure, and who on occasion vents his anger and hostility toward the source of his support. Colvin's superior tone exasperated and demoralized Stevenson. With the exception of Henry James, who was an infrequent correspondent, and E. L. Burlingame, who was after all his editor, Stevenson had little feedback about his work. He cannot have been blind to the effects that this absence of literary give-and-take, of disputation, had on him. Colvin received the benefit of Stevenson's extended and elaborate commentary, and he systematically diminished the value of all work that touched on the Pacific.[6] As Stevenson said to him in one letter (17 May 1892): "So you see you are like to hear no more of the Pacific or the XIXth century for awhile."

From Stevenson's point of view, Colvin was a trusted intimate, a belletrist who could be expected to judge and evaluate Stevenson's work. But Stevenson's letters to him suggest that Stevenson expected or requested evaluation on an essentially nontechnical level: he wanted Colvin to serve as a sounding board for his fiction, as a literate voice that might be expected to comment on the timbre or pitch of Stevenson's prose, to admire the method or originality of Stevenson's art, and to wonder at the departure in subject matter and style. I do not believe

6. Here is Stevenson's response (18 May 1891) to Colvin's criticism of the South Sea letters: "You may be sure, after the friendly freedoms of your criticism (necessary I am sure, and wholesome I know, but untimely to the poor labourer in his landslip) that mighty little of it will stand. I propose in the meanwhile to keep what you remarked (I fear in a strain of flattery) 'A.1' in the little copyright volume, and (I think it is) three more of the chapters with some overhauling. With your criticism of the last part received, I am more depressed; I could have bet my life, The Free Island was good. However, it is your business (and please understand this) to take these letters as they appear, and whenever a paragraph seems to you reasonably good, leave it; and whenever one does not delete it; and in this state, with as civil comments as your precision will suffer you to make, despatch them to the toiler, registered, to be ready when I come to try the book."

Stevenson ever thought of Colvin as a blue-pencil editor, although, without question, he extended to him blue-pencil privileges. Just how Colvin assumed those privileges, and how the assumption became the reality, is really a part of the story. Because of distance, Stevenson's friends, namely Baxter and then Colvin, had extensive relations with Stevenson's publishers. These friends, especially Colvin, became identified in the publishers' minds as Stevenson's surrogates. Turning to Colvin for advice or merely conferring with Colvin thus began to seem usual. In time—and given Colvin's own propensity to acquire more power and leverage with publishers through his association with Stevenson—Colvin became entangled with Stevenson's work. Gradually, and without real calculation, Stevenson ceded authority over his work to other people. He asserted himself arbitrarily on occasion to state his position: "I will not allow it to be called *Uma* in book form, that is not the logical name of the story. Nor can I have the marriage contract omitted."[7] But in truth he had become the source of production with little control over the final product. Stevenson was a machine whose creative workings were alien to all those around him. He supplied the art: a variety of producers were involved in its finishing, marketing, and distribution.

The distance that separated Stevenson from London and New York further contributed to his publishing difficulties. Serialization, trade announcements, synchronization of English and American book publication—all these details had to be managed separately and jointly by Cassell and Scribner's, with an author who was at least one month away by steamer mail. And at the center of this correspondence was Stevenson, whose capacity to remain consistent in his demands was never very considerable. Thus publishers like Cassell and Scribner's were left very much at the mercy of the latest directions they received from Stevenson's agents—directions that were frequently contravened by Stevenson himself. The further Stevenson got from his publishing centers, the more problems his manuscripts encountered.

Finally, Stevenson's own attitude toward his personal life and his writing exacerbated problems that had been evident in publishing his work at least since the appearance in 1889 of *The Wrong Box*. For one thing, he had a heightened sense of urgency about his finances, which was really a sense of urgency about supporting his family in the manner to which they had become accustomed. To this end he would engage himself in as

7. RLS to Sidney Colvin, "Friday night, the (I believe) 18th or 20th August or September" 1892.

many projects as he could, maximizing his profits as quickly as possible. He would arbitrarily raise his royalty rate, and when that was insufficient he would renounce royalty arrangements altogether and agree only to the outright sale of his copyrights. Furthermore, Stevenson, like most of his contemporaries, did not have an iconic view of the artist's work. Meticulous and conscious a craftsman as he was, he wrote for publication and whatever glory might come by the by. He was not one to hold back his text over a disagreement about language or contents. Then, too, Stevenson's imagination was extraordinarily fertile; he was brimming with ideas for stories that he was forever beginning, suspending, and returning to. Had he Henry James's work habits he might have completed St. Ives, The South Seas, or possibly even Weir of Hermiston. But then if he had James's work habits, he would not have been Robert Louis Stevenson.

These explanations of Stevenson's attitude are based largely on external factors with only a shadowy relationship to those private compulsions that undoubtedly hold the keys to the riddle. For Stevenson, like so many of his fictional creations, had a divided view of himself as an artist and of his art. He had no doubts about his capacity for fiction or about his place among novelists, past and present. He also had an absolutely clear and convinced sense of his craft as one of the few honest and honorable professions. But, paradoxically, Stevenson also wondered about the entire pursuit of art. He often reflected on the contrast between his family, builders of lighthouses, and himself, maker of fictions. The comparison invariably elicited a self-deprecating view of his own work. Surely a tension as deep as this, a division of identity so profound as to form the structure of all his major work, must have expressed itself in the indifference or possibly resignation with which Stevenson treated the publication of Falesá. He abandoned it to Colvin and the publishers, and by doing so he abandoned it to his readers.

2

The Context

Our story begins with Stevenson's first letter to Sidney Colvin from Vailima. Stevenson had just moved into his new and final home in Samoa. His travels through the Pacific islands, which had taken him from the Marquesas through the Gilberts, from Tahiti and Hawaii to Samoa, were copiously recorded in a journal. His fascination with all that he saw and explored was still fresh. Unquestionably he viewed his long letters to Colvin as a part of his Pacific diary, for he invested them with a descriptive beauty that is hardly equaled in writing of the Pacific. The initial letter (6 November 1890) describes his efforts in battling the growth on his property; it contains images that were to be incorporated in the novel.

My long silent contests in the forest have had a strange effect on me. The unconcealed vitality of these vegetables, their exuberant number and strength, the attempts—I can use no other word—of lianas to enwrap and capture the intruder, the awful silence; the knowledge that all my efforts are only like the performance of an actor, the thing of a moment, and the wood will silently and swiftly heal them up with fresh effervescence; the cunning sense of the tuitui, suffering itself to be touched with wind-swayed grasses and not minding—but let the grass be moved by a man, and it shuts up; the whole silent battle, murder and slow death of the contending forest—wieghs [sic] upon the imagination. My poem the Woodman stands; but I have taken refuge in a new story, which just shot through me like a bullet in one of my moments of awe, alone in that tragic jungle. . . . It is very strange, very extravagant, I daresay; but its [sic] varied, and picturesque, and has a pretty love affair, and ends well.[1]

Stevenson's wonder and humility before the majesty of the tropics, a wonder that induces his meditation on life and death, became the inspiration for his new story.

1. Stevenson's letters to Colvin were published by Colvin after Stevenson's death, appearing in 1895 under the title *Vailima Letters*. As noted above, the published versions are unreliable.

Yet no more is heard of this germ of *Falesá*, "The High Woods of Ulufanua," until the following year. Stevenson apparently put it aside for some time, for he wrote to Colvin on 29 April 1891: "I have taken up again The High Woods of Ulufanua. I still think the fable too fantastic, and far fetched. But on a re-reading, fell in love with my first chapter; and for good or evil, I must finish it. It is really good, well fed with facts, true to the manners, and (for once in my works) rendered pleasing by the presence of a heroine who is pretty. Miss Uma is pretty: a fact. All my other bitches have been as ugly as sin, and like Falconet's horse (I have just been reading the anecdote in Lockhart) *mortes* forbye." Stevenson here introduces a theme that he was to echo regularly in his comment on this story: its veracity, its realism.

Although there must have been some lapse in his work on the story, Stevenson was clearly enraptured with the South Seas as a subject. Responding to Colvin's suggestion that he control his material rather than let so much come out, Stevenson replied in early September 1891: "What ails you, miserable man, to talk of saving material? I have a whole world in my head, a whole new society to work, but I am in no hurry; you will shortly make the acquaintance of the Island of Ulufanua, on which I mean to lay several stories: The Bloody Wedding, possibly The High Woods—O it's so good, the High Woods, but the story is craziness, that's the trouble—a political story, The Labour Slave. Ulufanua is an imaginary island; the name is a beautiful Samoan word for the *top* of a forest, ulu—leaves or hair, fanua = land. The *ground* or country of the leaves. 'Úlufanúa the isle of the sea,' read that verse dactylically and you get the beat; the u's are like our double oo: did ever you hear a prettier word?" Stevenson dropped his title, for as he noted parenthetically in a line at the top of the letter subsequently expunged by Colvin, "I'm afraid I'll have to give up Ulufanua, they say it has a bawdy meaning!" But he was far from giving up his story.

I have just interrupted my letter and read through the chapter of the High Woods that is written, a chapter and a bit, some 16 pages, really very fetching; but what do you wish? the story is so wilful, so steep, so silly—it's a hallucination I have outlived, and yet I never did a better piece of work, horrid, and pleasing, and extraordinarily *true*: it's sixteen pages of the South Seas: their essence. What am I to do? Lose this little gem—for I'll be bold, and that's what I think it—or go on with the rest which I don't believe in, and don't like, and which can never make aught but a silly yarn? Make another end to it? Ah, yes, but that's not the way I write; the whole tale is implied; I never use an effect, when I can help it, unless it prepares the effects that are to follow: that's what a story consists in. To make another end, that is to make the beginning all wrong. The dénouement of a long story is nothing; it is just a 'full close,' which you may approach and accompany as you please—it is a coda, not an essential member in the rythm [sic]; but the body and end of a short story is bone of the bone and blood of the blood of the beginning. Well, I shall end by finishing it against my judgement; that fragment is my Delilah. Golly, it's good. I am not shining by modesty; but I do just love the colour and movement of that piece so far as it goes.

Not only does Stevenson declare his admiration for his tale, but he provides Colvin with some literary criticism on top of it. The truth or essence of the South Seas is what he aimed for. If the truth is "horrid," its artistic representation at least is not. Stevenson's aesthetic commentary, however, was lost on Colvin. In particular, his belief that there is an indissoluble link between all the incidents in a short story did not deter Colvin from excising a crucial interpolated yarn of more than two hundred words at the beginning of *Falesá*.

Before the month was out, Stevenson again wrote to Colvin, and this time he elaborated at length on his story (28 September 1891):

My dear Colvin, since I last laid down my pen I have written and rewritten The Beach of Falesá: something like sixty thousand words of sterling domestic fiction; (the story you will understand is only half that length); and now I don't want to write any more again for ever, or feel so; and I've got to overhaul it once again to my sorrow; I was all yesterday revising and found a lot of slacknesses and (what is worse in this kind of thing) some literaryisms. One of the puzzles is this: it is a first person story: a trader telling his own adventure in an island; when I began I allowed myself a few liberties, because I was afraid of the end; now the end proved quite easy and could be done in the pace; so the beginning remains about a quarter tone out (in places); but I have rather decided to let it stay so. The problem is always delicate; it is the only thing that worries me in 1st person tales, which otherwise (quo' Alan) "set better wi' my genius." There is a vast deal of fact in the story, and some pretty good comedy. It is the first realistic South Sea Story; I mean with real South Sea Character and details of life; everybody else who has tried, that I have seen, got carried away by the romance and ended in a kind of sugar candy sham epic, and the whole effect was lost—there was no etching, no human grin, consequently no conviction. Now I have got the smell and look of the thing a good deal. You will know more about the South Seas after you have read my little tale, than if you had read a library. As to whether anyone else will read it, I have no guess. I am in an off time; but there is just the possibility it might make a hit; for the yarn is good and melodramatic, and there is quite a love affair—for me; and Mr Wiltshire (the narrator) is a huge lark, though I say it. But there is always the exotic question; and everything, the life, the place, the dialects—trader's talk, which is a strange conglomerate of literary expressions and English and American slang, and Beach de Mar, or native English—the very trades and hopes and fears of the characters, are all novel and may be found unwelcome to that great, hulking, bullering whale, the public.

This letter illustrates Stevenson's habit of revision, his tendency toward concision as he revised, his insistence on the "fact" in the story, and finally, his special emphasis on the language and the authentic expression of the speech, so crucial to this tale. If there is anything central to Stevenson's argument here, it is the pride he expresses at having captured the truth of the South Seas. But Colvin was not the man to tell it to. At the best he was indifferent to the South Seas; at the worst he despised and resented what he considered its corrupting influence on Stevenson's art.

If Stevenson expressed his ideas about his work to Colvin, even knowing that Colvin's understanding and appreciation were limited, he wrote in a very different vein to Charles Baxter. Baxter was Stevenson's closest friend, their friendship going back to the days when they were both university students in Edinburgh, and the novelist could reveal himself in ways that he would never have considered doing with Colvin. Stevenson entrusted to Baxter all the details concerning the sale of his fiction. Baxter, unlike Colvin, never tried to contravene Stevenson's intentions. When Stevenson wrote to Baxter about *Falesá*, it was to tell him what he wanted done with the story. He dropped him a note on 15 September 1891: "Next month I shall have a story ready which should bring in some cash." True to his word, he wrote on 14 October:

I send you herewith a story: *The Beach of Falesá*. I have asked McClure to make you an offer for serial rights. If he offer less than £500, I am disinclined to accept; if less than £400, I refuse point blank. You should hear from him almost at once, and if he does not come to the scratch, it will be a fine problem what to do next. I believe it will be best to have it out as a small volume through Cassell's and Scribner's; I refuse [the] shilling touch, and incline to half-a-crown, but will accept two shillings if the Cassells force it: terms as usual, and better take some money down if I am behindhand, as I fear I must be. The Scribners must just please themselves as to price etc.; these conditions are for England. I fear we shall miss Christmass with it, so it will be a near thing if we catch it. I don't know though, you should get it early in November; it might still be doable. But then of course the volume is a gamble; and it might be worth while to find out what Lippincott would offer, or even Arrowsmith. I will of course sell nothing but serial rights; and these emphatically not for less than £400. I prefer the naked gamble to that. Even before you hear from McClure, you might make inquiries. But remember if McC. offers £500, it is his, even if you have found better, as I have offered it to him for that. Awfully sorry to bother you with this; but McC. is so little of a businessman and so much of a splasher, that I do not care to send him the copy direct. My hope is, he will give the sum asked, and there will be no more bother.[2]

2. DeLancey Ferguson and Marshall Waingrow, eds., *R. L. S.: Stevenson's Letters to Charles Baxter* (New Haven, Conn., 1956), pp. 286–87.

There was no reason for Stevenson not to assume he could demand such a substantial sum from McClure, who on 4 December 1890 had estimated Stevenson's earnings for the following year: "In regard to financial matters I think you can make yourself perfectly easy. . . . You can safely count on a sum in excess of $20,000 from me during the next eight or ten months." It is clear, too, from Stevenson's refusal of the "shilling touch," that he wanted the book publication of his story to do adequate justice to its artistic merit.[3] Finally, Stevenson's remarks about what other publishers might offer anticipate the method that Baxter later employed of putting the novelist's prospective books up for bid.

On 4 December 1891 William Ernest Henley—poet, editor, former friend and literary collaborator of Stevenson—wrote to Lemuel Bangs, Scribner's London representative: "My friend, Mr. Charles Baxter, . . . is anxious, as Mr. R. L. Stevenson's legal agent, to discuss the sale (for America) of Mr. Stevenson's new story. Let me express the hope that this introduction may be the means of sparing you much correspondence."[4] It must have struck Bangs as odd that Baxter would approach him, since he knew that Scribner's had cordial relations with Stevenson himself. Nonetheless, he wrote to Charles Scribner five days later (19 December 1891) about Baxter's visit.

With a letter of introduction from W. E. Henley a gentleman called named Charles Baxter,—"R. Louis Stevenson's legal agent"— He said he had instructions from Stevenson to arrange if possible on terms given first with McClure for the *serial* rights of publication of his new story "Beach of Falesá"— It is subsequently desired that it be published in Book form, & not being long enough for a volume, that other stories by him (or some one else) should be included, & that Cassell will arrange for it here; & he asked if we would arrange for it for America for simultaneous publication with Cassell— I told him your relations were very cordial with Stevenson & that in all probability he had already communicated with you about this for America but that in any event I would mention it & let him know, what you said.

Bangs could not have known that Baxter had signed an agreement that very day with Robert McClure, selling the world serial rights of *Falesá* for

---

3. Stevenson was determined to avoid the pejorative label of "shilling shocker" or "shilling dreadful." Earlier, for example, the *Athenaeum*, anticipating the publication of the *Strange Case of Dr. Jekyll and Mr. Hyde*, disclosed that "Mr. R. L. Stevenson is writing another 'shilling dreadful,' in which supernatural machinery will be employed" (14 November 1885, p. 638).

4. Baxter retained Henley's letter of introduction, for written in pencil in Baxter's hand is the notation: "Beach of Falesá—Serial or 'newspaper rights' are disposed of. It is desired to publish in Book form with other stories simultaneously here & in America." Beinecke Library.

£500. A week and a half later Bangs wrote again to Scribner (30 December 1891):

> Mr. Baxter (Stevenson's legal representative here) writes me that he has arranged as to the book publication here with Cassell; & that they will be prepared to give you every facility in the way of advance proofs & to make every arrangement as to keeping the American copyright secure. The matter is now understood to be between Cassell & you & I will see them when I receive your reply to my last on this subject. Baxter issued the clause agreed to between himself—Cassell & McClure viz: "That the said Charles Baxter shall be at liberty to authorise publication of this work in book form one week before publication of the last instalment (in serial form), and the said McClure agrees to give the said Baxter notice in writing one month in advance of said date."

Baxter's facility and authority in dealing with Stevenson's publishers cannot be overestimated. In mid-October Stevenson had forwarded him the manuscript, which probably arrived in mid-November. Within the next month, Baxter had established terms for both serial and book publication; and his demands for money had been clear and uncompromising.

Meanwhile, Charles Scribner, responding to Bangs's letter of 19 December, acknowledged the oddity of the *Falesá* proceedings (31 December 1891): "The Stevenson story is complicated and it seems strange that he has not written to us. We will gladly issue the book at any date to be decided upon and pay him a 15% royalty on all sales. This last is Stevenson's own suggestion for his new books and the terms on which we shall issue 'The Wrecker.' I don't think anything else is desired but if necessary we could make an advance; but, as I say, these terms we have every reason to suppose *entirely* satisfactory to Stevenson. I hope no one else's work will be mixed with his and yet I know of only one story of Stevenson's that has not been gathered into previous volumes." From Scribner's point of view, it was certainly odd that Stevenson had not written directly to him; but having recently agreed to a 15 percent royalty on all of Stevenson's new books, Scribner could only believe that Stevenson would be pleased with the terms. It is noteworthy, however, that Scribner mentioned his wish that there be no other author involved in the new work. He and Burlingame believed that Stevenson's collaboration with Lloyd Osbourne on *The Wrong Box* and *The Wrecker* was having a deleterious effect on sales: readers assumed that Stevenson was allowing his name to be used to help sell his stepson's work, or else that Osbourne's work was corrupting Stevenson's. In either case Stevenson was the loser—both in prestige and in his pocketbook.

With the start of the new year, then, all the elements were ready for the publication of *Falesá*. The manuscript was in the hands of Baxter, who had made arrangements with McClure and with Cassell and Company. Charles Scribner wrote to bring Bangs up to date on 29 January, quoting Stevenson's letter of 2 January and commenting: "This settles the question of its publication alone and we shall not apply for more stories for the volume. It will only remain to arrange later on for a date of issue with Cassell. Of course we will send them the dedication when it comes and shall be glad to have them mail to us copies of the proof of the book as ready with them, if any special arrangements have been made for the proof-reading." Of course Scribner assumed, as Stevenson had said, that the story was 50,000 words—sufficient for a single volume. But it is important to note Scribner's unquestioning acceptance of Stevenson's terms.

In the meantime Robert McClure had typewritten copies made of the manuscript. This was a regular practice of the McClure syndicate. Writing to Stevenson about his South Sea *Letters*, for example, S. S. McClure noted (31 January 1891): "I enclose you herewith 4 typewritten copies of the third batch of letters you sent me. When you correct them, if you will send one copy back to me here and two copies to Mr. Colvin, I will be obliged." That this is indeed what happened in the case of *Falesá* can be deduced from the letters. And it explains an otherwise inexplicable letter of Stevenson's. On 31 January 1892 Stevenson wrote to Colvin: "Understand, I send this brief scratch not because I am unfit to write more, but because I have 58 galleys of the *Wrecker* and 102 of the *Beach of Falesá* to get overhauled somehow or other in time for the mail, and for 3 weeks I have not touched a pen with my finger." The oddity is this: what could Stevenson have meant about correcting galleys for *Falesá*? The *Illustrated London News* galleys, which are the only ones extant, were probably set up in May or June 1892. They have no corrections by Stevenson at all. He must have seen instead a typewritten copy of *Falesá* prepared by Robert McClure—we can estimate that 102 pages would have been a reasonable length for a typed copy of the manuscript. McClure also included a letter in which he asked Stevenson to modify or alter the text, for on 1 February Stevenson wrote to Colvin: "The Beach of Falesá I still think well of, but it seems it's immoral and theres [sic] a to-do, and financially it may prove a heavy disappointment. The plaintive request sent to me, to make the young folks married properly before 'that night,' I refused; you will see what would be left of the yarn, had I consented." Although Stevenson here resisted the request to alter the marriage contract, the request itself constituted a form of pressure, and it had an effect on him. Gradually, in the face of admonitions and delays, his capacity to insist on the integrity of his text diminished.

Colvin, meanwhile, wrote to Baxter on 6 February: "Will you tell me what are the arrangements made with Cassell's about the publishing of the Beach of Falesá? I mean are they going to bring it out serially, & if so where?— And is there any arrangement for its coming out in book form afterwards, either by itself or with other stories (I should think it was too short to come by itself)? I ask the question because I want to know what sort of date it is likely to be done in book form, in order if possible to get 'Across the Plains' out first, as I think it desirable that this volume of pre-Pacific papers in his old vein should come out *before* any of the Pacific things appear in book form."[5] Colvin, far from disinterested, believed that Stevenson was glutting the market with his publications, and was convinced that the Pacific work was financially reckless—especially after the New York *Sun* canceled the remainder of Stevenson's South Sea *Letters*. Since Colvin was solely responsible for *Across the Plains*, he was well aware of the advantage of getting it into print first.

Until this time, however, there was very little discussion of the substance of the story. It is as if the contents were an afterthought, or more accurately, an irrelevant issue. What was important was the merchandising of the text—securing serial publication, arranging for book publication, adjusting for simultaneous publication in England and America, and establishing royalties and fees. Yet that the story itself was an issue became all too clear in two letters between Scribner and Bangs that crossed each other on their transatlantic journeys. Scribner first (19 February 1892): "Since writing to you last about Stevenson's story 'The Beach of Falesá' the situation has become complicated. We have read the story—lent to us by McClure—and find it one that we could not publish without modification and which we hope Stevenson will not issue at all in book form, particularly as it only contains 30000 instead of 50000 words as we understood his letter. When you see Cassell you might ask them whether they have read the story and tell them that we regard it as

5. The Colvin-Baxter correspondence at the Beinecke Library exists only in the form of typed transcripts of the original letters. These transcripts clearly present an edited version of the correspondence. A note to the collection speculates that the transcripts were made for E. V. Lucas "for his use in assembling material for his book on the Colvins." Lucas had access to the original letters, which were purchased from his estate and sold in turn to the Beinecke.

necessary to exchange letters with the author before publishing." And Bangs to Scribner, five days later and before receiving Scribner's letter:

I had sent word to Cassells about your letter from the author, & saw the man having charge of it today as he said there seemed to be some confusion about it; as they had received a letter from Stevenson, saying it was a short story but he did not wish it published as a 1/ book & would write another to make it longer; they could not find the letter, but are to look it up & write me the particulars to-morrow— Robt McClure has just called in, while I am writing, & says in relation to this story, that he has had copies made of it, but that as it stands it would not do for any firm to publish it, in fact that it is so "strong" he has sent a copy back to Stevenson asking him to modify or rewrite it—he has counted the words & instead of 50,000 there are some 30 to 35,000—as they do not expect to com-mence its serial publication before June or July—there will probably be further developments in the meantime.

But who would communicate with Stevenson? For Scribner's, Burlin-game received the assignment. On 25 February he wrote to Samoa.

The chief new thing that has come up since I wrote has been "The Beach of Falesá," of which I said only a preliminary word in my last, as all we knew then was that it would come in due time. Now that we have seen it, we feel that we ought frankly to advise you that we think it worth while to hesitate and to hear from you again about its publication; at all events alone and in the manner sug-gested. We have seen a proof of it, and its length seems to be only about 30,000 instead of 50,000 words. It would make an exceedingly small book, which pub-lished in that form, as if it were a very special thing upon which you laid great stress, would be received with an impression of its relative importance which we think would be unfortunate. Two or three other books of yours, as you know, are coming out almost at once,—"The Wrecker," the volume of Essays, and not long after the Samoa; and to make a special publication of this would we think be a serious business mistake apart from any other consideration. We wish we could persuade you to postpone it, at least, and feel that our advice is sound; and al-though I will not go at more length into reasons for it, but give just this statement of the thing from our special business point of view, I hope you will really consider it carefully.

Whether Burlingame shared Charles Scribner's qualms about the story, or merely reflected company policy, he unquestionably adopted a convenient line of resistance: single publication would be commercially imprudent. Stevenson's curt response, in late March, needs no commen-tary: "Do what you please about The Beach, and I give you carte blanch to write in the matter to Baxter—or telegraph if the time press—to delay the English contingent." Stevenson also wrote to Baxter (30 March 1892): "There seems a strong feeling against *Falesá* for a volume, so I consent to withhold it till there are more. God knows when that may be."

On 4 April 1892 Bangs wrote to Scribner: "McClure called in to-day & said his brother had received word from Stevenson in reply to a suggestion about altering the 'Beach of Falesa'—'that he would not change it in any way.' " Nearly three weeks later, on 22 April, Scribner wrote to Bangs and quoted from Stevenson's letter to Burlingame: "We have just received a letter from Stevenson from which I extract the following: 'Do what you please about the Beach (of Falesá), and I give you *carte blanche* to write in the matter to Baxter—or telegraph if the time press—to delay the English contingent.' This means indefinite postponement of the publication in book form." What had happened? After Scribner's and McClure's initial shock about the contents of *Falesá*, their strategy was to forestall publication in the hope of persuading Stevenson to revise the text. The letter to Burlingame gave Scribner's the authority to handle the publication as they pleased—or so it appears. Stevenson must have authorized Colvin to assume responsibility for the revisions. The procedure would not have been alien to Colvin, who assumed increased editorial responsibilities over Stevenson's work during these last years.

On 11 May Bangs wrote to Scribner about Cassell's prospective purchase of the electroplates for *The Wrecker*. He appended a note on *Falesá*: "This they understand has been put in the hands of Mr Colvin, to do what is necessary to make it acceptable for publication & is now being set up for the 'Illud News'— Cassell's want, or expect to publish it Oct 1st— This of course & the other dates to be arranged with you." Colvin had indeed been working on the novel, for a letter from Stevenson written on 17 May refers to the fake marriage certificate that gave Wiltshire license to bed Uma "for one night" only: "Yesterday came yours. Well, well, if the dears prefer a week, why I'll give them ten days, but the real document, from which I have scarcely varied, ran for one night." It is impossible to know whether Colvin himself was nervous about the document, or whether he simply conveyed the objections of Cassell's editors. But Stevenson clearly had little to do with the production of *Falesá* at this time. His explanation of the novel's manner to Colvin—"a piece of realism *à outrance*, nothing extenuated or adorned"—could be expected to fall on deaf ears. His approval of the change was mitigated only by his sarcasm. For all intents and purposes, Colvin received permission from Stevenson to proceed at his own discretion.

Meanwhile, Burlingame informed Stevenson (on 20 May) that *Falesá* was being held back by both Scribner's and Cassell, "according to the arrangement assented to by you, until after the present publication at least." Colvin, however, was trying to untangle Stevenson's arrangements with McClure about *David Balfour*. Writing to Baxter on 6 July, he stated that McClure could not arrange for *David Balfour*'s serialization until the summer of 1893: "This last point materially affects the question of the Beach of Falesá. To hold it over, as I was anxious to do, till after the appearance of David Balfour, would mean holding it for more than eighteen months. I am therefore the more inclined to favour Hamer's[6] proposition of bringing it out separately (or with the Bottle Imp) as soon as may be.—So, I suppose, will you be.—But in the meantime I have hopes that the sales of Across the Plains & the Wrecker together will be bringing a good sum of money into the till." Colvin's entire letter, of which this is a small part, is devoted to money, and the easy authority with which he suggests disposing of Stevenson's work invites comparison with Baxter's meticulous fidelity to Stevenson's instructions.

So, with Stevenson's approval, book publication of *The Beach of Falesá* was indefinitely postponed. Plans for the serial publication, however, continued apace. Colvin oversaw the necessary changes in the text, and galleys were presumably set up from a typewritten copy of the manuscript. Periodical publication in England began on 2 July 1892, in the *Illustrated London News*, and ran every week until 6 August, the date of the sixth and last installment. On 27 July, when the story had still two issues to run, Bangs wrote to Scribner from London:

The publication of this concludes in the "Illd L. News" on Aug 6th & I have seen Cassells people about it. They have been setting it up from the "News" copy, but Mr Colvin informed them that some changes or additions would be necessary in the book publication, & he is to supply these, when they will recompose it, & I have arranged for them to post to you direct the sheets as they are ready, *with* pulls of the illustrations they intend using— These illustrations they have reduced from those in the "News," & if desired they can supply you with electros of them; if you wish them please cable "send electros Falesa plates" & they will be prepared without delay— They will publish with the "Falesa",—"The Bottle Imp" by Stevenson—which was published in "Black & White." . . . They are in no special hurry to publish the book, but think Sepr 1st or thereabouts would be feasible & they will make it a 5/ volume—

Apart from illustrating how far into the background the manuscript had receded, and how many "texts" were serving as "copy-texts," Bangs's

6. Sam Hield Hamer, editor at Cassell and Company from 1886 to 1907.

letter carried the first official declaration that "The Bottle Imp" would be published along with the novel. Stevenson found out and replied—not to Colvin, but to Baxter—on 11 August: "Apropos of *The Beach of Falesá* I reply to you, although I believe it's through Colvin I have received the proposal. You will kindly communicate to him my answer. *The B. of F.* is *simply not* to appear along with *The Bottle Imp*, a story of a totally different scope and intention, to which I have already made one fellow, and which I design for a substantive volume. If on the other hand Cassell shall choose to publish it by itself, I would remind the lot of you that this was my own original proposal, which I have seen no reason to change, and which I should be rather glad to see come in operation."

Cassell and Company, in the meantime, had gone ahead and reset *Falesá* from the expurgated copyright issue that it had published on 23 July, and, at Colvin's urging, added "The Bottle Imp" to the volume. On 7 September they sent proofs of the volume to Scribner's: "We propose to publish the volume next month. If you would like plates, we would supply you with a set including cuts for £35." Scribner's replied on 16 September: "We have received the set of proofs of 'The Beach of Falesá.' We do not wish to purchase a set of plates, for it is necessary to reset the book here; but we do wish a set of the cuts and have telegraphed our Mr. Bangs to purchase a set from you, trusting that your price will be a reasonable one." Scribner's further noted the need for simultaneous publication, and the need for time to set up the book after the receipt of the cuts. On 24 September *Publishers' Weekly* carried the following announcement: "In 'The Beach of Falesá, and The Bottle Imp,' Robert Louis Stevenson will narrate two more thrilling tales of adventure in the South Seas."

Cassell accepted the order for the cuts on the 26th and added in reply: "As to date of publication, this is uncertain in consequence of a correspondence which has taken place with Mr. Stevenson as to some of the contents of the story. Please do not publish until we write or cable you." *Publishers' Weekly* thus had to announce the postponement of *Falesá* in its 29 October issue. Cassell had adopted Colvin's ideas and prepared a text of the two stories, but Stevenson had charged Baxter with halting any such publication. Baxter, after an apparent delay, finally notified Cassell of Stevenson's objection to the publication. T. Wemyss Reid, the director of the firm, wrote to Stevenson directly on 4 October.

We have just received from Mr. Baxter an extract from your letter to him regarding the Beach of Falesá, in which you refuse to allow that story to appear along with the Bottle Imp. Of course we shall respect your wishes in the matter; but I may point out to you that it is almost by an accident that we are able to do so. It was at the suggestion of Mr. Colvin that we arranged to publish the B. of F. & the Bottle Imp in one volume. That volume has not only been announced but is set up & I am able to send you a copy of it by this mail. We have not printed it off or issued it as yet because of the difficulty we were in regarding the wording of the sham marriage certificate. You must naturally have been very angry when you saw how that part of the book had been dealt with by the editor of the Illustrated London News. We of course never dreamt of taking such a liberty with your "copy," but I learned from Mr. Colvin that you had agreed to allow "one week" to be printed instead of "one night" in the certificate & after considering the matter we were prepared to issue the story with the certificate printed in that shape. But the consideration had occupied time, Mr. Colvin whom we had to consult being abroad, and it thus happens that the publication has been deferred & that we can consequently meet your wishes.

Under the circumstances the best thing will be to defer the publication of the book until we hear again from you; so that if you have any alterations you wish to make in the text they can be duly attended to. If you have a story or can let us have one which will in your opinion go well with the Beach of Falesá we should much like to have it, not only because the B. of F. is in itself so very short, but because it will have lost much of its freshness by the unavoidable delay in publishing it after its appearance in the I. L. N. This, however, we must leave entirely to you. Our wish is in every way to conform to your desires so far as we can understand them, & though difficulties occasionally arise owing to the distance between us we are happy to think that nothing serious has yet occurred.[7]

The copy of The Beach of Falesá and The Bottle Imp that Reid forwarded to Stevenson had no title on the binding. This was the book that Stevenson corrected and that became known as the "Trial Issue" in the comprehensive Yale bibliography, A Stevenson Library.

Meanwhile, as Reid was writing to Stevenson and trying to placate him in response to a letter written three months earlier, Colvin wrote to Baxter on 18 October: "[Stevenson] writes also about the Falesa and Bottle Imp book, no longer objecting at all to the publication, but giving me some corrections for the text and approving very much of the pictures.— I suppose the receipt of my letter and explanations had brought about this change of mind from his letter to you of August (of which I heard a few days ago from Cassell). Immediately on receiving the new letter I wrote to Cassells telling them the contents, as far as the Beach &, are concerned, and saying that they may go forward with the publication if they please."

7. T. Wemyss Reid to RLS, 4 October 1892; Beinecke Library. For the Illustrated London News and the marriage certificate, see below, pp. 83-88.

It is interesting to observe that Cassell and Company were apparently not confiding in Colvin at this point. They told him of Stevenson's objections only "a few days ago," or two weeks after their letter to Stevenson. Actually what is working here is a kind of confusion based on personalities and the long delays of the mail. Colvin undoubtedly believed that Stevenson's letter to him was an agreement to go ahead with the publication, that the letter was written after Stevenson's letter to Baxter, and that Colvin's letter of explanation had been the deciding factor. On 8 November Colvin again wrote to Baxter, trying to untangle the chronology:

You received in August (Cassell's tell me) a letter from L. strongly objecting to Falesa and the Bottle Imp being published as a book together—which letter I have not seen. But after sending it off, he received a full letter from me explaining our reasons for authorizing the proposed publication, and laying before him certain questions as to the text of Falesá, and apparently treating the book as a settled thing, but not explicitly mentioning the Bottle Imp question at all. Now, Cassells ask, may that be taken as a withdrawal of his objections, expressed to you, against putting in the Bottle Imp with Falesá: or are those objections to be taken as standing?

Someone at Cassell had apparently asked Colvin for advice—possibly in response to Colvin's having written Cassell in mid-October telling them to "go forward with the publication"—and Colvin was loath to make any definite statement. He clearly had no real sense of Stevenson's passionate objection to the publication of "The Bottle Imp" with *Falesá*. He continued to argue for the publication of the two together: "I don't feel that I quite know what to say.—Falesa by itself would make a miserably skimpy volume: the B. I. is just what is needed to give it reasonable bulk, and follows (I think) very well.—May the publication proceed under the circumstances, or must we wait till the great man's views after seeing a proof copy of the book can reach us—which would not be till January? What say you?"

The note of arrogant disdain that Colvin registered here is highly revealing. It is as if he considered Stevenson's opinions an irritating and time-wasting formality, a clog in the publishing process. Colvin's relations with Stevenson were marked by "secrecy and indiscretion," to use the novelist's terms, or by calculation and manipulation, to use more contemporary ones. He relished the role of paternal tutor and moral guide to this younger and somewhat disreputable writer, who supported a small tribe of in-laws and a larger tribe of brown savages. Colvin, in

Colvin's eyes, had a hard task keeping Stevenson up to the mark—and cleaning his manuscripts must have seemed, at times, an almost noble calling. It must therefore have been trying when, as in the case with *Falesá* and "The Bottle Imp," Colvin was forced to recognize that final decisions resided not with the editor-agent but rather with the imaginative artist.

Colvin was somewhat chastened by the recent experience. Baxter, who told him only what he felt was necessary, finally sent him a copy of Stevenson's letter of 11 August. On 21 November Colvin thanked Baxter for the "enclosures": "Not having seen the text of L's letter to you as to the Bottle Imp question,—when I got one of a month's later date from him, in answer to mine explaining the reasons of the publication, in which he gave me corrections for Falesá but said nothing about the Imp, I interpreted his silence to mean consent.—Now I have seen the text, I am doubtful on the point, and have written to Hamer to say I think the vol. should be kept back until they get his own explicit answer to Wemy Reid's letter of Oct 4:—which they cannot do until about Jan. 6."

Although book publication was now effectively stalled, Stevenson became confirmed in what had always been his belief: that periodical editors were opposed to *any* treatment of sexuality in fiction, irrespective of the context or the attitude expressed. Thus on 1 December, writing to Baxter about his new work, *Weir of Hermiston*, Stevenson remarked: "The heroine is seduced by one man and finally disappears with the other man who shot him. Now all this, above all after our experience with *Falesá*, don't look much like serial publication; if the worst comes to the worst we shall of course do without that." He had come to the point where he was writing about mature relations, and if he could not market serious fiction in magazines, then he would forgo serialization. This was an enormous step forward on Stevenson's part in assuming control over his work. His experience reflected what most important writers believed to be the major sensitive issue in magazine publication—sexuality. And there were good reasons for that belief. Thomas Hardy's problems with *Tess of the D'Urbervilles* occurred at this time. Even as late as 1905 Rider Haggard had a story returned to him by C. J. Longman: "I am afraid that I cannot run 'Renunciation' in the Magazine. The fact is that no minor alterations would alter the fact that, for good reasons, Rupert renounces sexual relations, except under marriage conditions. This is the basis of the book, which cannot be put in the background, and it is this particular relation which I think it is better not to discuss in magazines. I have been a good deal tempted by my desire to have another of your stories in the magazine, but there it is—we all have our cranks, and that I suppose is mine."[8] For Stevenson, *Falesá* reduced itself to a simple lesson: no sex.

On 10 January 1893 Colvin, waiting for Stevenson's reply to Reid's letter, complained to Baxter that the Samoa mail had not come. But in Samoa Stevenson seemed to have given up the entire matter. On 2 November he had written to Burlingame: "I note and sympathize with your bewilderment as to Falesá. My own direct correspondence with Mr. Baxter is now about three months in abeyance. Altogether you see how well it would be if you could do anything to wake up the Post Office." Stevenson had clearly resigned himself to the inevitable, as his letter to Colvin of 3 December makes apparent:

Now for a confession. When I heard you and Cassells had decided to print The Bottle Imp along with Falesá, I was too much disappointed to answer. The Bottle Imp was the pièce de résistance for my volume: Island Nights Entertainments. However, that volume might have never got done; and I send you two others in case they should be in time.
First have the Beach of Falesá:
Then a fresh false title: *Island Nights Entertainments*;
   and then
The Bottle Imp: a cue from an old melodrama.
The Isle of Voices.
The Waif Woman: a cue from a saga.
Of course these two others are not up to the mark of the Bottle Imp; but they each have a certain merit, and they fit in style. By saying "a cue from an old melodrama" after the B. I., you can get rid of my note. If this is in time, it will be splendid, and will make quite a volume.

This explains why Stevenson did not reply to Colvin, but instead expressed his indignation through Baxter, with whom he felt quite comfortable. But even at this stage Stevenson intended to separate *Falesá* from "The Bottle Imp" through the device of a title. *Island Nights' Entertainments*, which became the published book's title five months later, would serve as a covering title for "The Bottle Imp," "The Isle of Voices" (which Stevenson enclosed for Colvin with this letter), and "The Waif Woman" (which Fanny Stevenson insisted not appear). But the title was specifically not to cover *The Beach of Falesá*. How Stevenson imagined the design is hard to say; he was mainly concerned with protecting the aesthetic integrity of his major work. However, at the end of the letter he said, "Should you and Cassell prefer, you can call the whole volume

8. C. J. Longman to Rider Haggard, 30 January 1905; Huntington Library.

I. N. E.—though the Beach of Falesá is the child of a quite different inspiration. They all have a queer realism, even the most extravagant, even the Isle of Voices: the manners are exact." Thus he admitted, as far as the publication was concerned, that all the stories were of a piece. Such an admission, needless to say, was not a denial of the distinction he had been making all along about the *differences* among these stories. But as in all things, there seemed little he could do. Had he not added the codicil, there could have been a further delay of two or three months arguing about the complication of having four stories with a covering title for three. Stevenson must have realized this and therefore conceded the matter of the title—which was the last redoubt from the complete submersion of *Falesá* into a volume with works of a wholly different character.

Colvin received the letter on 11 January and two days later wrote to Baxter.

R L S agrees, in my letter received on Wednesday, to the publication of Falesa & Bottle Imp together as proposed, and sends me another story in the same key as the Bottle Imp—"the Isle of Voices"—to fill out the volume. It is about 9000 words long, and very good in its way.—Now of course I should like to get him a price for the serial rights of this. It should be worth—at the scale paid for the Beach, which was liberal—£100 or £120. I wrote to the Illustrated London News (not naming figure until I had consulted you) to ask whether they would have it. They answer yes, delighted,—for a June number: but that they could not publish it earlier.—This seems to me too late. With the David Balfour coming out in book form about October, The Beach ought certainly to come out in April (so also thinks Hamer). In order not to lose time, I am . . . trying in one or two other quarters to see whether they will publish serially by then.—If not, I think it would on the whole be best in L's interests to forego the serial publication, and let . . . L. bring it out fresh in the volume, which it will greatly improve, & increase to reasonable size.—What say you as to these points? and would your agreement with Cassells as to the Beach volume be valid and sufficient for it with this addition?

Stevenson never mentioned serial publication for either "The Isle of Voices" or "The Waif Woman." But between 17 and 21 January Colvin nevertheless fired off a series of notes in order to place "The Isle of Voices." He had offered the story first to the *Illustrated London News*. But they could not print it on such short notice. He then wrote to Thomas Joyce, editor of the *Graphic*, asking if the *Graphic* could print the story before Easter. Colvin sent a typewritten copy of the story on the 19th, marking "with a cross" the passages that might be good for illustration.

"The price which R. L. S. gets for serial rights of stories is about £15 per 1000 words: say in this £120." The *Graphic*, unfortunately, could do no better than the *Illustrated London News* in terms of time, and Colvin had to wire Baxter on the 21st that he was sending the story to W. E. Henley at the *National Observer*. Henley, of course, could not have paid the kind of money that Colvin was demanding from Joyce at the *Graphic*, but he did publish the first installment of the story on 4 February—less than a month after Stevenson's manuscript reached London. The "Voices" episode left Baxter with a low regard for Colvin's skill as a negotiator. Colvin was essentially a belletrist; he clearly lacked the hardheaded realism of the businessman.

Stevenson's letter to Colvin of 3 December climaxed the plans for the publication of *Falesá*. Approval to produce the volume with "The Bottle Imp" was the green light for the publishers. Bangs wrote to Scribner's on 28 January:

Cassells people asked me to call in relation to Stevenson's new volume— They have from him through Mr Colvin, the additional story "The Isle of Voices," which with the "Beach of Falesa" & "The Bottle Imp" they will publish under the general title of "Island Nights Entertainments"—as the "David Balfour" will be ready in the autumn they are anxious to have the first published as soon as possible—as quickly as they can (probably by this post) they will give me sheets of the "Isle of Voices" to send you— The illustrations they are having prepared by Hatherell & Gordon Browne. . . . Some of them at least will be text illustrations, therefore if you set up the type before their receipt, it should be kept in "galleys" & not stereotyped,— They wish to work for publication on March 27th & will of course arrange for simultaneous issue. I have told them if you get all the material there will be no unnecessary delay in being ready.

Within a week *Publishers' Weekly* announced the volume in a note on the author. On 25 March Scribner's advertised the volume in the same periodical, and on 8 April *Island Nights' Entertainments* was listed under the weekly record of new publications. Finally, after eighteen months (from Stevenson's forwarding the original manuscript to Baxter in 1891) *The Beach of Falesá* saw print in book form for commercial distribution.

In January, however, Stevenson was still querying Colvin about the proposed volume (he was unaware how quickly the new book was being prepared).

Consideranda for The Beach.
I. Whether to add one or both the tales I sent you?
II. Whether to call the whole volume "Island Nights Entertainments"?

III. Whether, having waited so long, it would not be better to give me another mail, in case I could add another member to the volume and a little better justify the name?
If I possibly can drum up another story, I will. What annoyed me about the use of the Bottle Imp, was that I had always meant it for the centrepiece of a volume of *märchen* which I was slowly to elaborate. You always had an idea that I depreciated the B. I.; I can't think wherefore; I always particularly liked it—one of my best works, and ill to equal; and that was why I loved to keep it in portfolio till I had time to grow up to some other fruit of the same *venue*. However, that is disposed of now, and we must just do the best we can.

Stevenson began this letter by noting: "You are properly paid at last, and it is like you will have but a shadow of a letter." He also informed Colvin that he had "written to Cassell & Co. (matter of *Falesá*) 'you will please arrange with him' (meaning you) 'What he may decide I shall abide.' So consider your hand free, and act for me without fear or favour." Stevenson went on to praise the pictures in the copy of *The Beach of Falesá and The Bottle Imp* that Wemyss Reid had sent him on 4 October. Thus Stevenson must have corrected this book sometime between November and January and returned the text directly to Cassell. It is odd that he never mentioned correcting the copy to Colvin—of course there was so little done in the way of correction. There was, however, a nicely barbed comment—one recalls Stevenson's insistence on the novel's realism—about the illustrations ("It is very strange to a South-Seayer to see Hawaiian women dressed like Samoans, but I guess that's all one to you in Middlesex"), as if the provincialism of the English was to be placed on Colvin's shoulders, as in a sense it was, since Colvin had become responsible in Stevenson's eyes for the entire *Falesá* affair. Yet there was also resignation and the sense that, after all, it really did not matter: "none will sleep worse for it."

By the end of 1892 Stevenson was over his head in dealing with publishers and agents. In late November he received from S. S. McClure nearly eight single-spaced typed pages detailing the financial wranglings that McClure had had with Baxter over *David Balfour* and *Falesá*. McClure was turning to Stevenson for support and justification. It would have required a skilled business manager merely to unravel the accusations, accounts, and almost daily telegraphic give-and-take between Robert McClure and Charles Baxter. On top of that Stevenson was as ever worried about the expenses at Vailima—and reluctant to kill any goose as profitable as McClure. On 1 December he wrote to Baxter:

"[McClure] has put a vast deal more money into my hand than ever I had before, his offers having been the first thing to make me raise my charges." Stevenson finally did what it took him two and a half years to discover he needed to do—two and a half years into the Pacific and away from New York and London. "As thus. Now that I understand you are going to make me pay something at least for all your trouble, I propose in any case of the least difficulty to plump the business right into your hands. As soon as I hear that you are agreeable to this arrangement I shall refer everybody to you and be done with this three[-]month-answer-and-reply business for ever." Stevenson recognized that he could do no better than allow Baxter to assume control over all his future business arrangements with publishers and syndicators. And he was right. As it turned out, Baxter was virtually responsible for introducing the auction into Stevenson contracts. He felt no loyalty to Scribner's, as Charles Scribner noted acidly on 26 May 1893 in a letter to Bangs: "We have suddenly received a letter from Stevenson—quite out of a clear sky—following the receipt of his last royalty account, that he is dissatisfied with the amount of money he receives under the present arrangement and that he wishes to sell outright his American rights in 'David Balfour.' " Whether Stevenson's unhappiness with Scribner's was justified is beside the point, although it is true that Charles Scribner had little enthusiasm for *Island Nights' Entertainments*. The issue is the way that Stevenson perceived his position vis-à-vis his publishers and what he decided or finally acknowledged to be the most useful course of action.

But turning over all his business affairs to Baxter was only one result of the *Falesá* affair. Whetted by his work on *Falesá*, Colvin now saw the prospect of a continued activity on Stevenson's behalf. Reading manuscript copy (he was already adept at Stevenson's hand), obtaining typed transcripts, seeing and correcting proofs—not to mention, through it all, taming the indelicacies—all this service Colvin could be counted on to perform, for a price. In his letter to Colvin of January 1893, Stevenson dealt with this crucial issue of editorial duties (in a paragraph that Colvin deleted from *Vailima Letters*):

I had just last mail placed all my business in C. B's hands, and determined to be quite done with negotiations. Your very welcome proposal (it seems to me) ought therefore to go to him; I do not like to give one month and seem to take away the next; so all I have done, or care to do, is to write to him announcing your willingness to help in what is such a strange business to him; and if you please, I would have you two arrange grounds and responsibilities between the twae o' ye, and without my intervention. If this is not all right communicate again, and I will do otherwise. But if you and C. B. can arrange between you, it would please me best. I have written him that in any case, the financial aspect should be his: which I think right.

Without the original letter, it is unclear exactly what Colvin proposed. Stevenson, it is worth repeating, never for a moment questioned Baxter's ultimate authority, and in his reply to Colvin he made this clear. It is interesting that in handling a situation so delicate—the adjustment of relations between two separate friends—Stevenson resorted to a playfulness that made light of the serious issues involved. The phrase in Scots served to defuse a potentially awkward confrontation. Colvin probably wanted to be involved with financial negotiations, but Stevenson clearly let him know that Baxter was the businessman. And that was how it was to remain. Prior to writing to Colvin, Stevenson had written to Baxter on 28 December: "O, by the way, Colvin would like to have a finger in the pie, and I believe about proofs, forms, etc. he would be very useful and relieve you of all sorts of distasteful little higgling details. If it seem well to you, will you make use of him? Of course in all the financial part you will be absolute and single." We may speculate that Stevenson was placating Baxter and Colvin in turn. In truth, whether consciously designed or not, Stevenson was acknowledging the interests of both men, as well as confirming a fait accompli. Baxter's reply was predictably straightforward: "I think with you that Colvin should certainly be asked to do the editing work, but as you will see from *The Isle of Voices* business, he is not much use at selling. And it would, I think, be the best plan to send all MSS *here*: in the first place I am in touch now with all the necessary people, and after I have made the bargain and arranged for the cash business, Colvin can start in and do his part."

What Stevenson did was to rationalize and codify the situation that existed during the publishing of *The Beach of Falesá*. Although the loose arrangement between Stevenson, Colvin, and Baxter may not have begun, exactly, with *Falesá*, it assumed a pattern with that book. There was probably no reason to believe that any other work would be so controversial, that any special editing problems would emerge. But if Stevenson believed that, then it was naiveté on his part, or else indifference. Colvin shared in the mutilation of *Falesá*, and Stevenson was now making him responsible for his proofs. He wrote to Baxter on 16 April 1893:

It is understood that Colvin has nothing to do with the Business.
" " " 		 " 	Baxter " 	" 		 " 	" 	" 	" 	Proofs.

Again, casual comedy in the most serious of issues. To place his financial affairs in Baxter's hands was the mark of prudence, if not necessity; to place his literary materials in Colvin's hands was the mark of friendship run riot. Nothing that passed through Colvin's hands emerged without retouching: of this I am convinced. And Stevenson himself knew it. The "cuttings and carvings in my immortal text" that he complained of to Baxter in 1894 sounds as if it were an unexpected discovery. *The Beach of Falesá* alone should have prepared Stevenson for the Edinburgh Edition.

3

The Accidentals

Stevenson was the first modern novelist to be assiduously pursued by collectors. Almost nothing seems to have escaped detection and preservation—notebooks and journals, letters, jottings on folio scraps, drafts and fair copies of novels, poems and stories—and nearly everything made its way to libraries from Edinburgh to California. Yet these materials did not become a resource for scholars. They were, for one thing, controversial. So many manuscripts and books were disposed of by Stevenson's own family that it appeared his writing was being promoted simply to drive up auction prices. Secondly, Stevenson's reputation collapsed during the 1920's, a victim of the period's antipathy toward all Victorian writers and the special hostility reserved for one whose life, transformed into hagiography, completely overwhelmed his hard-earned achievement. Further, Stevenson's "works" were readily available in every variety of printed text, from elegant limited sets to mass-produced pulp editions. There was no need to turn to manuscripts and archives to study his artistic development. And who would have thought verification of his texts important? He was not, after all, the magus of *Esmond* or *Bleak House*. He was merely the author of *Treasure Island*. Nonetheless, Stevenson had always been widely regarded as a meticulous craftsman. George Meredith, writing to Stevenson of *Catriona*, said it best: "As for the writing I say nothing more than that I trust it may be the emulation of young authors to equal it."[1] Thus the recovery of Stevenson's manuscripts is the first step toward the restoration of his art. In the case of *Falesá*, the manuscript affords us an unmediated view of Stevenson's habits and practice as a writer. Perhaps more significantly, a comparison of the manuscript with the printed

1. C. L. Cline, ed., *The Letters of George Meredith* (Oxford, 1970), III, 1153.

texts enables us to see precisely how a finished and artistically sophisticated novel was reduced to a vulgar and meretricious shadow of itself.[2] The simplest way to begin is with the manuscript itself. Stevenson's hand, in all his writing, runs from clear and pleasing to absolutely unreadable. Fortunately, *The Beach of Falesá* is in excellent condition, legible throughout, with only a very few words that cannot be deciphered easily. But the script is small, even tiny. Stevenson was quite aware of the problem his hand presented, and he was determined to leave nothing to chance or to the compositor's imagination. Therefore he printed in capitals, directly above his cursive writing or in the margin, anything he thought might be misread, particularly Samoan place-names and vocabulary, and slang expressions. Indeed, Stevenson was more than meticulous with his copy for *Falesá*: he was fussy almost to the point of fanaticism. Experience had taught him to be cautious with his texts. A decade earlier he had written to William Dean Howells, who was publishing a poem of his in the *Atlantic Monthly*: "May I hope for proofs? I am one who never was yet correctly printed, even under the supervision of a synod of intelligent friends. My mind is not sympathetic with that of the Average Printer."[3]

Although Stevenson was aware of the problems in transcribing his handwritten script, nothing angered him more than wholesale butchering of his punctuation. He wrote to Burlingame in late 1887: "Herewith the proof, which I trust will put your printers on their mettle. Possibly a word from you might help: depict me as a man of a congested countenance and the most atrabilious disposition: you will only anticipate the

2. For bibliographers and textual critics, *The Beach of Falesá* figures as one of Stevenson's most fascinating works. The most obvious reason is the number of extant texts: a minimum of six printed texts, if one includes the English and American first editions of *Island Nights' Entertainments*. But even more telling is the variety: there are two sets of galley proofs; the story as it appeared in the *Illustrated London News*; an issue that was "expurgated" and printed solely for copyright purposes; a text that was bound with "The Bottle Imp" (only two known copies exist); and finally the English book edition published by Cassell and Company, and the American book edition published simultaneously by Charles Scribner's Sons. What adds a touch of spice to all this is the fact that the "Bottle Imp" version was sent to Stevenson and bears his own corrections, a detail that encouraged one collector to print privately a slim booklet listing the corrections for the delectation of other bibliophiles (*Unique; or A Description of a Proof Copy of The Beach of Falesá Containing Over 100 Manuscript Changes by Robert Louis Stevenson* [Chicago, 1914]). Finally, there is the manuscript itself, now in the Huntington Library. This consists of 58 pages of text, beautifully bound by Sangorski and Sutcliffe of London in crushed brown Morocco and titled in gold.

3. RLS to W. D. Howells, undated (ca. 1880); Houghton Library.

truth, for if they go on making hay of my punctuation, I shall surely have a stroke. I am up to the neck in attempted papers; three of them, no less; and not one will come off. Well—better luck!—but this warning has gone to your printers and to the composition of insults to the reader. I hope he is a man of a sensitive vanity. Then I shall have touched him on the raw."[4] Stevenson had ample justification for his complaint. James Dow, one of the proofreaders for *Young Folks*, the pulp weekly that first published *Treasure Island*, *Kidnapped*, and *The Black Arrow*, wrote years later about his experience with Stevenson's texts.

> The first instalment of a new adventure story, which was afterwards called *Treasure Island*, came into my hands in galley proof just after my return from my holiday, and when I was "reading" it I was impressed by the story and by the style.
> "Who is this new writer?" I asked the "copyholder." "His work is much better and more literary than anything else in the paper."
> We did not know anything about the author, but from that moment I took a great interest in his work, and I did my best to ensure very correct "reading" of the proofs; and I must emphatically deny the statements which have been made, inferring that I amended the syntax and corrected the punctuation. Throughout the three stories that I "read" for him I had no occasion to do either. In no instance did I alter the text, and I did my utmost to preserve the author's punctuation. In syntax he needed no coaching, and of punctuation he was a Master. The difficulty I had was to induce the compositors to "follow the copy," and to refrain from trying to improve the punctuation so carefully prepared for them.[5]

Stevenson was concerned with the aesthetics of the printed page. Someone who corrects the punctuation on the title page of a book (including the publisher's name and place of publication), who worries over the maps and the color of the ink ("Where is the map of *Kidnapped*? I must have my map, when you next issue it; a book of mine without a map, ye Gods!"[6]), who prefers the "look" of a word spelled one way rather than another ("the chief of the short stories got sucked into *Sophia Scarlett*— I give you the two Ts, though I prefer the look of it without"[7]), can hardly

4. Received by Burlingame on 7 November 1887.
5. James Dow, "Robert Louis Stevenson and the *Young Folks* Reader," in R. Masson, ed., *I Can Remember Robert Louis Stevenson* (Edinburgh, 1922), p. 207. On 24 February 1888, S. S. McClure wrote to Charles Scribner: "I have heard Mr. Stevenson talk especially about the proof-reader, who read his stories which appeared in 'Our Young Folks,' and he says that no proof-reader in the world ever read his proofs so well. I would, therefore, infer that if the printers follow this copy [*The Black Arrow*] absolutely, they will probably get punctuation &c. just as Mr. Stevenson would desire." Princeton University Library.
6. RLS to E. L. Burlingame, received 26 October 1887.
7. RLS to Sidney Colvin, 17 May 1892.

be thought of as indifferent to minor details. Like most modern writers, Stevenson wanted the physical details of the printed text to illuminate and reinforce the substantive meaning. This is nowhere more clearly illustrated than with the punctuation of *Falesá*, which Stevenson saw as organically related to the story's purpose and meaning. Wiltshire, the semiliterate trader who narrates the tale, was not schooled in English grammar. Stevenson deliberately chose a point of view that would enable him to use an oral and colloquial style, free and familiar in its language and rhythms, a style that served the main objective of replicating the Pacific world that he knew so well. The punctuation was an integral part of that aim.

PUNCTUATION

Since all the printed editions of *Falesá* reveal a pattern of punctuation markedly different from that of the manuscript, the immediate task is to determine the extent of the corruption and its effect on the story. My procedure will be to examine in sequence each device (comma, semicolon, etc.) altered by the printers. For the most part I have selected examples that were changed in all the printed versions. Thus if a comma was deleted in the copyright and Cassell editions, but remained intact in the galley proofs and periodical issue, I have not cited it in my commentary. Furthermore, I have restricted my examples wherever possible to those that illustrate only the general alteration under discussion.

Commas deleted. One feature of Stevenson's style is the separation of a brief introductory phrase from its main clause by a comma, a practice that extends on occasion to phrases following fuller stops within the sentence. All these commas are systematically deleted from the text, undoubtedly on the assumption that they are excessive punctuation, stopping the thought after it has barely begun. But for Stevenson the stops are both a means for emphasis and a way of conveying the oral tone of the narrative itself. "With that [,] I gave him the cold steel for all I was worth." With the comma deleted, the entire sentence becomes the unit of meaning. The comma is used to focus attention on both parts, heightening the phrase that refers back to a previous incident and placing weight on the main clause, with its dramatic intensity.

One of Stevenson's commonest tactics is to use *and* to introduce a complex sentence, and to separate the clauses with a comma: "And that was all I saw of that precious gang [,] until what I am about to tell you."

The conjunction could also appear in the midst of a longer sentence: "My conscience smote me when we joined hands; and when she got her certificate [,] I was tempted to throw up the bargain and confess." In each instance the comma slows the narrative, keeps us connected with Wiltshire (whose delivery of the story we are always aware of), and focuses attention on the syntactic element that precedes the comma. Stevenson's pattern is to suspend the main element until the end of the sentence, thereby building tension and suspense. The pause implies a causal connection between the separate elements, and it directs attention to Wiltshire's thinking. It is not happenstance that a story dealing with the education of a derelict trader should turn so prominently on a syntax in which the "I" is a key device and the thought expressed is encountered or discovered in the process of the narration. For this reason alone the comma is an essential and supple device. It allows us access to Wiltshire's mental process, the way he tries to understand what is going on around him. The removal of commas blurs distinctions between clauses and runs them together, thus distorting the effects that Stevenson intends.

In our examples so far Stevenson's use of the comma is conscious and calculated. Its removal was not a correction so much as an elegant improvement. But other cases are less problematic. Stevenson uses a comma before *that* clauses as a matter of course, offending all the compositors, who carefully remove every one of them. "It was in one of these still times [,] that a whole gang of birds and flying-foxes came pegging out of the bush like creatures frightened." The separation strikes the reader as odd and just slightly disturbing, for it divides the main clause from its defining subordinate clause, thus causing a disjunction in the reader's mind. Yet the pause is not an eccentricity of Stevenson's; it is a mental pause, invoking the preceding sentence through the repetition of the word "still," then moving forward to the new incident—the interruption of the quiet. And if we recall that Uma, who has related the story to Wiltshire, is also one of those frightened creatures, then we can see that Stevenson's punctuation, far from being eccentric, contributes to the mood and tension of the scene.

In all Stevenson's *that* constructions the same method is at work—a subordinate clause is separated by a comma from its main clause, thus acting as a conclusion or reflection that derives from or is attendant on the main clause. The technique fixes Stevenson's overall method of making gradual yet methodical connections between details that eventually lead to a conclusion. The pauses, unexpected from a grammatical point of view, are crucial from a rhetorical and psychological one.[8]

Stevenson also employs commas to set off a prepositional phrase from its main clause, thus freeing it from its moorings and allowing it a degree of autonomy: "But of all this [,] on the first morning [,] I knew no more than a fly." The statement begins a new paragraph, and Wiltshire summarizes, through the pronoun, the preceding paragraph's description of Case and Randall. The phrase, which Stevenson virtually makes parenthetical, becomes suspended and reflective, implying more than its statement that Wiltshire learned all these things about Case after that morning. The pause, with its hint of knowledge that Wiltshire was later to discover, teases the reader into wondering what happened to create such a reflective mood in Wiltshire. There is a sense of innocence thoroughly ended, or converted, and a sense of despair, even bitterness, in the simile. What we witness is Wiltshire recounting his hard-won knowledge, trying to start at the beginning, yet not being able to begin with a blank sheet since the events already have happened—he has been a party to them all—and he is no longer an innocent. Stevenson's freeing of a clause or phrase from its controlling element, making it no longer restricting in function, gives it a suggestiveness that contributes to the uncertainty of the narrator's dilemma.

Stevenson sometimes uses a comma to separate a compound predicate: "I went home [,] and asked Uma if she were a *Popey*, which I had made out to be the native word for catholics." Or: "There I sat [,] and had a meal which was served us by Case's wife." It is as if the going home and the asking Uma a question, or the sitting and the eating, were separate and unrelated events, and in a sense they were—in Wiltshire's mind. In his narration he breaks down the events into single entities and then tries to reconnect them. In this way he attempts to establish some order among events, some causality or sequence that will suggest a degree of control, or a semblance of rationality.

But Stevenson appears to destroy any order when he employs clearly eccentric punctuation. "Now to see these two when they came aboard [,] was a pleasure." The disjunctive character of this sentence is not funda-

8. An enormously popular handbook on punctuation declared: "Commas are properly used, not for the purpose of showing where pauses are to be made in reading, but to present to the eye the proper grammatical instruction of the sentence, so that one reading a new book or a newspaper cannot fail to perceive the meaning at first sight." (Marshall Bigelow, *Punctuation and Other Typographical Matters* [Boston, 1893], p. 9.)

mentally altered by removing the comma that splits the subject from the verb. The syntax itself is striking and not a little unsettling, the inversion of the normal order making us take special note of the statement. "Now," a weak introductory element, inserts doubt into a statement that seems to be unambiguous. And by splitting the subject from the verb with the comma, Stevenson leaves us momentarily suspended, suddenly rendering questionable whether it was in fact a pleasure to see Case and Randall when they came aboard.

In the following example the deletion of a comma simply softens the emphasis. Wiltshire is incensed at Case's ally, Black Jack. " 'Here, you [,] nigger!' says I." The comma enforces the racial slur, making it more dramatic and vicious. We are aware of Wiltshire's own consciousness of Black Jack as a "nigger," and of his willingness to resort to such a vile epithet. The importance for the characterization of Wiltshire, not to mention for the theme of the story, in which slavery is a prominent motif, is shown by Stevenson's changing "Black Jack" in the manuscript to "nigger" in a subsequent sentence.

Stevenson's use of the comma throughout his text is calculated and deliberate; its persistent and systematic deletion diffuses and distorts his meaning in particular cases and in the overall artistic scheme.

Commas added. In the second sentence of *Falesá* Stevenson writes: "The moon was to the west, setting [ ] but still broad and bright." By supplying a comma after "setting," the dynamic picture that Stevenson creates is diminished and a static one introduced. Stevenson's aim is to sustain a tension between two opposing ideas, a tension captured in this illustration descriptively and expressed throughout the text with the same conjunctive device in various ways. "She agreed with this [ ] but kept considering"; "the five chiefs looked at me civilly enough [ ] but kind of pointed." Since a central concern of the novel is epistemological, what Wiltshire knows and how he comes by that knowledge, it is not hard to understand why Stevenson would weave into the texture of the narrative a pattern that suggests things are never quite what they appear to be. Wiltshire contends with this throughout, and Stevenson's omission of the comma in these conjunctive sentences enforces that tension, perhaps even ambiguity. Adding a comma not only separates conflicting ideas and behavior, but makes them seem artificially separate and therefore logically appropriate. What is lost is the uncertainty in Wiltshire's mind, the ambiguity inherent in the process of trying to accommodate these contradictions.

Commas were in fact added extensively to Stevenson's text. The seventh rule in Bigelow's well-known typographical handbook proclaimed that "adverbs and short phrases, when they break the connection between closely related parts of a sentence, should be separated by commas from the other portions of the sentence."[9] Stevenson, however, rarely used a comma after introductory conjunctive adverbs or adverbial clauses. *However, indeed, moreover, altogether,* and *now* are all given their supportive stops by the printer. The pauses not only slow the sentences but impart a formal and artificial tone to the writing. Wiltshire's speech is an effort to be gentle and fluent; the adverbial introducers are merely devices that tie the sentences to their previous connections. And indeed these terms do confirm the logical semblance of the story. It is as if the more Wiltshire uses words like *however* or *altogther* or *indeed* or *now* the more he declares his understanding and control over the events described and experienced. Yet it is an irony that the more Wiltshire declares his control the less he actually possesses. The sense of a deductive process or method, of a man attempting to understand his surroundings, is further exhibited in a series of words and phrases that become a leitmotiv throughout. "I let him go [ ] of course, for I had passed my word"; "and [ ] besides [ ] I was blazing to that height of wrath that I could have bit into a chisel." Commas are supplied around *of course* and *besides* on at least ten occasions, thus strengthening otherwise weak words. The printer's emphasis calls attention to them as devices, and actually converts them into bookish intrusions.

There is no question that the additional stops in *Falesá* alter the impact and the meaning of the story. *Perhaps, doubtless, maybe, I suppose*—these not only capture the natural and fluent rhythm of Wiltshire's mental journey, but they contribute to the doubt and uncertainty that dominate the novel. Doubt is diminished when words that serve to suggest it are converted into mere stage directions. Furthermore, in cases where there is a dramatic or heightened action, and the sentence is short for the purpose of emphasis, to add a comma can be counterproductive. " 'I *am* tabooed [ ] then?' I cried." Stevenson's emphasis is effectively neutralized by the comma, which creates an emphatic "then" and a sentence that would sound thoroughly unnatural if it were spoken. And since it *is* spoken by Wiltshire, the alteration is an especially dismal one.

As a matter of aesthetic principle Stevenson tended to avoid commas

9. Bigelow, p. 15.

where the sense of the language could be clearly understood. But the printers disregarded this. Where *or* functions as a common coordinating conjunction, a comma is regularly added: "whether it was Case stubbing his toes within a few yards of me [ ] or a tree breaking miles away, I knew no more than the babe unborn." The absence of the comma before "or" yokes together two nearly antithetical details, and thus identifies Wiltshire's fear and anxiety as he waits in the darkness for his enemy. Stevenson binds elements together that are then unbound in the printed texts. "That's Falesá [ ] where your station is, the last village to the east"; "where she had come with a white man [ ] who was married to her mother and then died"; "and her red flowers and seeds [ ] that were quite as bright as jewels." The addition of commas alters more than the tone of the colloquial address. In the second example Stevenson insinuates ambiguities that the printed version omits. Without the comma the white man and Uma's mother and his death are linked in the reader's mind. It is as if the white man married Uma's mother and as a consequence died. Separated, the man and his marriage are distinguishable, signifying only that Uma's stepfather was white. But that is not really the point; it is not uneventful to be a white and to marry a native woman; it separates one from everyone else, and it may have dire consequences. Therefore it is not a white man, *comma,* married to a native girl. The restrictive construction and absence of commas serve to fashion the equation linking the white man with death. Furthermore, the equation has a dramatic irony since Wiltshire is himself a white man who marries a native girl. He does not die, of course, but he comes close. Stevenson is setting up the terms by which white and brown relations function in the Pacific, and these terms are reflected in Wiltshire's syntax and punctuation.

Stevenson's working conjunction in *Falesá* is *and*. With unerring regularity the printers alter its effect with commas. "For all that he is very shrewd, and [ ] except in politics or about his own misdemeanours, a teller of the truth." The missionary is here describing Faiasao, "an old rascal of a chief." By linking the conjunction directly to the qualifying phrase and forcing the phrase between the main and subordinate clauses, Stevenson introduces doubt into the whole question of Faiasao's veracity. At the least it makes us aware that Mr. Tarleton takes nothing for granted, that he takes Faiasao's story for its information and utility, but that he is well aware of the limitations of the storyteller. With the additional comma the text loses its ambiguity, no longer holding the contradictory elements in suspension.

And may connect elements that are directly related, united, or only apparently related. For Stevenson, it is an all-purpose device, and his use of it reveals a good deal about his methods and aims. For one thing, it allows him to add details to Wiltshire's narrative by a process of accretion. The following example completes a long interpolated story that Uma has told Wiltshire of six young men, all but one of whom lost their lives to women devils. "Against all expectation, they came safe in a dreadful tempest to Papa-mālūlū, where the palms were singing out [ ] and the cocoanuts flying like cannon balls about the village green; and the same night the five young gentlemen sickened [ ] and spoke never a reasonable word until they died." Stevenson's description of the storm is made vivid through his images of the swaying palm trees and the coconuts that are dropping off them as if they were shot from cannons. The ferociousness of the wind through the trees is expressed through the sound made by the leaves and the falling coconuts. To separate the two elements by adding a comma after "singing out" diminishes the sense of their simultaneity and connectedness. Similarly in the second half of the sentence, the five men did not simply sicken and then die, which is the effect conveyed by adding a comma after "sickened."

Stevenson's habit of eliminating (or rather avoiding) excess punctuation is in part related to his desire not to call attention to common modifying expressions. Yet it seems that neither compositors nor proofreaders ever missed an opportunity to create a parenthesis where Stevenson avoided one. Conventional intrusions that Stevenson tried to emphasize by minimizing punctuation are converted back to stage directions: "He spoke eager [ ] I thought, and that surprised and pleased me." These changes are endemic to all the printed texts of *The Beach of Falesá*. And they occur as well, in a minor though exasperating way, in those passages where Stevenson attempts to capture the native pidgin dialect. " 'White man [ ] he tell me you no got.' " "White man" is at least a descriptive phrase as Uma uses it; and it is also a reference to a particular white man, Case. The revised form sacrifices Stevenson's ambiguity in a vain effort to correct an alien syntax.

Commas altered. Commas were also changed to dashes, exclamation points, periods, and, most often, semicolons. Some of these alterations are strictly grammatical; for example, an exclamation point is substituted for a comma after an interjection: " 'O [,] well, I suppose he was ashamed to tell the truth,' says Case." Stevenson, however, does not use punctuation for grammatical purposes alone. In matters of emphasis, he prefers to let the language and context create the drama, rather than to impose it arbitrarily with an exclamation point. " 'Damn Ese,' she cried," is a lot less obtrusive, both aurally and visually, than " 'D—n Ese!' she cried," as it was rewritten. Stevenson's aim, to be unobtrusive in his punctuation, can be seen when the dash is substituted for the comma: "The moon was up, a tropic moon," becomes "The moon was up—a tropic moon." The beauty of the sentence, which depends on repetition as well as on a slightly exotic word and barely audible softness in the speech, is vitiated by the obtrusive dash. Stevenson's style depends on a fine adjustment of the ear to both word and rhythm; altering his punctuation creates a different and far less supple voice.

Although dashes are most frequently substituted for commas—nearly two dozen examples can be cited—periods and semicolons are also substituted regularly. Either might be used when a comma separates one clause from a second one beginning with *I*. A period was supplied with "He was rich as well as powerful [,] I suppose that man was worth fifty thousand nuts per annum." A semicolon was supplied with " 'That's so,' said I [,] 'I had forgotten.' " Stevenson's intention is to leave as little separation as possible between his statements, so long as the connections are apparent; and the comma offers a casual and loose means of relating elements. "My leg was broke, my gun was gone [,] Case had still ten shots in his Winchester [,] it looked a kind of hopeless business." The speed of reflection and the immediate danger of the moment are what Stevenson captures. He is not bothered by the use of commas in an unparallel series, or by the inequality of the elements that are ungrammatically connected. But printers and proofreaders were bothered. Although Stevenson's version is not stream-of-consciousness prose, it effectively reveals Wiltshire's quickened perceptions at a moment of mortal terror.

The substitutions of periods, semicolons, dashes, and, in two cases, colons for commas all serve to reduce the informality and ease of the narrative, and at the same time slow its movement. Where Stevenson prefers loose connections—for the sake of tempo, rhythm, verisimilitude, and psychological realism—the compositors and proofreaders prefer full stops for the purposes of clarity and consistency. Clarity, however, means nothing more than regularity, or punctuation according to rule. There is absolutely no concern in these alterations for meaning or context. Far from being slipshod, the printers that Stevenson railed against were exceedingly careful and unerringly consistent. But it was a consistency antagonistic to the aims and methods of Stevenson's art.

Semicolons. There are indications, especially in Stevenson's correspondence, that his use of the semicolon was habitual in his writing, and not peculiar to his fiction. But my concern is the use of the device in *Falesá*, and how it was regularized and changed by the compositors and proofreaders. By far the major alteration was the substitution of a comma, particularly where Stevenson deploys the semicolon before a conjunction. "It's a cruel shame I knew no native [;] for (as I now believe) they were asking Case about my marriage." Wiltshire here is caught in a quandary. He does not know the native language, which is a crucial point since this declares his isolation and estrangement from his environment. Furthermore, it puts him at the mercy of Case, whose interest is clearly antithetical to his own. In retrospect, Wiltshire believes that Case and the chiefs were talking about his sham marriage. But Wiltshire does not *know* this; he simply believes it. What is known, and what does require emphasis, is the initial statement. The semicolon gives weight and voice to the declaration, providing it with an independent existence and in effect an independent integrity.

As we would expect, the conjunction most frequently used in tandem with the semicolon is *and*: "Then it came back [;] and the first thing I attended to was to give him the knife again." Together the conjunction and semicolon imply a connectedness between syntactic elements that is more arbitrary and capricious than logical. *And* links the syntactic units in a chain that seems coherent and rational. But the semicolon is the triggering device, revealing Stevenson's habit of stringing together details in a loosely punctuated sequence. Through the lucidity of his prose Stevenson discloses a fundamental irony: that things in the world are *not* clear and lucid; that the more one aspires to express their coherence, and is successful at it, the more one recognizes the futility of the pursuit; that language itself, and the way in which we organize and build our sentences, provide an illusion at odds with reality. The semicolon, with its pause—virtually a full stop, yet not the end of a sentence—fits Stevenson's scheme beautifully: it is neither a terminal mark, like a period, nor an intermediate device, like a comma. This ambiguity is apparent even in simple compound sentences, where Stevenson almost invariably uses the semicolon. He does not separate the clauses with periods, nor does he use commas. It is as if he were not sure whether to make his statements independent or to connect them. There is an uncertainty built into his style that is encouraged or assisted by his use of the semicolon. There are physical details, incidents (including the behavior of people), and emotions that need to get written down. These are transcribed by Wiltshire (Stevenson) and duly reported to the reader. They are presented in sequence, and sequence, as we have seen, suggests causality or the semblance of order. Yet the semicolon is Stevenson's great dissembler. For it is opposed to order and sequence. It can apparently be placed wherever the narrator prefers: "but the shell went off (in the usual way) before he threw it [;] and where was papa's hand?" The final element, a question attached at the end, has no grammatical relation to the statement that Papa Randall lost his hand while dynamiting for fish. Yet Stevenson is so accustomed to the semicolon, to employing it where sentences are uncertain about their beginnings or endings, that it is no oddity to find it here. For the compositor, however, the substitution of a comma whenever a semicolon stopped a final clause that began with *and* was an unalterable rule. And so in this case, when the comma aims at diminishing the eccentricity of the anacoluthon, the change is regularly adhered to.

The semicolon can also be used as a functional means to set up contrast within a sentence. The concluding sentence of the first paragraph of Chapter II reads: "It was mortal still and solemn and chilly [;] and the light of the dawn on the lagoon was like the shining of a fire." In this case the two clauses seem to have a relationship to each other that depends upon their descriptive functions. The night is cold and the dawn casts a glow over the water. But it is neither night nor morning; it is both dark and light. Here Stevenson clearly envisions a connective between the parts of this sentence. The scene is a miniature of hell—the cold and the fire that exist simultaneously, as in Milton's "the parching Air / Burns fire, and cold performs the effect of Fire" (*Paradise Lost*, II, 594–95)— and Stevenson does not want that picture made obvious through the use of a comma, which would spoil the rhythm and deflect from the two distinct images, both of which join to form a powerful vision. The sentence is the whole unit, but within that are two separate syntactic units, and it is these that need to retain their integrity.

The semicolon before the conjunction connects elements that are bound together through sense, but it is frequently a connection that is loose and sequential. "Uma asked me in the morning if I was going to 'pray'; I told her she bet not [;] and she stopped home herself with no more words." The affection, or rather devotion of the wife to her husband, is emphasized through the virtual isolation of the final clause; it stands as a separate statement, commenting upon and completing Wilt-

shire's declaration. The comma eliminates the long pause and thus reduces Wiltshire's consciousness of the impact of the act, and makes it
appear as if he assumed it the most natural thing in the world for Uma to
stay home because of him. Thus the punctuation mark can aid in the
delineation of character, in conveying motive and perception.

In all these examples the semicolon has preceded a conjunction and
been altered to a comma. This represents the great majority of semicolon
alterations in the novel. But other instances are equally illuminating.
"He was yellow and smallish [;] had a hawk's nose to his face, pale eyes,
and his beard trimmed with scissors." Or: "This was the first time, in all
my years in the Pacific, I had ever exchanged two words with any missionary [;] let alone asked one for a favour." In both cases Stevenson
clearly disorders our sense of grammar and even our expectations of what
is normal or logical. Yet it reveals how his style is linked to his narrator's
character, to the verisimilitude he strives to develop. The semicolon
provides the narrator with a reflective or meditative delivery. It is as if a
statement led him to pause, and then continue on with a supplementary
statement—connected to be sure, and not separated by periods, but not
so linked as they would be by a comma, where the supplementary statement is not so much additional as integral to the primary clause. The
initial clause establishes the declarative observation—that Wiltshire
had never spoken to a missionary in the Pacific. The semicolon stops that
clause; then, almost as an afterthought, although clearly significant since
it indicates how far Wiltshire has come around in his attitude towards
missionaries, Wiltshire adds: "let alone asked one for a favour." This pattern supports what we have already seen of Stevenson's punctuation,
namely that it creates the sense of a mental process both orally (as it is
articulated by the narrator) and mentally (as the narrator recalls it in the
process of narration). "Her fingers nestled into mine [;] I heard her
breathe deep and quick [;] and all at once she caught my hand to her face
and pressed it there." The removal of the stops and the substitution of
commas veil both the emotion and Wiltshire's effort to recreate it. Each
of the first two clauses has its own sentiment and its own memory that
Wiltshire recalls, dwells on, and uses to build to the climactic act of
Uma's devotion. To put them all in a sequence that glides over them and
makes them part of a facile and quickly delivered sentence is to do an
injustice to the emotion. Wiltshire knows this—his first coming to know
Uma, his appreciation of her love for him, his gradual awareness of her

respect for him as a man—and he cherishes the recall that his narrative allows him.

If the change to a comma is the most frequent semicolon alteration, the change to a period is also common. This occurs most often when a semicolon precedes a personal pronoun, as in Uma's declaration to Wiltshire of her love and respect for him because he is not concerned that she is a native: "Now you come marry me [;] you big heart—you no 'shamed island girl." By separating the statements, as a period does, the continuity between them is sacrificed. The period breaks the two thoughts and gives each a visibly distinct emphasis that is actually false to the psychology of the situation.

Stevenson uses the semicolon as a loose connective, a device for tracing the narrator's reflections and for representing speech and thought as accurately as possible. The connections never show up as sharply as they do in native dialect, when they often seem odd and incongruous. The following sentence is part of a comic exchange between Uma and Wiltshire on island devils: "Victoreea he big chief, like you too much [;] no can help you here in Falesá; no can do, too far off." The contradiction between Queen Victoria's being a "big chief" and her powerlessness to do anything about the devils in a remote Pacific island does not trouble Uma in the slightest. She placates Wiltshire by acknowledging the Queen's partiality for him (thus undercutting Wiltshire's patronizing manner toward Uma's provincialism), and the repetition later on in the sentence underlines the reality that Uma sees sharply but Wiltshire chooses to ignore—that his being a British subject is of little use in the distant Pacific. Thus the positive (Victoria's liking for Wiltshire) and the negative (his helplessness in Falesá) are fused in a single sentence that is appropriately stopped by semicolons, rather than by an additional period. The unity of thought and style is built up through the language, the repetition, and the irony and playfulness that turns back upon Wiltshire, as well as through the larger irony that it is Uma, an illiterate native girl, who sees this all.[10]

Colons and dashes. Stevenson uses the colon for clear and unambiguous ends. Emphasis is among the most immediate of these: "Yes [:] that's

---

10. There are two other minor changes: in a few instances semicolons were altered to colons, and in nine instances to dashes. The revised punctuation creates an emphasis that is not Stevenson's and functions intrusively, halting the narrative in order to remind or inform the reader of the action's significance. This is especially true with the alteration to the dash.

Case, sure enough, and the darkie." Or: "Thinks I to myself [:] 'I must find some way of fixing it so for Master Case.' " In both cases the colons are changed to commas. In the first example, the short pause makes the sentence smooth in its delivery but deprives it of the suspense and even awe implied in the long pause following the word "Yes." Stevenson gives the affirmative the tone of a declamation, and the colon draws our attention to it: an attitude is conveyed in the "Yes" that the captain announces as he looks through the telescope at the approaching boat, an attitude that shapes the reader's response to the character. In the second example the colon draws our attention to a stage direction that Wiltshire makes a number of times in the novel ("Thinks I to myself," "I thought"), a stage direction that exhibits Wiltshire as a reflective agent. The colon is thus Stevenson's means of calling the reader's attention to the statement that follows the device as well as the one that precedes it: "But I do know now, and I don't mind [:] I love you too much." Wiltshire's apology to Uma, when he discovers that she was an innocent victim in Case's scheme, prompts his declaration. The colon sets the declaration off more emphatically than the substituted punctuation, maintaining its dramatic integrity, impact, and meaning in the context of Wiltshire's character and his understanding of the events.

The dash, although used less frequently than the colon, is allied with the latter in Stevenson's style. It provides an extra pause, longer than a comma, yet not so long as a colon. It functions more as a rhetorical device, adding or introducing a statement that supplies more information or elaborates upon the preceding statement: "Here's a pretty mess to have made [—] as if I wasn't bothered enough anyway!" The substitution of a comma minimizes the emphasis that the dash conveys by its suspension, and reduces the angry tone that Wiltshire carries with him. The voice is actually quieted with the comma, whereas the dash keeps the pitch up, a pitch that begins with the opening charge of Uma's messiness. Stevenson himself indicates that the dash is a device for heightened emotion in the following quotation: " 'E le ai!' says she [—] she always used the native when she meant 'no' more than usually strong" (the alteration is to a period). Here, as elsewhere, Stevenson aims for the most fluid narrative consistent with realism and suspense. That is, he wants to provide the plot details that are essential for moving the story forward or revealing character. Thus the statement above tells us something about Uma: that naturally enough when she is excited she reverts to her own language. But it tells us that almost parenthetically. Stevenson first indicates that the "*E le ai!*" is a response to Wiltshire's query about whether Uma is a Catholic. Since the reader cannot be expected to know what the expression means, Wiltshire's pause enables him to translate it for us, almost matter-of-factly, as a bystander, without halting the action and thus drawing attention away from the main concern—which is Uma's view, and indirectly the islander's view, of Roman Catholicism.

Dashes contribute to the effective pacing of the story. The substitution of commas creates shorter pauses and reduces the emphasis, the heightened emotion occasioned by additional discovery; and the substitution of periods stops the action and separates elements in the sentence that are in fact intimately connected. Taken as a pair, the dash and colon bear nowhere near the burden of work assigned the comma and semicolon, and consequently they are not as thick in the text or as often tampered with. Yet they are not immune. The tampering that I have described demonstrates that even among infrequent devices the pattern of revision thrives, affecting style and meaning, altering tone, disturbing rhythm, and undermining Stevenson's artistic methods and achievement.

Terminal punctuation. It is clearly easier to tamper with internal than terminal punctuation, since changing the latter requires a decision tantamount to rewriting both the original sentence and the subsequent one. Nevertheless, terminal punctuation marks were changed, the period receiving the most attention. The simplest change is from a period to an exclamation point. There are fewer than a dozen instances in the novel. The following example comes from Case's cynical and amused description of a derelict's death. " 'Get the priest,' says he, 'get the priest, don't let me die here like a dog [.]' " Of course, the substitution of the exclamation mark indicates emphasis. But it also creates an inflection, a tone of voice that is unduly heightened and melodramatic, and thus it diminishes the emotion that Stevenson aims at conveying. The plea by Buncombe for absolution, although mediated through the scurrilous voice of Case, is a genuine one, and is meant to be heard as such by the reader. The emotion comes through the language and our visualization of the scene—Buncombe in convulsions, lying in filth, thousands of miles from any home that he might have once known, and a South Seas life to atone for—and it is not meant to be diluted or, in effect, mocked, as the intrusion of the exclamation mark indeed accomplishes.

The two other alterations of the period are to semicolons and to commas. Thus sentences are extended, with pauses substituted for final stops. The first change comes when a semicolon precedes a clause introduced by a conjunction: "She told me the thing was well known, and with handsome young men alone, it was even common [.] But this was the only case where five had been slain the same day and in a company by the love of the women devils." The full stop allows Stevenson to emphasize the statement that precedes the conjunction, and the conjunction then introduces a qualification. The separate sentence highlights the qualification by giving it an independent status; with the semicolon it is grafted onto the first sentence and made a little less dramatic. Thus the terminal period gives Stevenson an opportunity to focus a comic point: Uma's intuitive knowledge of sexuality is contrasted with her naive and almost blissful acceptance of the most bizarre superstitions. The full stop is necessary for the timing of the narrative, for the full comedy of this story.

In a number of cases where a semicolon is substituted for a period, the sentence following the period begins with a conjunction. As I have already said, Stevenson had no objection to beginning a sentence with "But" or "And" or "For," although the compositors and proofreaders were often hesitant to do so. Stevenson's practice, however, speeded the narrative forward. Although a period is a terminal stop, and a semicolon a partial stop, the period reduces the length of the sentence and builds shorter, staccato-like syntactic units: " 'All right,' said I [.] 'Stay where you are.' " Or: " 'Look here,' I said [.] 'You're pretty sick.' " In these cases the revision is always toward the substitution of a comma for Stevenson's period. What is lost is the drumbeat of the narrative and the dramatic effect that Wiltshire always maintains. He is aware that he is relating a narrative, and his "said I" or "I said" serves as a punctuation mark for himself as a storyteller. It is analogous to the omniscient narrator's "I say" that slips into his sentence, often bracketed by commas, and that reminds the reader the storyteller is never far from his story. The final punctuation of the personal stage direction reminds the reader of Wiltshire's involvement in the events. By placing this within commas the revision makes it nothing more than a stage direction, and it obliterates its function as an element to characterize the narrator.

HYPHENS

Stevenson uses hyphens sparingly, to the point where they function as devices that carry aesthetic meaning. Yet the sparsity of the hyphen could never be gleaned from a reading of the printed text of *Falesá*. Hyphens abound—and there is no question but that conventional printers' practices are largely responsible. Theodore Low De Vinne, one of the most influential printers of the day, declared: "When to set up two meeting words as two words, when to consolidate them in one word, when to connect them with a hyphen, are problems that the compositor has to decide almost every hour. He finds it very difficult to get authoritative instruction. There are not many authors who compound words uniformly, and the dictionaries differ, and sometimes are not consistent in rendering words or phrases of similar class."[11] In line with contemporary practices, printers simply adopted rules that they consistently applied in their particular houses or magazines. The practice of compounding through hyphenation was an ingrained one, and it represented a conservative printing stance.

Stevenson's style was realistic and colloquial, and it drew on a speech that inevitably contained a large number of compound words. But his instinct was to write them as single words, without a hyphen. *Figurehead, cockfighting, topknots, seabathing, treetops, duckshot, toyshop, secondhand*—these all had hyphens supplied by the printers. Words that Stevenson pronounced or heard as single words were written that way, like *cocoanuts* or *cocoapalms*. He wrote with his ear tuned to the language, aiming toward greater ease and flexibility in idiom, and away from the "literary" or the conventional. But printing conventions often get the better of art. The following is the native chief Maea's final comment to Wiltshire: " 'No talk. Go up tomollow. You my friend?' " Even in Stevenson's time, the hyphenation of *today, tonight,* and *tomorrow* was something of a vestigial practice. Yet, analogically, if *tomorrow* is *to-morrow,* then *tomollow* should be *to-mollow.* The added hyphen gives a non-word legitimacy, and the verisimilitude of the scene, through the replication of the dialect, is effectively undermined.

By far the largest number of alterations in Stevenson's text came about through the printer's creation of compound words where Stevenson used two separate words. The briefest comparison of the manuscript journal that Stevenson kept at Silverado with the printed text of *The Silverado Squatters* illustrates this well: "At sunrise and again late at night the scent of the sweet bay trees fills the canyon. . . . Azaleas make a big snow bed just above the well. . . . Some sort of red flowering stone plant clings about the overhanging rocks."[12] This passage was rewritten and devel-

11. Theodore Low De Vinne, *Correct Composition* (New York, 1901), p. 61.

12. John Jordan, *Robert Louis Stevenson's Silverado Journal* (San Francisco, 1954), p. lxvi.

oped for the book, and "bay trees," "snow bed," and "stone plant" all appeared with hyphens. Stevenson's departure from convention is evident throughout. De Vinne states, for example, that "first-rate, second-rate, and other terms signifying degrees are compounded."[13] Stevenson writes: "He was accomplished too; played the accordion first rate." De Vinne declares that "compounds that end with *boat, house . . . room,*" among others, "are frequently printed with a hyphen."[14] Stevenson writes: "the crew were singing and the paddles flashing in the missionary boat." Or: "My public house?" These are all hyphenated in printed versions.

For Stevenson, hyphens are a form of punctuation that not only alter rhythm but change pronunciation. A compound word is not the connection of two words so much as the creation of a third word. Overall the pattern of creating hyphenated compounds makes substantives where they do not exist. In effect, the alterations create a heavier style than Stevenson's more moderated and suggestive one: "wedding-nights," "land-crabs," "deck-cargos," "fruit-trees," and "banjo-strings" are far more substantial with hyphens than without. What for Stevenson are descriptive phrases become transformed into absolute objects. The addition of hyphens is so pervasive as to lead to clear-cut gaucheries: "The night was nearly come; the village smelt of trees, and flowers and the sea, and breadfruit cooking." Instead of "breadfruit" functioning in a series with "trees," "flowers," and the "sea," "breadfruit-cooking" becomes the fourth item in the sequence.

If the sentence is spoken aloud, one sees how the rhythm is disrupted and the sense distorted: "breadfruit-cooking" might be a special kind of cooking, like Italian or Chinese cooking, rather than what Stevenson intends, the aroma of breadfruit while it is being cooked. Perhaps Stevenson's avoidance of hyphens, of compounding words as prolifically as the printers, exhibits a more acute and a fresher perception of the objects in the world, or of the language necessary to describe those objects.

We can see in Stevenson's manuscript and in the printed versions of the text two distinct styles, each in conflict with the other: the one easy, idiomatic, and oral, the other formal, conventional, and written. It is clear that the production of a book demands, on the part of compositors

13. De Vinne, p. 67. Also: "Ordinal numbers compounded with the words *rate* and *hand* are usually written with a hyphen; as, first-rate, fifth-rate; second-hand, fourth-hand, etc." (Bigelow, p. 62).

14. De Vinne, p. 73.

and proofreaders, a uniformity that strips the individual text of its uniqueness. In the case of *Falesá* this process runs counter to the artistic aims of the author. Stevenson's restraint in his use of the hyphen is consonant with the rest of his punctuation. *Falesá* is a story of process and discovery, and the freer and sparer the punctuation, the less fixed and encased the story.[15]

SPELLING

Stevenson suffers an undeserved reputation as a poor speller. Colvin considered him constitutionally unable to spell correctly, as he implied in a letter to Baxter on 10 January 1893: "Had he any kind of excuse for spelling Simon Symon [in *David Balfour*], or is it only part of his general vagueness in orthography?" John Jordan, who worked with Stevenson's holograph manuscript in preparing his edition of the *Silverado Journal*, came to a similar conclusion.[16] Both judgments reflect an attitude toward Stevenson's spelling that exhibits itself in the alterations in *Falesá*. And both neglect the obvious factor of Stevenson's background. Whereas everyone applauded his use of Scots material in "Thrawn Janet" and the major novels, no one recognized how this might extend down to the spelling. For Stevenson, a Scots spelling was often more natural than an English one. In the manuscript of *Kidnapped*, for example, he titles one chapter "The Muir." It emerges in the first edition as "The Moor." This is not to say that there was anything approaching a uniform Scots spelling in the last half of the nineteenth century. But it is clear that Stevenson's perfectly understandable and coherent spelling was anglicized by the printers to make it more accessible to a primarily English and American audience.

Stevenson had a tendency to double consonants in some words—

15. Unlike the printers, Stevenson employed hyphens sparingly, and with deliberation and artistry. An example is found in Wiltshire's reference to the beachcomber who carried Uma and her mother around with him, "one of these rolling stones that keep going round after a soft job." Wiltshire's contempt for this beachcomber (whom he hears about only through Uma) comes out in the next sentence: "If a man wants an employment that'll last him till he dies, let him start out on the soft-job hunt." Stevenson has taken a perfectly apt phrase and, through the hyphen, converted it into a substantive that ridicules a derelict Wiltshire has reason to despise, if only for his past relationship with Uma. By the third sentence the phrase becomes an image for the fraud and hypocrisy of the man: "Anyway, this beachcomber carried the woman and her daughter all over the shop . . . where there were no police and he thought perhaps the soft-job hung out." Needless to say all the printed texts delete the hyphen, robbing Wiltshire both of his irony and his contempt.

16. Jordan, p. lxxii.

murmurred, obeissance, jackalls, gunfull—and those were all corrected. Other changes, however, appear more arbitrary: *galoshes* becomes *goloshes* in the British editions, but is restored to *galoshes* in the American text; *ricketty* is rewritten *rickety*, although both forms are acceptable in the *NED*; *waggon full* is changed to *wagonful*. But a number of Stevenson's spellings are phonetic transcriptions of what he hears. "These she fixed upon me with a wrapt expression that I saw to be part acting." The printers supply "rapt." Although the *NED* lists a source for "wrapt" as late as 1809, it describes the form as obsolete and erroneous. But in Scots dialects the "w before r was still pronounced in words like *wright, wrong, wrote, wrought* . . . till well on to the end of [the nineteenth] century."[17] Similarly, in "Case and the negro were parasytes," the spelling of the final word is justified by Scots practice, where *y* commonly represented the diphthong *ai*. On one occasion Stevenson's phonetic transcription proved more accurate than the standard form: "and behind her ears and in her hair, she had the scarlet flowers of the hybiscus." The change to "hibiscus" lost the sound still heard in the islands today, which was undoubtedly what Stevenson tried to imitate. He was clearly tuned to the sounds of speech, and he made every effort to reproduce them as faithfully as possible.[18] Indeed, his sole criticism of Melville as a writer of the South Seas was that he was deaf to the languages of Polynesia.[19]

Stevenson's desire to convey pronunciation accurately appears in his use of macrons and accents. "She was a Sāmoa woman, and dyed her hair red, Sāmoa style." The macrons are eliminated here and in the final reference to "the Sāmoa woman" at the end of the novel. If the *NED* is our guide, not only does it fail to print the word with the macron, but it gives an essentially different pronunciation, *Sămoa* instead of Stevenson's more accurate *Sāmoa*. As for accents, the following line of dialogue by Case is illustrative: "It's half empty to this blesséd hour." Given the heat of Case's retort, the accent is essential not merely to convey the pronunciation but to emphasize the imprecation. Case's language is not meant to be tamed or softened; it is as much a key to his character as an expression of the milieu. "Blesséd" is a curse—a shorthand for *damn* or its equiv-

17. *The Scottish National Dictionary* (Edinburgh, n.d.), I, xxiii.

18. As early as 1879, in *The Amateur Emigrant*, Stevenson supplied this footnote to "Arkansas": "Please pronounce *Arkansaw*, with the accent on the first" (ed. James D. Hart [Cambridge, Mass., 1966], p. 106). In *Falesá* he again called attention to an American pronunciation during his proofreading of the "Bottle Imp" version: "Please pronounce *pappa* throughout."

19. *The South Seas* (London, 1890), p. 26.

alent. Removing the accent strips the harshness from the word, muting Stevenson's portrait of Case's brutality.

Stevenson's ear for language as it is spoken is especially evident in the following example. Talking to a French priest, Wiltshire says: " 'Don't you speak any English?' said I. 'Franch,' says he." The spelling is nothing more than Stevenson's effort to approximate the sound of Galuchet's response; yet the conversion to the appropriate "French" flattens the voice and obliterates Stevenson's realism. What is particularly distressing about this example is that Stevenson anticipated just this error on the printer's part, and protected against it. Although his cursive "Franch" is clear and incapable of being misread, above the cursive he printed in unmistakable capitals "FRANCH." There is no excuse for the change—no misreading, no judgment required for the spelling of an alien or Scots word, and of course nothing in the word itself to encourage censoring. Not twenty words later Stevenson uses "French" appropriately, when Wiltshire says "He tried me awhile in the French."

The habit of correction is so ingrained in all the stages of book production that the author's clear text is powerless against its force. That this subversion of Stevenson's intention might only reveal the assiduous care given his text by compositors and proofreaders—the proofreader "is always adjudged in fault if he passes any misspelled word that can be rightly spelled"[20]—is ultimately beside the point. For it nonetheless betrays the paternalistic attitude toward the writer that is built into the entire process of preparing his copy for print.

CAPITALIZATION

"The first word of every full sentence should begin with a capital letter."[21] Stevenson occasionally defies this dictum of De Vinne: "Talk about meat and drink! to see that man lying there dead as a herring filled me full." Wiltshire's glorying in Case's death is conveyed by tying together the two sentences as if they were one and not allowing for a pause between them. In instances where there is emotional excitement or rhetorical questioning ("Where should I look for a better? how was I to find as good?") Stevenson deliberately avoids capitalizing in order to simulate the quickness of speech and maintain the pace of the narrative.

The avoidance of capitals serves the realism of *Falesá*. Stevenson

20. De Vinne, p. 300.
21. De Vinne, p. 108.

writes: "It seems she was born in one of the Line islands." The capitalization of "Islands"[22] creates the impression that Wiltshire thinks of "Line Islands" as a compound noun lifted off the pages of an atlas—when it is nothing more than a part of his unconscious and habitual speech. In fact Stevenson is unerring in reproducing the easy, casual way that islanders do indeed talk about their homes. Further, the uncertainty of the sentence is underscored by the lowercase letter: Uma comes from *one* of the Line islands (not from the substituted collective noun), and these are among the smallest and most isolated in the Pacific. Wiltshire's vagueness about her background only deepens the mystery that characterizes the story.

The absence of capitals also plays a role in characterization. Case, in his victimization of the drunken Captain Randall, regularly refers to him as *papa*—with a lowercase *p* that underlines his contempt for the man. This is always raised by the compositors. But the most interesting example concerns Wiltshire, and involves a key word in the novel—*kanaka*. The term, common throughout the Pacific, is generic for *man*, and is defined by Webster's as "a native of the Sandwich Islands."[23] Thus it qualifies as a proper noun and is capitalized in all the printed texts. Yet the word is not nearly so neutral as this definition implies. Used by non-Polynesians, and occasionally by Polynesians themselves, it can be a scurrilous epithet. As early as 1865 Lorrin Andrews listed as the fourth definition of the term: "In a *vulgar, low sense* as sometimes used by foreigners, a Hawaiian, a native, in distinction from a foreigner."[24] And years later Bret Harte provided a graphic illustration of the word in his story *The Heritage of Dedlow Marsh*: " 'So,' he said, facing her quickly, 'for the sake of a lot of riff-raff and scum that's drifted here around us—jest for the sake of cuttin' a swell before them—you'll go out among the hounds ez allowed your mother was a Spanish nigger or a kanaka.' "[25]

For Wiltshire, whose livelihood depended upon the exploitation of brown labor, the word rolled off his tongue at every turn: "You know what kanakas are," or "I know how to deal with kanakas," or "You don't find me turn my back on a parcel of kanakas." Yet against all his experi-

22. "Names of all geographical zones or sections of the world, when used as proper nouns, take a capital, as the Arctic, the Tropics, the Levant, the Orient" (De Vinne, p. 119).

23. *An American Dictionary of the English Language* (Springfield, Mass., 1890). All subsequent references to this dictionary will appear as *W* 1890.

24. Lorrin Andrews, *A Dictionary of the Hawaiian Language* (Honolulu, 1865), p. 256.

25. Bret Harte, *The Heritage of Dedlow Marsh and Other Tales* (Boston and New York, 1889), p. 33.

ence he comes to love and marry a native girl, someone who refers to herself as "no common kanaka."[26] Wiltshire's slow recognition that *kanakas* might be the equal of whites is made all the more dramatic because of the superiority he exhibits toward them throughout. By capitalizing *kanaka* the epithet is muted—as is Stevenson's rendering of Wiltshire's transformation.

Not only is characterization affected, but also the tone and forcefulness of the story. The harshness and violence that border the narrative at all turns are conveyed through the casual disgust exhibited toward all proper authorities. Throughout, the major authority, the only one that offers a moral or ethical basis for judging conduct—religion—is treated with contempt. Falesá is a place where Catholics vie with Protestants and where all missionaries are condemned by the traders. And it is the traders, for the most part, who report the action and whose speech we witness. Yet throughout the book not only are the generic words like *Catholic* and *Protestant* given initial capitals by the printers, but the epithets as well. " 'Hillo!' says I, 'are you a papist?' " The anti-Catholic sentiment augments the anti-Christian theme in the novel, a theme as fundamental to the traders as their greed for copra. The traders' distrust of Christianity, which is also a distrust of missionaries, is reflected in Wiltshire's bargaining with Mr. Tarleton: "I want a service, I want two services in fact; and if you care to give me them, I'll perhaps take more stock in what you call your christianity."

The contempt and hostility expressed by Wiltshire toward religion is weakened if religious terms are dignified through capitalization. The conventions of printing promote a typography that is indifferent to the interpretive demands of the text. There are, for example, two instances where *bible* is printed with a lowercase *b* in the galleys. "Talk all-e-same bible. Bring out a bible here, Uma, if you've got such a thing, and I'll kiss it." Clearly the lowercase *b* was transcribed because it was unmistakable in the manuscript. Yet it was quickly altered by the proofreader for the *Illustrated London News*. And after that all references to *bible* are printed *Bible*, although many of them appear in one of the most comic scenes in the novel and are the occasion for broad humor. For the proofreader, however, the proprieties must be observed. Instead of portraying the way religion functioned on an island in the Pacific in the last years of the nineteenth century, the simple expedient of supplying capitals every-

26. Near the end of the novel Stevenson wrote: "Uma had stuck to her tree like a sensible kan"—he quickly deleted the anticipated "kanaka" and substituted "woman" instead.

where introduced an entirely different religion. For a reader in 1892, *catholic* would not evoke the same response as *Catholic*. Only an illiterate or bigot would write *catholic*. Yet that is precisely what Stevenson is driving at—the education of a bigot: how Wiltshire comes to be delivered of prejudices that are so ingrained he cannot consciously rid himself of them. Indeed, part of the point of Stevenson's method is to reveal the discrepancy between what we believe and what we feel, between what we know in our minds and what we understand through our hearts.

Stevenson's lowercase letters represent nothing more than the language and attitudes of the novel's protagonists—crude, vulgar, and violent as they are. All the major epithets—*papists, nigger, kanaka*—are emblematic of the abuse of men and the exploitation of women that form a major theme of the story. They are a means of subjugation and humiliation. The racial and religious slurs are a part of the language of *Falesá*. And language is Stevenson's central theme. For it is language that defines the self, and just as Wiltshire struggles to find his own identity through the language, so the profane and scurrilous language helps to define the world of Falesá. The alteration of Stevenson's lowercase letters is in fact the substitution of words that call forth other meanings: *dissenters* are not pious mourners in their chapels, hypocrites in Wiltshire's eyes, but rather *Dissenters*, a group with a history and a respectability that runs counter to the linguistic context in which Stevenson places them. The raising of the letters deprives the story of its integrity and introduces instead a scheme of values that are unquestionably more acceptable, appropriate, and tolerable than Stevenson's.

The correction of Stevenson's spelling, the hyphenation and de-hyphenation of his compounds, the capitalization and de-capitalization of his words—all are efforts to impose uniformity, to stamp the work out according to a mold. This is an abuse of art as surely as the cancellation of a word, or the substitution of another one. In *Falesá* the appearance of the printed text not only subverts Stevenson's meaning, but contradicts it, presenting a smooth surface, a veneer of rationality that belies everything the story itself says: that chance and fortune are facts in human life, that we are all victims of our past and of ourselves, and that the unknown, perhaps the unknowable, is always with us, indeed is embedded in our language.

4

The Language

Fascinated by languages, Stevenson found a paradise of tongues in the South Seas. The names of places, of plants and fruits, held an exotic charm for him. In *Falesá* he possessed a subject that allowed him to meld the array of dialects and idioms that he had absorbed in his travels as an "emigrant" across the continental United States, and on his cruises through the Pacific. At his command were American slang, Samoan, pidgin English (what the professional linguists called Beach-la-mar), and the ubiquitous sailor's talk, a range of terms and expressions that were commonplace at one extreme and required a glossary at the other. The reviewer for the *New York Times* was riveted by the language: "An older school which read Herman Melville and his 'Typee' may have had its blood quickened, but Mr. Stevenson gives one a vertigo. Where or how did he ever catch the roughness of the beach comber, words of the past and present that are the slang of Seven Dials or Five Points, such as are vollied from the mouths of the toughest of the tough?"[1]

The *Times* reviewer was quick to recognize that Stevenson consciously sought to use everyday language. He also saw that it was a tactic enabling Stevenson to reproduce vividly the Pacific world during the closing years of the nineteenth century. Thus the language of the sailor, Polynesian, and trader, however violent and crude, was an integral part of the novel's themes of racism, colonialism, sexism, and cultural disintegration. If realism was the aim, a realism that depicted the savagery of Pacific history, a savagery linked to white behavior rather than Polynesian practices, then language became the appropriate embodiment for that realism. And

1. *New York Times*, 9 April 1893, p. 19. Seven Dials is in London, Five Points in New York.

just as realism in art was considered offensive by many late Victorians,[2] Stevenson's realism in *Falesá* was particularly reprehensible. It subverted widely held prejudices about the superiority of white European civilizations to brown-skinned peoples; it raised a violent, semiliterate Englishman to the level of a hero; and it connected the white and brown worlds through the illicit coupling of the hero with a native girl.

There was no simple way a compositor, proofreader, editor, or publisher could contravene the meaning of the story, short of destroying it altogether. The most reasonable procedure was therefore to manipulate the language, which was systematically gutted through additions, deletions, and substitutions. Although in each case there is a clear reason for the alteration, the overall effect is to contain Stevenson's criticism of imperialism and to domesticate, as far as possible, the violence and vulgarity of the narrative. These intentions were not, of course, at the front of each compositor's or proofreader's mind. But a pattern was operative, and the result was a tamer book.

The manipulation of Stevenson's language begins with the deletion of the letter *s* at the ends of words. There are at least a dozen instances, of which the following are representative. "Pretty soon after, the nigger was turned out of the island[s] for stealing from white men." Or: "It's my belief a superstition grows up in a place like the different kind[s] of weeds." The first change subdues the decisiveness of Black Jack's banishment from all the islands, and the second creates an illiterate expression. Both changes detract from the colloquial authenticity of the speech. On the other hand, dropping the *s* from "hilts" ("he shook hands with me up to the hilts") modernizes an old-fashioned expression and obscures the fact that Wiltshire's language is laced with archaisms.

But if dropping an *s* can deflect the tone, the addition of an *s* can alter the meaning: "The first thing I lighted on was a case of gin . . . and partly for the girl's sake, and partly for horror of the recollection[s] of old Randall, took a sudden resolve." Randall's degeneracy, recalled to mind, terrifies Wiltshire. Revised, however, the sentence reads as if Randall's stories, or recollections, are responsible for inducing the horror.

2. On the problems that Henry Vizetelly, Zola's British publisher, faced with censors, Samuel Hynes writes: "It is not surprising that Vizetelly found himself in Criminal Court . . . charged with publishing an obscene libel titled *The Soil: A Realistic Novel.* . . . Vizetelly had made another mistake when he attached that subtitle to the book: in 1888 'realistic' was almost an obscenity in itself, and certainly in many minds it was a promise of obscenity to follow." (*The Edwardian Turn of Mind* [Princeton, N.J., 1968], pp. 259–60.)

A story as colloquial as *Falesá* contains numerous contractions: these have frequently been expanded, including those that are attempts to capture the slurred speech of the alcoholic Captain Randall. When Case maliciously tells Wiltshire that "Papa's pretty full this morning"—from gin—Captain Randall objects: " 'Never took such thing my life!' cried the captain, indignantly. 'Take gin for my health's sake, Mr Wha's-ever-your name. 'S a precaution'ry measure.' " The reality of Randall's alcoholism is revealed through his dropped words and slurred syllables. Yet in the printing Randall is sobered up. He does not become a teetotaler, but his speech improves with a little help from the compositors and proofreaders. "Never took such thing my life" becomes "Never took such a thing in my life," and "precaution'ry" becomes "precautionary."

Although there is no way to decide in every case why particular alterations were made, it is clear that they were largely implemented on an ad hoc basis. Syntax, context, structural relation—these had no relevance to the effort to impose order on the copy. As one expert proofreader, T. J. Venn, advised his fellows, "The object of adopting a certain 'style' where a number of compositors are employed is to secure uniformity or consistency in the setting of matter."[3] Venn was talking specifically about accidentals: but the habit of imposing order spread itself to all aspects of the text, and especially to those forms of expression that plainly lacked gentility. Stevenson's realism offended the notions of correctness that were the essential technical and moral equipment of the compositors and proofreaders. And those notions proved more powerful than Stevenson's own style. Thus even the pidgin English was revised: "Suppose I drink gin, my little wifie he 'fraid." Here Wiltshire's fond mimicry of Uma's language is corrected by changing "he" to "be," a change that makes syntactic sense for an English speaker but not for a South Sea islander.

In small ways, then, the revisions aimed at softening the roughness of the realism. That they could not do so without distorting the nature of the story is beside the point: there is no other explanation for changes as arbitrary as those just described. Or the following: " 'You see, you get copra,' says she, the same as you might offer candies to a child." In this example "said" replaces "says." The *NED* states: "The 3rd singular present is often substituted *colloquially* for the past tense *said*. Hence in vulgar speech or jocular imitations of it, *says I, says you* = 'said I,' 'said you.' " But this is not exactly what happens in *Falesá*; that is, "says" does not

3. T. J. Venn, *Manual of Proofreading* (Chicago, 1897), p. 28.

function solely as a vulgar use of the third-person present for the past tense. It actually works to give a degree of intimacy and realism to the dialogue, by placing the speech in the present, although the action occurred in the past. Of course we know, as does Wiltshire, that it is all past action. But the use of the present tense gives immediacy to the narrative, contributing a sense of current action that makes the story more intense and dramatic. It also highlights Stevenson's belief that the past, forever being fashioned and refashioned in our thoughts, never really leaves us.

An interesting turn on this alteration appears once in the text: " 'Well,' said I, 'you're a nice kind of a white man!' " This is the only occasion where Stevenson's use of the past tense is converted to the colloquial "says." Although it is dangerous to speculate on a single example, the fact that this is the only conversion of "said" to "says" suggests that the change had something to do with the content. Wiltshire's remark is both ironic and reflective: that is, he accuses Case of abandoning him without any knowledge of the local language or customs. He charges him with betraying a fellow white man for a "parcel of kanakas." The common bonds that connect all whites, Wiltshire realizes, prove no more durable than a sand castle. That discovery is startling for the reader as well: the alteration reduces the authority of the narrative voice and blunts Stevenson's exposure of the spuriousness of white superiority.

The alteration of individual words is consonant with a pattern of change aimed at formalizing Stevenson's style. In "I could have tore my hair," the reader is given "torn." In "I suppose it might be eight o'clock when I took the road, loaden like a donkey," the reader is given "laden." Stevenson was quite conscious of his linguistic inelegancies, as his manuscript revisions indicate. Initially he wrote "I could have torn my hair out," blotted "out," then went back and put a line through "torn" and wrote "tore" over it. He was dissatisfied with "out," for that made the sentence a cliché, and he changed "torn" to avoid a hybrid that was formally correct but ludicrous in tone. All the printed texts disregarded Stevenson's correction.

Stevenson's familiarity with American speech, and the problems it posed for the printers, is evident throughout *Falesá*. An example involves the Americanism "hollered": "At that she ran, and the pig after her, and as the pig ran it hollered aloud, so that the place rang with it." Again: "I guess that pig would have hollered so as to surprise himself." The word, variously described as a corruption of *hollow* or *halloo* or *holloo*, appears regularly in American slang dictionaries with Stevenson's spelling as its

"Yankee pronunciation." Compositors, however, ordinarily do not use slang dictionaries as their office authorities. Hence they printed *hollaed*, assuming the form *holla* and putting it in the past tense. But *hollaed* can only have looked odd to any reader, a printed word with no relation either to the context or to the sound of the expression. In subsequent editions, therefore, *hollaed* was contracted to *holla'd*, presumably on the theory that the *e* was silent and the apostrophe might suggest something of its colloquial intention.[4]

Style is the bone and sinew of Stevenson's story. Slang, colloquialism, obsolete diction—these join together in forging a bastard idiom that makes *Falesá*, linguistically, Stevenson's most original book. The compositors and proofreaders, whose first obligation was the reputation and respectability of the publishing house, attempted to legitimize the language by correcting it. Often they added or supplied words to the text. In some cases these were restorations of Stevenson's own deletions. Wiltshire is admiring the missionary boat that has just arrived with Mr. Tarleton: "and I considered it for half a minute with a bit of envy perhaps, and then strolled towards the river." Originally Stevenson wrote "down towards the river" but crossed "down" out. It was reinstated in print. Or: "and though I am not due at this end of the island for a month, I will see what can be done." Stevenson's first version read: "I must just see what can be done." The printed text was "I will just see what can be done," a form that incorporates his final decision on the holograph page, and half of his original phrase.

Although it is difficult to explain this, the following example presents no problem: "The same night of our marriage, Galoshes called round, made himself mighty civil, and got into a habit of dropping in about dark and smoking his pipe with the family." Stevenson deleted "and" before "made," and the compositor again revived the deletion, thus giving an independent status to Father Galuchet's civility and reducing the sense of manipulation that is implied in his behavior without the conjunction. There is no deeper reason for the restoration than the desire for symmetry and balance. Stevenson's own deletions in his manuscript are consistently geared to pruning the style to its barest and hardest lines. For him it was a matter of both art and attitude, a desire to capture and create a poetic voice in the most unpoetic of settings.

4. M. Schele de Vere, *Americanisms* (New York, 1872), p. 489. The galleys, the *Illustrated London News*, and the copyright issue printed *hollaed*; the "Bottle Imp," Cassell, and Scribner's editions substituted *holla'd*.

Even the smallest additional word can tarnish the effect. "The sun was now up, but it was still behind the cape of woods: say quarter of an hour had come and gone." The compositor for the galley proofs made two sentences ("The sun was now up, but it was still behind the cape of woods. Say quarter of an hour had come and gone"), and the proofreader for the *Illustrated London News* added a word ("Say a quarter of an hour had come and gone") that was picked up in all subsequent editions. Another example is in the missionary's chilling recital of Underhill's live burial. "Namu, my pastor, whom I had helped to educate, offered up prayer at the hateful scene." The change to "offered up a prayer" alters the meaning, for Namu is offering *prayer*, a generalized plea for surcease from the evil that is felt by all at the burial site. The alteration to a single prayer cheapens the feeling at the burial scene and virtually dismisses the native pastor's devotion as a cynical sop to convention. And this merely by the addition of an article.

One of the curiosities about the additions is that a number appear to be efforts at clarifying what seem to the compositor or proofreader vague or lax constructions. There is always the desire for grammatical correctness: "others swore there was no sorcery at all" becomes "others swore that there was no sorcery at all." Stevenson's avoidance of *that* clauses makes his style more open and less stilted than the revised version. However, the printer's desire to avoid confusion—to make exact what Stevenson deliberately makes ambiguous—resulted in genuine oddities. Here is Wiltshire describing his marriage by the missionary: "So we had in two of the crew to witness, and were spliced in our own house." This is corrected to read: "So we had in two of the crew for to witness, and were spliced in our own house." Of course Stevenson's ambiguity, suspended in the infinitive of the verb, becomes a mirror of the moral ambiguity in the story. Wiltshire believes he is doing the decent thing by marrying Uma. But the crew cannot testify to that, and their serving as proper witnesses to a Christian ceremony is an irony not to be missed. The service after all is conducted in the native language, to please Uma, but the whole intent of the ceremony is white and Christian. What is a Christian ceremony to a woman who believes in island gods and devils? What does it mean to Wiltshire, who has clearly rejected Christianity? And yet the forms bind, and insofar as Wiltshire believes he is doing the honorable thing, then the marriage is useful and good. The compositor's discomfort with Stevenson's elliptical manner, his effort to straighten out a disturbing syntax, leads directly to the awkwardness of the revision.

A final example of the effect of adding to Stevenson's text should suffice to indicate just how determined the compositors were to alter what they considered inexact and vague. "Case had as good as said he would pot me if ever I got copra." This goes through two revisions. In the first (galleys, *Illustrated London News*, and copyright issue) it becomes "if ever I got my copra." And in the second (the "Bottle Imp" volume, Cassell's edition, and Scribner's edition), it reads "if ever I got any copra." Both revisions make specific what Stevenson implies. The character of Wiltshire is altered in the first instance, and the plot is reduced to the level of a sensational adventure in the second. Stevenson's version leaves unstated the precise stage at which Case might let Wiltshire survive with a piece of the copra market. Doubt is built into the sentence. The function of the additional word is to justify Wiltshire in the eyes of the readers—even a caged animal will fight to preserve himself—and therefore authorize the violence that he commits against Case at the end of the novel: "and the best thing I thought I could do was to get in first with the potting."

Deletions of words and phrases throughout the text demonstrate the continuing vigilance of the compositors and proofreaders. One of the common expressions subjected to correction is the comparative *kind of a*.[5] Here, for example, Wiltshire suddenly realizes Uma's great beauty: "It came over me she was a kind of a countess really." The deletion of the indefinite article formalizes the colloquial voice and makes the noun phrase more restrictive. Stevenson's form is open and tentative, dramatically appropriate since it supports the theme that appearances are deceptive: a *kanaka* girl looks like a countess; a rough trader hides a gentleman (" 'I'm the sort of a man God made me,' says I"); and a mysterious sickness conceals a murder (" 'Some kind of a sickness,' says the captain"). The mystery of the plot, which is Stevenson's emblem for our lives, is diminished by the deletion of the indefinite article.

The compositors and proofreaders, trained on manuals and textbooks, were expected to revise for correctness and grammatical propriety. But *Falesá* presented them with a more complex problem: it substituted ambiguity in language for certainty. Yet efforts to resolve ambiguity failed because the ambiguity was not merely that of an occasional word or syntactic construction but that of method and manner, a function of the colloquial style itself. The slang that Stevenson employs elicits an am-

---

5. *W 1890* defines *a kind of* as: "Something belonging to the class of, something like to;—said loosely or slightingly."

bivalence in the reader, who presumably knows the correct forms—what Mark Twain called "the sacred proprieties"[6]—but is forced to repudiate them in the act of reading the novel. He is asked to ally himself with a man who swears like a sailor, distorts the English language, and peppers his talk with words and expressions drawn from different jargons. The reader stands in almost the same position to Wiltshire's language that Wiltshire is in with respect to the natives' language: each is mystified by the other's tongue.

Henry Bradley, in his entry on "Slang" for the *Encyclopaedia Britannica*, states that "a slang expression . . . may be used for the purpose of concealing the meaning from uninitiated hearers, or it may be employed sportively or out of aversion to dignity or formality of speech. The essential point is that it does not, like the words of ordinary language, originate in the desire to be understood."[7] Nothing could be more ironic, nor more brilliantly realized from an artistic point of view, than Wiltshire's repeated declaration that he wants to be "plain," when the instrument for his plainness, his language, is itself a device for concealment. The irony must be further compounded when we consider that Stevenson himself was an admirer of the plain style. As he said to Henry James, he wanted to create a style that was a cross "between a ledger-book and an old ballad."[8] Yet as Stevenson knew, and as his successors like Kipling and Hemingway discovered through his example and their own discipline, plainness has its own kind of opacity, and the farther one goes toward capturing that elusive goal, the farther one seems to be from it. It is as if the effort to communicate by mastering a clear style is contravened by the realization that the style may not be a means for discovering any truth at all, except, paradoxically, that ambiguity and irresolution are the conditions of life.

For simplicity's sake, it would be convenient to turn to unequivocal bowdlerizations of the text, since these would need no explanation. Yet the principles for deleting oaths or objurgations are neither simple nor consistent. "He was in a hell of a taking was the priest" comes out "He was in a rare taking was the priest." The alteration almost disguises the meaning. "Taking," of course, is the key word—not "hell." The expression is colloquial, defined in *W 1890* as "agitation; excitement, distress

6. Mark Twain, *Roughing It* (Berkeley, 1972), p. 305.

7. *Encyclopaedia Britannica*, Eleventh Edition (Cambridge, 1911), XXV, 207.

8. Janet Adam Smith, ed., *Henry James and Robert Louis Stevenson* (London, 1948), p. 233.

of mind," and in Wright as "a fit of petulance or temper."[9] We can assume that the meaning is not apparent to all readers, and the oath therefore helps to define it in context. Here the complete distress of the priest (as Case tells the story), "hammering on the door outside . . . and singing out it was a soul he wished to save," is undermined by the colloquial inappropriateness of the language. Stevenson shows the cynicism and callousness of Case, who in the next breath describes Adams's death in sailor's slang—"Johnny had slipped his cable"—as if Adams had killed himself rather than been murdered by Case. On another level Stevenson demonstrates the duplicity of language. The oath is hardly an oath; Case is not using strong language. By turning the incident into a jocular account Stevenson illustrates how language can be used against itself, serving different purposes simultaneously. The priest was not petulant: he was truly terrorized by Randall and fearful that he would not save Adams's soul, not a small thing to the Frenchman, although a matter of complete contempt to Case. Thus Stevenson's language serves both to characterize the speaker and to expose more profoundly the uses and misuses of language itself. The bowdlerization alters the impact of the statement and reduces the snide mockery of Case's tone, thus forcing us to try and think what "taking" might mean and deflecting our recognition of Case's evil. *Priest* and *hell*—the sanctity of the church and the language of the gutter—should not be conjoined on the printed page.

If "rare" was substituted for an expression more ironic than objurgatory, then what happens in the reverse case? Is *hell* always deleted? In fact it appears sporadically throughout the text. Consider the following two examples: "Wha' 'n hell's he want Uma for?" and "He was nipping gin all the while . . . and every now and again he would ask me why in Hell I wanted to marry Uma." For Billy Randall, soaked in gin and lying in filth, the oaths coming out of his mouth are profane in the extreme. They indicate a man low enough to frighten even Wiltshire, who has seen his share of Pacific low life, and they exemplify the casual profanity that characterizes this world. What happens in the revision? In the first instance the offending expression was removed, and the sentence succeeded in making no sense. The error, however, was picked up in the

9. Joseph Wright, *The English Dialect Dictionary* (Oxford, 1898–1905). Wright cites S. R. Crockett, an effervescent admirer of Stevenson, for *rare taking*: "Well—then I tell you the fat wench was in a rare taking" (*Little Anna Mark* [London, 1900], p. 364). Crockett conceivably lifted the phrase from his idol, unaware that it was spurious, and in turn became the acknowledged source for Wright.

"Bottle Imp" volume, and "hell's" was restored to its proper place. Yet ten sentences down the page this same edition deletes "in Hell" (our second example). One principle of textual censorship can be stated: censor profanity if it can be done without disturbing the commonsense reading of the sentence. Thus to delete "in Hell" from "he would ask me why in Hell I wanted to marry Uma" proved a simple task for the compositor. He did not need to exercise his ingenuity to invent a substitute phrase that would retain the syntax and meaning.

It is not altogether accurate to call the compositors censors, although they are engaged in bowdlerizing Stevenson's manuscript. In their eyes they are cleaning the text up and making it palatable for a mass audience. Although the distinction might seem a nice one, there is no other way to explain the utter inconsistency in deletions and bowdlerizations. Early in the novel Wiltshire says of Case: "He had the courage of a lion and the cunning of a rat; and if he's not in Hell today, there's no such place." There is nothing in the least puzzling here. The capitalization of "Hell" works both as a means of identifying the place and as an intensifier of Wiltshire's attitude. Readers, who know nothing at this point of Case, cannot but be struck by the word and its capitalization. Wiltshire's hatred cannot be gainsaid. The revisers do not delete "Hell" for a good reason: it is crucial to the syntax. They do, however, lowercase the initial capital. The alteration reveals the dilemmas facing them. Their instinct was to delete and censor all profanity. Yet in every instance the problem was different. In one case, they could not remove *hell* without destroying all sense; in a second case, they deleted the word and substituted a neutral one; in a third case, they eliminated it with no one the wiser; in a fourth case, they removed it despite the resulting nonsense, and restored it in a later edition when the need for sense overcame the desire for purity. In an effort to control the objectionable material the compositors resorted to an essentially ad hoc censorship—one whose main aim was to delete all offensive language, and, if that proved impossible, to reduce the offensiveness of the language and minimize its impact.

I have not considered the question of whether Stevenson himself might be inconsistent. At the end of *Falesá* Wiltshire observes: "But I'm bound to say he gave a pretty sick view of the dear departed's prospects, and seemed to have his own ideas of hell." The meaning here is the same as in Wiltshire's earlier quotation ("if he's not in Hell today, there's no such place"). But the tone is decidedly different. Stevenson is so attuned to voice in his writing that he instinctively capitalizes or lowercases let-

ters, depending upon the voice of the speaker. In the last quotation Wiltshire is understandably quieted by the occasion of the burial and the
anticlimax following the violent night. He sticks to his belief that Case
went to hell, but he makes no special plea for it. In the first example,
when Wiltshire begins the story, the recall of Case activates his intense
hatred for the man and the episode that he is about to narrate. It is as if
the memory of the past is sufficient to revivify the experiences of the past.
Yet by the end of the story the narrative has a way of calming even the
most intense hatreds. The storytelling purges Wiltshire of the animus
that is evident throughout—and thus hell is not so powerful an idea in
Wiltshire's mind, or rather its force, its stipulated meaning, does not
require the emphasis that he gives it at the beginning.

That Stevenson's characters use so much profanity is not unusual. The
world he draws is not picturesque but brutal, and the verbal violence is
merely part of the general violence of the novel. " 'Damn Ese,' [Uma]
cried," and Wiltshire himself says, "You might think it was funny to hear
this kanaka girl come out with a big swear. . . . [She] meant the word
simple and serious." In other words, Uma is not using "damn" as a profanity but rather in its theological meaning, condemning Case to hell.
But the mere prospect of profanity is sufficient, and the word is printed
"D—n." The *NED* in its definition of the word "used profanely" says:
"Now very often printed 'd—n' or 'd——'." The casualness with which
Wiltshire uses *damn* is concealed perhaps by the fact that he frequently
uses the term *damfools*. " 'I never saw such damfool kanakas as you people
here,' I said once to Uma, glancing out of the window at the starers."
And the sentence emerges: " 'I never saw such fools of kanakas as your
people here,' I said once to Uma, glancing out of the window at the
starers." The revision naturally separates Uma from the rest of the kanakas, and thus obliterates the fact that in Wiltshire's mind, at this time,
Uma and the "damfool kanakas" are one and the same.

Wiltshire's violent speech to the missionary contains a similar con-
demnation: "I'm just a trader, I'm just a common, low, god-damned white
man and British subject, the sort you would like to wipe your boots on."
What is important about Wiltshire's declaration is the view of the white
trader that he exhibits, a disgust and contempt that shocks even the
missionary, whose view of traders is not very favorable to begin with. The
idea that "god-damned" might be more than an imprecation, that it
might contain Wiltshire's own deeply ingrained view of his future life, of

the punishment he can expect as a result of the life he has lived, is validated by the contexts in which "hell" and "damn" are used in the story. We have seen how instinctive is Wiltshire's belief in hell and the punishment it offers the wicked of the world, a belief unrelieved by notions of mercy or forgiveness of the sort that temper the missionary's Christian preaching. It is crucial to Stevenson's story that we understand this: for the profanity that offends compositors and proofreaders has a dual purpose in *Falesá*. It creates and intensifies the violence and squalor of the milieu and is thus an expression of the unrestrained viciousness of the island's white inhabitants. At the same time it sets up an entire eschatology that is felt and adhered to by these same unredeemed sinners, living outside the pale of the church. From a dramatic point of view Stevenson offers the whites' profanity as a mirror image of the natives' belief in devils or *aitus*: the eschatology is in both cases equalized, although neither group puts any stock in the other's system. Stevenson thus reveals in another way the relativism of cultural attitudes or myths. Though the natives believe in their superstitions, the whites have no faith in their own. Yet the whites submit to their superstitions as a means of imprecation or objurgation. What is so profound about Stevenson's perception is how essential a Calvinistic system of rewards and punishments appears to be even to the most debased. The desire for justice (which in the story is a desire for revenge), in however primitive or brutal a fashion, survives among people living completely outside any social restraints. Stevenson uses profanity to conjure up a semblance of justice that will rationalize the world. This, of course, is the underlying quest of Wiltshire throughout the novel—to discover meaning and order, and to find some vindication for his own life. That he cannot is one of the basic ironies of the story.

But in the printed versions, *hell* and *damn*—not to mention the whole range of religious terms from *christianity* to *dissenter* and *papist*—are bowdlerized and normalized without regard for their function in the text. It does not matter whether Stevenson was always consistent in his capitalization or even spelling. The effort to circumvent his own practice and impose another, which is inconsistent in itself, creates a false impression of regularizing the style. That swearing and profanity are endemic in the novel and integral to the story is the central fact: the printers and publishers in Stevenson's day were simply unequipped to realize that there could be a structural and artistic purpose to profanity.

We have been examining additions and deletions, but there is still another category of changes that affect Stevenson's text: the substitution of words for Stevenson's own. At first glance the number of alterations is so large, and the kinds of changes appear so trivial, that one wonders why such an effort was made. A significant number of substitutions seem guided simply by a sense of correctness or appropriate form. "And she threw herself in a corner on the floor, and began to cry." "Of" is substituted for "on," and the effect is to mute the violence of the action. Stevenson's sentence has Uma throwing herself *both* in the corner *and* on the floor; it exhibits his keen sense of detail and his continuous avoidance of cliché. Many other alterations seem capricious: *may* becomes *might*; *could* becomes *would*; *I said* becomes *I cried*. Of course a number of changes could have been the result of misreadings or errors in transcription. "There she stood" turns out "Then she stood." "I was brought to a clean stand" appears as "I was brought to a clear stand."

That each of these changes alters the meaning in some way is incontestable. What is more interesting is the conscious and willful substitution of apparently trivial words. "O, that's part of a yarn I want to tell you" appears as "that's part of the yarn I want to tell you." Then there is the reverse: "*Ese* was the name the natives had for Case; it may mean foreign, or extraordinary; or it might mean a mummy apple; but most like it was only his own name misheard and put in the kanaka spelling." The final phrase appears in print as "put in a kanaka spelling." In both examples Stevenson's diction is precise and accurate. In the first instance Wiltshire is responding to the missionary's statement that he was sorry to see Wiltshire fighting. Wiltshire informs him that the fight was a part of *a* story that he is going to relate. The change refers to *the* story, as if there was one that the missionary was privy to beforehand or prepared for by some earlier reference. Logically of course "the yarn" has no antecedent, and thus is inaccurate, a syntactic suspension that has no moorings.

But more importantly, "a yarn" conveys an ambiguity that we have already seen as integral to Stevenson's novel. What yarn, precisely, does Wiltshire want to relate? The story of his relations with Case? Of his experiences on Falesá? Of his love for Uma? Of his attitude toward *kanakas* and missionaries? Of exile and loneliness? Of language? Conversely, when Wiltshire digresses on the word *Ese* and indicates that it could mean anything in the native tongue, his use of "the" consigns the entire question to the impenetrable world of foreign idiom. Wiltshire is not referring to any specific *kanaka* spelling: for him it is all a kind of non-language, a world of words with no meaning that he dismisses with a vague and offhand expression. By altering the article to "a kanaka spelling," the revision makes it more accessible and less ambiguous. That is, if we can discover the *kanaka* spelling that *Ese* corresponds to, then the prospect of finding out exactly what the word might mean becomes plausible. Yet the point of the digression, besides dramatizing Wiltshire's frustration and bewilderment in the face of the islanders' language, is to enforce Stevenson's theme that words can be understood differently ("it may mean foreign . . . it might mean a mummy apple . . . most like it was only his own name misheard") and that meaning may only be provisional.[10]

If changes of this sort are exasperating in their capriciousness, there is still a rationale behind them. Cleansing the text through grammatical improvement is one means of segregating Wiltshire, and the whites, from the brown people of the island. Thus when Wiltshire, describing his lonely stay on one of the Line islands, refers to "buying gin, and going on a break, and then repenting; sitting in my house at night with the lamp for company," and the revision, from the copyright edition onward (which meant that it was introduced after the text had been in print), reads "sitting in the house at night," we can surmise there was a desire to remove the stigma of a white man possessing a home in a nonwhite world. Even though most of the whites in Stevenson's tale are virtual outlaws ("And will you please to observe that almost all that is ugly is in the whites?"[11]), they are still white and therefore distinguishable from, and superior to, browns. Surely one of the ironies of the history of *Falesá* is that a story rooted in an exposure of white racism should become a victim of that racism, a racism expressed in the minutiae of altered indefinite articles and personal pronouns. One might grudgingly admire the tenac-

10. Although Wiltshire was not prepared to entertain the multiplicity of Polynesian languages, Stevenson himself was quite aware of them: "In the small isle of Tana, Mr. F. A. Campbell counts no fewer than six languages; and on New Caledonia I was assured there were not less than fifty; the latter figure struck me with incredulity. M. Gallet (who gave it me for a round number) immediately called into the office one of his native assistants, asked the lad what languages he could understand and which he could not, and as each was named, showed me its territory on the map. The boy spoke three; he mentioned (I think) four of which he was quite ignorant; and they were all close neighbours in a narrow belt across the island." (*The South Seas*, p. 9.)

11. RLS to Sidney Colvin, 17 May 1892.

ity with which compositors and proofreaders, and ultimately editors and publishers, proceeded to drive a wedge between the language and the story, to cover up the implications of the text from the text itself, to tone down the diction so that the latent and provocative meanings would be voided.

These seemingly innocuous and insignificant words that were substituted for Stevenson's own vocabulary illustrate the pervasive character of the alterations made to his text. What we have seen are substitutions for words that are utterly inoffensive in themselves. But in the hands of a stylist like Stevenson, the smallest words carry his meaning, and often they carry it through the tone, whose colloquial manner is itself part of the meaning. Indeed, through Wiltshire Stevenson transforms a vernacular into a poetic language, raising it from its low origins and giving it a dignity and respectability that match his own view of its functional utility. Stevenson had no superior or contemptuous attitude toward the language he was so careful to transcribe and invest with beauty, a language that never has the dullness and falsity of the rhetoric that passed for educated speech and belletristic prose (which Stevenson brilliantly mocked and parodied in *St. Ives*). Indeed, Stevenson's passionate love for language is reflected in the fact that the word "Beach" in the title of the story refers not merely to a place but to the language of Falesá, the Beach-la-mar that Stevenson prophesied would become "the tongue of the Pacific."[12]

But he was singularly thwarted in *Falesá*, as I believe he was in all his later work, by a mentality that could not see what his aims were and could not think, linguistically, in his terms. The subtleties of Stevenson's articles and pronouns, which help to chisel character and distinguish meaning, and which authenticate his style, were lost on the compositors and proofreaders. They supplied substitutes, which insured that a reader, when he passed over a sentence, would not have to pause or give a special ear to sound and meaning because a familiar word appeared in an unorthodox context. Instead he could glide gracefully over the page, automatically filling out the words and, on occasion, the clichés. The smallest changes, by offering an essentially placid substitute, significantly alter

12. *The South Seas*, p. 10. According to William Churchill, the name "Beach-la-mar" derived from a common sailor mispronunciation of *bêche-de-mer*, a name given to the edible trepang, or sea cucumber (*Beach-la-Mar: The Jargon or Trade Speech of the Western Pacific* [Washington, D.C., 1911], p. 4). For another interesting early discussion of Beach-la-mar, see Llewella Pierce Churchill, *Samoa 'Uma* (New York, 1902), p. 234.

Stevenson's text. The authority of the voice is compromised, and thus the statement loses its integrity.[13]

In the following example Wiltshire has a sudden recollection of his childhood, after he discovers Case's ingenious deception in the bush to fool the *kanakas*. "I remembered a boy I was at school with at home, who played the Case business." To revise the preterit to "remember" does more than distort the dramatic situation: Wiltshire is narrating a story, and in his narrative he is describing how at a specific moment he *remembered* an incident from his childhood. The alteration makes it seem as if he remembered the incident only now, at the time of his current narrative. The past tense is essential for consistency. But more than creating a grammatical inconsistency, the alteration destroys the quality of memory that is introduced through "remembered." Stevenson's form deepens Wiltshire as a character and presents the reader with a side that is so human as to belie the harsh and violent trader. Wiltshire at no time becomes sentimental; the memory ends with the boy being "flogged" by the master. Yet the recollection, the vignette of Wiltshire as a young boy, draws for us an ever wider picture that spreads out from the small scope of *Falesá* with its traders and *kanakas* and at the same time makes distant parts of the world seem very much alike: both *kanakas* and English boys have to grow up and see their fears exposed as groundless, and their superstitions revealed for what they are. Wiltshire's ability to make connections, to move from his idea that *kanakas* are like fifteen-year-olds to the memory of one fifteen-year-old at school, is what gives him the imaginative freedom he possesses and enables him to play the role he does in the novel. To flatten that out, as "remember" does, is to blunt the point of the story.

The flattening, as we have seen, takes different guises, although patterns are nonetheless evident. "The morning before my arrival, Vigours had been set on board the *Lion*." Vigours was carried on board because he was blind drunk. Yet "set," with its associations with objects—"to *set* a house on a wall of stone; to *set* a book on a shelf; to *set* a chest or trunk on its bottom" (*W 1890*)—clearly upset the printers' sense of decorum: the picture of Vigours deposited like cargo is too stark and graphic. The revision has him "sent" instead, thereby sobering him up, restoring his

13. There were also alterations in meaning from misreadings, probably with no motive behind them. "I made out he didn't think much of you or Captain Randall," Wiltshire says to Case. This was printed as "I made out he didn't think much of your Captain Randall." For Wiltshire's "and we cracked jests together, mostly through Uma for interpreter, because he had mighty little English," the compositors give us another character, printing "mostly through the interpreter."

dignity, and eliminating Stevenson's unorthodox and inexplicable bad taste. At the conclusion of the novel Mr. Tarleton, the missionary, is responsible for the paperwork, seeing that all the legal matters are taken care of (in the Pacific islands the missionary often functioned both as legislator and administrator): "That done, he took down my evidence, and Uma's, and Maea's, wrote it all out fair, and had us sign it." The printed version: "wrote it all out fine, and had us sign it." Stevenson's script in this instance is not problematic. The only explanation for the change is that "fair" sounds odd and "fine" seems an adequate alternative. But Stevenson's term has at least three meanings, all of which are appropriate. The missionary wrote everything down impartially, legibly, and in a manner that did not require correction. The term thus tells us something about Tarleton as a man (he is honest) and as an administrator (he attends to the compiling of documentary evidence). It does this by the meanings already disclosed and by its placement in the sentence. But the impulse on the part of the reviser is to remove the odd and unorthodox note, even where there is no racial, sexual, or political content.

Other changes are clearly the result of a squeamishness that cannot abide graphic descriptions. "He fixed his teeth in my forearm like a weasel" is changed to "he fastened his teeth in my forearm like a weasel." "Fix," an Americanism with an almost universal applicability, is cited at length in all the dictionaries of the period. It is also a word that Stevenson was partial to. Yet this alteration is not so startling as what I take to be the most remarkable change of an individual word in the novel. Wiltshire is describing Case: "He could speak when he chose, fit for a drawing room; and when he chose he could blaspheme worse than a Yankee boatswain and talk smart to sicken a kanaka." If we consider what "talking smart to sicken a kanaka" might mean, we can only imagine talking smart-ass. But why would this sicken a *kanaka*? And *sicken* for Stevenson is a powerful word that he uses almost literally ("the things [Uma] set her hand to, it would have sickened an entire horse to eat of"—changed, by the way, to the incomprehensible "an honest horse to eat of"). Naturally enough Stevenson never wrote "smart" but "smut"—which dictionaries of the period classify as slang and define as obscene language. Additionally, all the dictionaries cite "talking smut" in their sources, the NED quoting Goldsmith ("The gentlemen talked smut, the ladies laughed and were angry"), and W 1890 quoting Addison ("He does not stand upon decency in conversation, but will talk *smut*, though a priest and his mother be in the room").

The imagined sensibilities of the reader are not nearly as important as the reviser's own distaste for writing that is indelibly graphic in its expression. But the language is crucial to an adequate picture of just how low Case is: how else do you characterize a man who murders with impunity and lives among the outcasts of the Pacific islands? The portrait is essential if the reader is to understand what sort of man Wiltshire is up against—the kind of man who has monopolized the copra trade and tyrannized the natives. Case's ability to move back and forth from the language of the "drawing room" to the language of the "Yankee boatswain," and then to the language of the "kanaka," and to excel in each area, says a good deal about his abilities and the danger he presents to Wiltshire. Although Wiltshire's great trait as a narrator is his unflinching honesty before the coarser truths, even he, subjected to an uncensored dose of Case, has moments of revulsion. "Smut" is artistically right, dramatically appropriate, and truthful. But truth is not the essential factor for the compositors. If one considers the language of Stevenson's friends in their own writing—the language of Sidney Colvin or Edmund Gosse, for example—then clearly Stevenson's language is so coarse as to be repulsive. Yet it is Case's language that is repellent—Case talks smut, not Stevenson. But that distinction means nothing: the word itself is objectionable and must be expunged. What we see is an effort, possibly unconscious, to deny verisimilitude by rejecting language, as if the ugliness of Case will disappear if we refuse to say how he talks. We must recognize that from start to finish there was nothing in *Falesá* that could truly please the people who were responsible for the production of Stevenson's books and for the promotion of his reputation. They could not do anything explicit about his chosen story, his *donnée*, but they could, and they did, eviscerate it.

The larger changes reveal nothing new: motives are inconsistent and at times contradictory; attitudes fluctuate; excisions in one edition are restored in subsequent editions; and details retained in earlier texts are removed in later ones.[14] These changes are noteworthy only because the marriage certificate—a document deleted entirely from the *Illustrated London News*—has a kind of titillating interest for writers on Stevenson who believe they are making something new available to their readers. Joseph Furnas, in an edition of *Falesá* published in 1956, declared that

14. What can be said is that there was less interference at the periodical stage than at the book stage, a crucial point in evaluating the reliability of serial versions of novels as opposed to first editions.

he was restoring the novel to its original form by printing the marriage certificate in its accurate text. The Penguin edition of *Falesá*, edited by Jenni Calder, declares on the cover that it is "unexpurgated." That Furnas and Calder are not textual scholars is no sin. But they contribute to the easy, uncritical acceptance of a mutilated text. Had none of the alterations about to be discussed been made, and had the marriage certificate remained intact, Stevenson's art would have been no less abused. With a single major exception—the excision of an interpolated yarn of more than two hundred words—there were not many alterations made on a scale larger than a phrase of two or three words.

On the simplest level, a change in paragraphing to conform to composition requirements has the effect of undermining the text's purposes. Stevenson writes: "I stopped in the door, and she looked at me, not speaking, with eyes that were eager and yet daunted. Then she touched herself on the bosom. 'Me—your wifie,' she said." From the copyright edition on, "Me—your wifie" begins a new paragraph. Stevenson, especially in sensitive or poignant moments, aims for an understated and quiet treatment. He distrusts above all else language that calls attention to itself. And the same holds for gestures or behavior. For all the brutal and grim realism of *Falesá*, there is a beauty and dignity achieved through the subdued underplaying of both language and gesture. In a small way this method of Stevenson's is realized in Uma's unobtrusive yet dramatic declaration of self. She is someone—not an outcast from an alien island, chattel to be disposed of by hard traders like Case, but Wiltshire's "wifie," a status that confers on her a position almost akin to royalty.

But none of this is what Wiltshire thinks, although all of it shoots through him as a revelation, and the discovery of his love for her is made in the very next sentence, containing one of Stevenson's most striking images: "It had never taken me like that before; but the want of her took and shook all through me, like the wind in the luff of a sail." In the printed texts, this entire sequence (beginning with Uma's assertion) stands as a separate paragraph. In Stevenson's text, it is merely the climax of the paragraph that takes Uma and Wiltshire into their house after the sham marriage—and becomes in a symbolic sense their true marriage. Uma's declaration, with "the lamplight shining on her skin," is a profession of her love, a vow that is as sacred as any made on a Bible and sanctioned by a priest. To set it off in a new paragraph is to separate it from its context, from the house and the shadow and Uma's "bright" figure. On the surface the meaning has not been altered, but in a subtle way it has; through the device of a new paragraph, we are ever so slightly jarred from the illusion of reality created within the paragraph and returned to the reality of a bound book and compositional conventions. The low-keyed mood that Stevenson builds up in his work comes from his imaginative involvement with his characters and their story. Despite the violence of *Falesá*, the profound action, the discoveries crucial for character and destiny, come in quiet, reflective, and almost surprised moments. Stevenson was a psychological novelist all the time, and nowhere does this fact demonstrate itself more clearly than in a moment like this one, when Uma, half child, half woman, betroths herself to Wiltshire.

One deletion that occurred only in the *Illustrated London News* version illustrates the capriciousness of many other examples. In the first paragraph of Chapter III, Wiltshire describes the arrival of the missionary boat. "She was a long whale boat painted white . . . and the missionary under the awning, in his white clothes, reading in a book, and set him up!" The proofreader was baffled by the last phrase and deleted it. That it can be unclear is testified to by a query from Grant Richards tipped into one of Princeton University's copies of *Island Nights' Entertainments*: "Sir,— . . . Now what, I have asked myself do the last four words mean? I cannot make head or tail of the phrase. One allows for the fact that Wiltshire, the narrator, a trader, cannot be expected to use literary English; but even then the words seem to me to mean nothing in this place and in this connexion." The reply by Macmillan is quite simple: " 'And set him up' is excellent and familiar Scots and may be roughly rendered—'And isn't he fond of himself too!' In Wright's Dialect Dictionary 'Set one up' is described as 'an ironical phrase used in contempt of any one; only used in imperative,' and the following quotations are given; . . . "[15] Wright's *Dictionary* cites *Catriona* as a source for the expression. The phrase in context ridicules the missionary, whom Wiltshire is naturally resentful of even before he meets him. The phrase is restored in the copyright and all subsequent editions, indicating how closely each edition of *Falesá* was read against a copy text.

Despite this attention mistakes occurred. The galley proofs and the *Illustrated London News* both include the following passage from Chapter I, where Wiltshire is emptying the gin bottles.

I prized the lid off; one by one, I drew the bottles with a pocket corkscrew, and sent Uma out to pour the stuff from the verandah.

15. Copy 3, listed in *Robert Louis Stevenson: A Catalogue* (Princeton, 1971), p. 31.

She came back after the last, and looked at me puzzled like.

"Why you do that?" she asked.

"No good," said I, for I was now a little better master of my tongue. "Man he drink, he no good."

With the copyright edition Uma's question disappears, and the reader is left to wonder what Wiltshire is responding to with his "No good," or whether he is simply declaring a newly discovered virtue in abstinence. Uma's complete unfamiliarity with decent behavior is reflected in her look and question. The deletion is nothing more than an inadvertence, the loss of a line in setting up the text for another edition. It is, however, another small example of how *Falesá* has been distorted.

Another alteration appears in the following dialogue. Tarleton, the missionary, is reporting to Wiltshire the conversation he had with his native pastor Namu. The problem is one of quotation marks within quotation marks, at least initially. But after that the problem becomes one of absolute bungling through the entire paragraph, a job of botched transcription that is more amusing than upsetting. The entire paragraph follows, as it should have appeared:

" 'And I explain it, Misi,' said Namu in this way. 'The country in Europe is a Popey country, and the devil of the Evil Eye may be a catholic devil, or at least used to catholic ways. So then I reasoned thus; if this sign of the cross were used in a Popey manner, it would be sinful; but when it is used only to protect men from a devil, which is a thing harmless in itself, the sign too must be harmless. For the sign is neither good nor bad, even as a bottle is neither good nor bad. But if the bottle be full of gin, the gin is bad; and if the sign be made in idolatry, so is the idolatry bad.' And very like a native pastor, he had a text apposite about the casting out of devils.

Stevenson aims at a number of things at once in this marvelous little paragraph. On the one hand he is presenting a comic portrayal of an islander's confused yet apparently logical explanation for behavior that he, Namu, knows is unacceptable to Mr. Tarleton—the adoption of Catholic practices by the congregation. Stevenson of course really insists upon exposing the artificiality of an alien religion grafted onto island beliefs and superstitions. This theme runs through the novel, and it is the occasion for some sharp comedy, especially in the later chapters between Uma and Wiltshire.

What Stevenson points out here, however, is how readily Namu will accommodate any practice that appears to be directed against devils, even if the practice goes against the doctrines of the missionary in charge, in this case a Protestant. Yet the islander is knowledgeable enough to recognize that his superior Christian European will not accept any such accommodation with Catholic doctrine and practice, so he employs the technique or instrument that he knows will be acceptable to the missionary—white logic. That the logic is illogic makes no difference: it has the form and appearance of rationality and, from Namu's point of view, is immune to the criticism of being mere superstition. Stevenson recognized what many white missionaries refused to see, that the adoption of Christianity by the native islanders had little effect on their beliefs and superstitions. The alien religion was a cloak that the natives frequently wore at the missionaries' expense. And when it came down to a basic superstition, like fear of the dark, no amount of Christian doctrine could dislodge it.

In this paragraph Stevenson reveals both the innocence of the native pastor and his shrewdness. Namu argues that the sign is nothing more than the form or shell of a doctrine; and one would as soon hold the sign of the cross responsible for sinful practices as hold an empty bottle guilty of promoting drunkenness. So much seems clear in the paragraph. Yet what comes out in print? The first correction is in the opening statement, and it may have been encouraged by one of Stevenson's errors. " 'And I explain it, Misi," said Namu in this way." Stevenson erred in using double quotation marks after "Misi." He should have used a single quotation mark, because he is identifying Namu's speech, as reported by Mr. Tarleton, who provides the stage direction "said Namu in this way." All the rest of the paragraph is in Namu's words, until the final sentence. The revision, pouncing on Stevenson's use of the double quotation mark, removes the double quote from "Misi," then inserts a single quotation mark before "in this way." The sentence thus reads: " 'And I explain it, Misi,' said Namu, 'in this way: . . .' "

The revision creates a different voice altogether, reduces the sense of the native manner (the Beach-la-mar inflection), and inserts an ordered rationale where Stevenson avoids one. It is as if the logic that the paragraph mimics is in fact introduced by figures outside the story in order to demonstrate the validity of Stevenson's observation within the story. Namu, according to the revision, will "explain . . . in this way." Yet it is Tarleton who is commenting to Wiltshire on the manner of Namu's speech and explanation, a manner that symbolizes for Tarleton the linguistic and cultural impediments to converting the native to a Christian-European way of seeing or perceiving. By removing "in this way" from

Tarleton and giving it to Namu, the revision slurs Stevenson's point and gives a specious coherence to Namu's argument. The phrase, used by Tarleton, could refer to Namu's manner of calling Tarleton "Misi," a detail which points up the linguistic difficulties that are pervasive in the story, illustrates Stevenson's accuracy at recording native expressions, and serves as a comic contrast to the sober and serious purport of the explanation. Furthermore, the weight of the revision, with the added comma, falls on "in this way," rather than on "And I explain it." The latter keeps the emphasis on Namu as narrator, where Stevenson intended it.

Another badly mangled passage occurs when Wiltshire, unseen by Case, watches his enemy go past: "He was in deep thought; and the birds seemed to know it, trotting quite near him on the sand or wheeling and calling in his ears. Where he passed nearest me, I could see by the working of his lips that he was talking in to himself, and what pleased me mightily, he had still my trademark on his brow." In examining the printed version, one might first suspect that "Where" was simply misread as "When"; but the deletion of "nearest" three words later suggests something other than a misreading. The matter is made clear by the removal (in the same sentence) of "in" from the expression "talking in to himself": the revisions were intended to make the language more orthodox and comprehensible, even at the expense of the logistics of the scene. What do the revisions in fact achieve? They destroy the privacy of Wiltshire's view of Case, and they remove as well Case's touch of neurotic behavior ("talking in to himself"), so nicely registered in Wiltshire's own idiosyncratic speech.

Two other alterations are perfectly clear in their purport. The first is nothing more than the deletion of an imprecation that is handled gingerly at best. It comes in the midst of one of Wiltshire's most explosive speeches, when he identifies himself to the missionary: "I'm no missionary nor missionary lover; I'm no kanaka nor favourer of kanakas: I'm just a trader, I'm just a common, low, god-damned white man and British subject, the sort you would like to wipe your boots on. I hope that's plain." The speech provides an extraordinary view of Wiltshire's attitudes toward others and toward himself: his antagonism toward missionaries, his consciousness of the racial distinction between himself and Polynesians, and his ingrained contempt for the class that he represents. Indeed, the anger he exhibits toward missionaries and *kanakas* is more than equalled by the contempt he visits upon himself. When he says he is a "god-damned white man and British subject," that is exactly what he means—that he is condemned by a system to perdition and he knows it. The only admirable thing about the statement is its honesty of feeling and expression. To Wiltshire being "plain" is a virtue.

What Stevenson provides here is not merely an oath offensive in its clarity and unrelieved plainness, but an attack on the entire class system, economic and political, that is at the center of *Falesá*. Common, low, white, British, *kanaka*, trader, missionary—these terms are critical in the novel; indeed they are what the novel is all about. Wiltshire is at one and the same time a representative of the system (dispensing rubbish to the natives, exploiting their copra, trafficking in their women) and a rebel against it (marrying a *kanaka* girl and upholding an elemental standard of decency and honor). The "god-damned"—deleted in two editions and softened in three others[16]—does not speak to all these issues. But in a way, along with the capitalized "kanakas" and the insertion of "low-down" for the more derisive "low," the deletion is a means, albeit unconscious, of taming or subduing an attack whose truth hits too close to home.

Another alteration whose purport is very clear was the deletion of the expression "mother naked." The puerility of this change particularly struck Stevenson—he mentioned it in a letter to James Barrie. The original passage read:

Three little boys sat beside my path, where I must pass within three feet of them. Wrapped in their sheets, with their shaved heads and bits of topknots, and queer faces, they looked like figures on a chimney piece. Awhile they sat their ground, solemn as judges; I came up hand over fist, doing my five knots, like a man that meant business; and I thought I saw a sort of a wink and gulp in the three faces. Then one jumped up (he was the farthest off) and ran for his mammy. The other two, trying to follow suit, got foul, came to ground together bawling, wriggled right out of their sheets—and in a moment there were all three of them, two mother naked, scampering for their lives and singing out like pigs. The natives, who would never let a joke slip even at a burial, laughed and let up, as short as a dog's bark.

The *NED* defines "mother naked" as "stark naked," citing Ruskin as its only nineteenth-century source; Wright notes various dialect uses in Scotland, Ireland, and England; and *W 1915* calls the phrase "rare." That it should be found offensive is hard to understand, even given the sensibilities that we are now familiar with. The picture of two children with-

---

16. The oath appears in the galley proofs, is deleted in the *Illustrated London News* version and the copyright issue, surfaces in the "Bottle Imp" volume as "God-d-ned," is restored by Stevenson to "God-damned" for Cassell, and is so printed in Scribner's.

out clothes on can hardly have threatened Victorian readers. Yet the phrase must have had a force sufficiently strong to be noticed and expunged. The deletion spoils the point of Stevenson's little vignette, since it is precisely the uncovering of the children that upsets the solemnity of the occasion and breaks the natives up with laughter. The contrast (although not a part of Stevenson's text) between the natives' ease with naked children and the Victorians' squeamishness with the printed statement cannot be left unnoticed.

It is important to note, however, that when Stevenson explicitly aimed at restoring an excised passage, the restoration was made. In this case, working solely from memory, Stevenson inserted "mother-naked" after "sheets" in the margin of the "Bottle Imp" volume. What emerged in the Cassell edition is the following: "The other two, trying to follow suit, got foul, came to ground together bawling, wriggled right out of their sheets mother-naked, and in a moment there were all three of them scampering for their lives and singing out like pigs." A bastardized restoration, to be sure, but an effort to get his phrase back into the text.

Nakedness might well have been an image that invited expurgation automatically. In the manuscript of *Catriona*, for example, David Balfour declares: "I am thanking the good God he has let me see you naked." The printed edition reads: "I am thanking the good God that he has let me see you so."[17] To call attention to an unclothed body is practically taboo: for children it is questionable; for young women it is absolutely prohibited. Undoubtedly this explains the censoring of the portrait of Uma on her first appearance in the book. Wiltshire has been looking "like a Bashaw" among the crowd of girls at the beach who had come to see the boat's arrival. Case points out Uma to him: "I saw one coming on the other side alone. She had been fishing; all she wore was a chemise, and it was wetted through, and a cutty sark at that. She was young and very slender for an island maid, with a long face, a high forehead, and a sly, strange, blindish look between a cat's and a baby's." The galley proofs, *Illustrated London News*, and copyright edition all eliminate the entire clause "all she wore was a chemise, and it was wetted through, and a cutty sark at that." With the "Bottle Imp," the final clause is restored except for the final phrase, "and a cutty sark at that." Finally, the *Illustrated London News* and all subsequent editions print "shy" for "sly." The passage appears in Cassell as: "I saw one coming on the other side alone. She

17. *Catriona* (London, 1893), p. 331.

had been fishing; all she wore was a chemise, and it was wetted through. She was young and very slender for an island maid, with a long face, a high forehead, and a shy, strange, blindish look, between a cat's and a baby's." It is plain that the censorship is designed to tone down the portrait of Uma as a truly seductive woman, conscious of her body and her capacity to affect behavior through its manipulation.

Stevenson is of course using nothing more than good Scots in his description; "cutty sark" is both a short shirt and a saucy wench. The double meaning is further underlined by the use of "sly" in the final sentence. Uma is thus a lovely innocent island maid, yet sensual and conscious of her seductiveness at the same time. Certainly Stevenson was not inventing the character. He was drawing from nature, and specifically from what he observed in his travels through the South Seas. Here is a passage from his unpublished journal in the Marquesas Islands: "Last of all there came a little cutty of thirteen or fourteen, draped in a white Holoku and smoking her pipe like an ancient mariner. And how pretty she looked in the moonlight! and how saucily she imitated my wife, nodding her head and saying 'Yes, yes' with high delight." And a bit later: "Then these young giggling ogling misses in the least clothes I had yet seen, in fact in so little that I can find no language to describe it in."[18]

The "cutty" that Stevenson refers to in his journal—the offender against chastity, the slut, perhaps the playful "cutty-sark" of Burns[19]—is transformed into the "cutty sark" in *Falesá*. To remove the chemise, and the way it clings to Uma's body, is not only to alter her character, but to eliminate as well Wiltshire's conscious observing of her. For Stevenson is not brooking any ambiguity in the role that sex plays in his novel: it is the force that drives Wiltshire to go along with Case's plan to take Uma as a "wife," just as it is the means by which Case can manipulate Wiltshire for his own ends. In simple terms, then, the portrait of Uma that Stevenson sketches in these few lines is realistic and subtle; she is innocent and experienced, childlike yet mature. The ambiguity of the character is augmented by the details in the final sentence that set off Uma's "look"— somewhere between "a cat's and a baby's." The revisions create an inconsistency in characterization and thereby falsify the reality on which Stevenson bases his work.

We turn now to the marriage certificate, a document that certified, in

18. Entry for 22 July 1888; Huntington Library.

19. "Whene'er to drink you are inclin'd, / Or cutty-sarks run in your mind" ("Tam O' Shanter," *The Poetical Works of Robert Burns* [London, 1811], II, 10).

effect, that Uma could be legally kept by Wiltshire for one night and then sent to hell the next morning. The notoriety of *Falesá*, if that word is appropriate, has to do with the excision of this certificate in the *Illustrated London News* and in the 1892 copyright issue, and its inaccurate wording in subsequent editions. It is the marriage certificate that prompted J. C. Furnas to declare he was restoring the document in its original form and publishing *Falesá* "exactly as R.L.S. wrote it." It is again the marriage certificate that encouraged Penguin to call its edition "unexpurgated." This is all that critics have noticed as an issue in the text of *Falesá*. For readers today the issue hardly seems worth the battle; the bowdlerized matter is so unexceptional that it is hard to imagine how late Victorian readers or editors could have become so worked up over it. It is much the same problem that occurs when students are exposed to *Sister Carrie* for the first time: how could publishers have been upset at Carrie's merely sleeping with two men and rising by her behavior, rather than falling by it? Yet the issue is not so innocuous as people who were intimately involved in the matter, like Clement Shorter, would have us believe in retrospect.

Let us start from the beginning. Case is intent on getting Wiltshire connected with Uma. Since she is ostracized from the local population, along with her mother, anyone connected with her also becomes tabooed. By joining Wiltshire with Uma, Case effectively neutralizes his rival in trade and forecloses any possible competition for the copra. He tells Wiltshire to take a wife; Wiltshire of course demurs; and Case merely laughs and says not to worry, it is not really legal at all. It is a joke at the expense of an ignorant *kanaka* girl. So a marriage ceremony is contrived: presiding are Papa Randall, the chronically drunk derelict, and the black who performs the ceremony (and whose signature on the certificate in all the printed texts is "BLACKAMOAR," instead of "Blackamoor"). The certificate reads as follows:

This is to certify that <u>Uma</u> daughter of <u>Faavao</u> of Falesá island of ———, is illegally married to <u>Mr John Wiltshire</u> for one night, and Mr John Wiltshire is at liberty to send her to hell next morning.

John Blackamoor
Chaplain to the Hulks.

Extracted from the register
    by William T. Randall
      Master Mariner.

It was clear from the start that Stevenson was going to have trouble with this. Although the certificate itself is not mentioned in any correspondence I could locate, Stevenson responded to the matter explicitly in the letter to Colvin already quoted (17 May 1892): "Yesterday came yours. Well, well, if the dears prefer a week, why I'll give them ten days, but the real document, from which I have scarcely varied, ran for one night."

The document Stevenson refers to can be found in his own writing. Chapter VII of *In the South Seas*, "Husband and Wife," concerns the relations between white traders and native wives in the Gilbert Islands. I quote from the Chatto & Windus edition, published six years after Stevenson's death.

The trader must be credited with a virtue: he often makes a kind and loyal husband. Some of the worst beachcombers in the Pacific, some of the last of the old school, have fallen in my path, and some of them were admirable to their native wives, and one made a despairing widower. The position of a trader's wife in the Gilberts is, besides, unusually enviable. She shares the immunities of her husband. Curfew in Butaritari sounds for her in vain. Long after the bell is rung and the great island ladies are confined for the night to their own roof, this chartered libertine may scamper and giggle through the deserted streets or go down to bathe in the dark. The resources of the store are at her hand; she goes arrayed like a queen, and feasts delicately every day upon tinned meats. And she who was perhaps of no regard or station among natives sits with captains, and is entertained on board of schooners. Five of these privileged dames were some time our neighbours. Four were handsome skittish lasses, gamesome like children, and like children liable to fits of pouting. They wore dresses by day, but there was a tendency after dark to strip these lendings and to career and squall about the compound in the aboriginal *ridi*. . . . The fifth was a matron. It was a picture to see her sail to church on a Sunday, a parasol in hand, a nursemaid following, and the baby buried in a trade hat and armed with a patent feeding-bottle. The service was enlivened by her continual supervision and correction of the maid. It was impossible not to fancy the baby was a doll, and the church some European playroom. All these women were legitimately married. It is true that the certificate of one, when she proudly showed it, proved to run thus, that she was "married for one night," and her gracious partner was at liberty to "send her to hell" the next morning; but she was none the wiser or the worse for the dastardly trick. Another, I heard, was married on a work of mine in a pirated edition; it answered the purpose as well as a Hall Bible.[20]

The remark that "some of the worst beachcombers . . . were admirable to their native wives" is precisely what is said of Case in *Falesá*: indeed, the one good thing said of him was that "he was fond of his wife and kind to her." Moreover, Stevenson depicts these native wives as "gamesome like children, and like children liable to fits of pouting." Yet they are not

20. *In the South Seas* (London, 1900), pp. 267–68.

children; they are married and bearing babies to their husbands. They are treated with great respect by the shipping captains, although they may have no standing among their own people.

One of the ironies of this particular example is that Stevenson's description of island wives and white traders in the Gilbert Islands appeared as early as 1891, in the serial publication of *The South Seas*. Thus a major New York newspaper, *The Sun*, carried the description on 11 October 1891—a good ten months before Clement Shorter believed it his "duty" to delete the marriage certificate from the *Illustrated London News*:

All these children were legitimately married. It is true that the certificate of one, when she proudly showed it, proved to run thus, that she was "married for one night," and her gracious partner was at liberty to "send her to hell" the next morning; but she was none the wiser or the worse for the dastardly trick. Another I heard was married on a work of mine in a pirated edition; it answered the purpose as well as a hall Bible.

Stevenson, interestingly enough, is not judgmental in his criticism of the traders: the deception is mean and unfair, but the main point is that it serves a beneficial purpose. It is telling that *The Sun* printed "children," whereas the book, posthumously published, substituted "women." The prospect of children engaging in sexual intercourse was undoubtedly too unnerving for a late Victorian publisher. Its survival in the newspaper may indicate either the haste of newspaper serialization or the possibility that nobody paid close attention to Stevenson's letters from the South Seas as they appeared. As we know, the New York daily ended up canceling the series before its conclusion. The linguistic change, along with the revision of "hall Bible" to "Hall Bible" (introducing a successor to Gutenberg?), is further evidence that the serial publication of Stevenson's later writing was more faithful to his original versions than the book editions.

At issue in the matter of the marriage certificate, as throughout *Falesá*, is the distance between Stevenson's attitudes and perception and the attitudes and perception of the people instrumental in publishing his novel. Clement Shorter is a good example. Twenty-two years after the publication of the novel in the *Illustrated London News*, Shorter brought out a thin pamphlet in which he published four short notes from Stevenson. His Foreword attempts to justify this self-flattering publication as well as account for "an episode which seems quite entertaining enough to be worth putting on record." Shorter's note exhibits neither regret nor remorse over his behavior in the affair. "Although it is true in a sense that the whole story hangs upon the bogus marriage certificate between a South Sea trader and a girl of the Island of Falesá, I felt it my duty, as the editor of a family newspaper, to omit it altogether. . . . Some of the greatest things in literature cannot be published in journals for general family reading, and no editor who knows his business would worry himself about the feelings of an author, however great, when he had such a point for decision."[21]

Judged within the context of the times, Shorter's attitude is perhaps exculpatory. After all, he says nothing more than a television executive might say about a network's obligations to its viewers. But there is a cynicism in the attitude that should not be overlooked, an open contempt toward the artist that translates itself into a contempt for art itself. The fractious relations between authors and publishers depicted in Gissing's *New Grub Street* (1891) was not the manufacture of paranoid, hypersensitive artistes, but a response on the part of writers to their perceived antagonists. And in this battle the writers were at a distinct disadvantage. They fought with words—the ridicule and sarcasm of Stevenson's "if the dears prefer a week, why I'll give them ten days"—whereas the editors used paste and scissors. Power was in the hands of the distributors of fiction rather than in the hands of its practitioners. It is hard to know which was the more reprehensible attitude: viewing the craft of fiction as a trade, or trading (and profiting) on the esteem and popularity of the craftsman.

Shorter made a sharp distinction between newspapers and books, the latter serving as appropriate vehicles for the publication of controversial material. "There is scarcely a publisher in London who is in the habit of issuing fiction who would hesitate to-day to print the Stevenson story exactly as he wrote it." *Exactly as he wrote it.* The recurrent phrase takes on the aura of an incantation, appearing first in a handwritten note by Edmund Gosse appended to the galley proofs of *Falesá*, now at Yale University, and repeated as recently as 1956 by Joseph Furnas. Yet what does it mean? The *Illustrated London News* and the copyright issue deleted the marriage certificate altogether. The "Bottle Imp" and Cassell's edition substituted "one week" for "one night" and "to hell when he pleases" for "to hell next morning." Scribner's cut "for one night" completely and

21. Clement Shorter, ed., *Letters to an Editor* (1914), pp. i–ii, iv.

offered "to send her packing when he pleases" for "to hell next morning."
Furnas was clearly using Scribner's *Island Nights' Entertainments* and was
thus unaware that Cassell's edition was closer to the original.

But these variants mask the main issue exemplified by the marriage
certificate: the revulsion felt toward the depiction of aspects of life considered vulgar or debasing. The problem that Hardy encountered with
Tess is instructive not merely because Stevenson repeatedly referred to
Tess, but because both novels dealt directly with sex and were censored.
In each case the editors censored material on the grounds of their own
convictions or beliefs. Shorter's decision was motivated by his opinion
about what was appropriate for a "family newspaper." I quoted earlier
C. J. Longman's rejection of a story by Rider Haggard because it dealt
with "sexual relations," a subject Longman felt belonged outside magazines. The ease with which these editors (think, for example, of Richard
Watson Gilder's famous refusal of Stephen Crane's *Maggie*) arrogated the
right to censor any author who wrote about sex cannot be excused by the
plea that they feared prosecution. They were the arbiters of the word,
and they decided what the public could read.

The effect on Stevenson was particularly hard. The controls were
tightened on his fiction just as he came to power in his art, and as he
confronted for the first time the role of sex in an adult world. Stevenson
was well aware of this.

As for women, I am no more in any fear of them: I can do a sort all right, age
makes me less afraid of a petticoat; but I am a little in fear of grossness. . . . This
has kept me off the sentiment hitherto, and now I am to try: Lord! Of course
Meredith can do it, and so could Shakespeare; but with all my romance, I am a
realist and a prosaist, and a most fanatical lover of plain physical sensations
plainly and expressly rendered; hence my perils. To do love in the same spirit as
I did (for instance) D. Balfour's fatigue in the heather; my dear sir, there were
grossness ready made! And hence, *how* to sugar? Of course, I mean something
different from the false fire of Hardy—as false a thing as ever I perused, unworthy
of Hardy and untrue to all I know of life. If ever I do a rape, which may the
almighty God forefend! you would hear a noise about my rape, and it should be
a man that did it. [22]

The quality that made Stevenson enormously popular in his own lifetime, and that has kept him alive for readers always, has been his ability
to write so clearly that all could see what he was saying. This is not to say

22. RLS to Sidney Colvin, "Wednesday," ?18 May 1892.

that all could understand what he was about. But he was never opaque or obscure. His prose was lean and limpid. And he recognized this. The deception that Henry James could manage in his writing about sex, and that was indeed his way with language, was foreign to Stevenson. Stevenson could no more hide what was going on in his fiction than James could express it plainly.

Part of the problem of course is that Stevenson's story was raw and coarse in the extreme. It is not only sex that disturbs editors in the bridal scene, but also Stevenson's contempt for forms, for Christian practice, and for matrimony as a sanctification. It is easy to label sex as the issue, but Stevenson, like Hardy, suffered from being blatant in his criticism of religion. As Samuel Hynes says, religion, politics, and sex are the taboo subjects for Victorian censors, and all are the warp and woof of *Falesá*. The marriage certificate is merely the instrument in a scene that disquiets the Victorian reader (or rather the late Victorian editor) by disturbing his most profound prejudices: race, miscegenation, and colonialism. The drunken Randall on a corner of the floor, the black performing the ceremony, Case as the manipulative devil in the background, Wiltshire contemptuous and a bit superior—all these are caught, in an almost miraculous fashion, by Gordon Browne in his illustration of the wedding ceremony for the *Illustrated London News*. It is not so much that the certificate is "bogus," as Shorter puts it, but that the entire ceremony is bogus, and this is entirely too close to the fears and anxieties that preoccupied the late Victorian reader.

Nowhere is the discrepancy between Stevenson and his producers more apparent than in this scene. For Stevenson, as we see in his letters, the problem is one of execution. How do I draw my women so that they are plausible, so that their beauty and their physical sensations are made apparent? How do I manage this without destroying the love that cannot be discovered through physical beauty alone? How do I avoid "grossness"? And the more he is able to answer these questions, the more he diverges from the editors and publishers who respond not to the art, but to the fears and anxieties that the art uncovers. Perhaps Stevenson touched too closely on areas that were taboo. But as Hardy claimed for *Tess*, and Dickens for *Oliver Twist*, truth was the object. A man so passionately devoted to the truth could never understand a mind (like Colvin's or Shorter's) that did not have the same conviction. And this I believe was one of Stevenson's small blindnesses. He gloried in his ability to create

Wiltshire, and in *Falesá* as an artistic achievement: "And I think perhaps you scarce do justice to the fact that this is a piece of realism *à outrance*, nothing extenuated or adorned. Looked at so, is it not, with all its tragic features, wonderfully idyllic, with great beauty of scene and circumstance?"[23] Stevenson's art, like his truth, was simply too plain, too tough, for its own good.

23. RLS to Sidney Colvin, 17 May 1892.

5

Conclusion

Why did Stevenson allow it to happen? Writing for him was after all the sole area in his life over which he maintained absolute control. This is one reason he despaired of writing to deadlines: not only did they cheat him of the time required to alter and revise, applying a pressure that, ever the moralist, he felt intensely, but they stole from him the power he sought to retain over his compositions. In fact, Stevenson's power over his writing was severely restricted—it extended no further than the pen and paper he held in his own hands. The moment he gave over his manuscript to the mails his ability to manage events collapsed altogether. What happened to *Falesá*, though mainly a consequence of the nature of the story, was also a function of the procedures for handling Stevenson's work and of Stevenson's response to those procedures. In large measure he was responsible for the corruption of his text. When I began this study I was convinced there would be a villain—Colvin appeared accommodating—and a hero—the self-styled "exile of Samoa," enduring the martyrdom of his art by philistines who neither admired nor understood it. But that scenario proved utterly simplistic. To begin with there was the bound volume entitled *The Beach of Falesá and The Bottle Imp*, a copy of which, with no lettering on the spine, had been sent to Stevenson to proofread. Receiving it admittedly put him in a defensive position and ruled out any major changes to the text. Nevertheless, and without having a manuscript copy to read, Stevenson made more than a hundred corrections, almost all of them simple restorations of the punctuation that existed in the original manuscript.

Yet this was nothing more than the merest trifle. By proofreading the volume that served as the text for *Island Nights' Entertainments*, Stevenson accepted the gutting of *Falesá* as an accomplished fact. And it is not as if he were unaware or forgetful of what he had written. When he saw, for example, a copy of the *Illustrated London News* with the first installment of *Uma*, he wrote immediately to Colvin.

. . . and the thing is full of misprints abominable. "The STAVE (*store*) was in front full of the finest" (which should be, as the context clamours, *poorest*). Then "ignorant of the native*s*", instead of the NATIVE, which is the point of the story. Also your omission of the little copra story seems to me very illogical; that is the preparatory note to Case, and the whole tale: the reader must be shown how far men go, and Case has gone, to get copra; and though you dislike the name of that merchandise, you might have borne ten lines for so obvious a purpose.[1]

But it was not only during the serial publication that Stevenson acknowledged what had happened to his novel. Responding on 1 November 1892 to a letter from James Barrie, in which the playwright had commented on Hardy's problems with *Tess*, Stevenson revealed his deep conviction that he had been hurt by the devastation visited upon his work:

Yours was an exquisite story about the barrow, but I think I can beat it. In a little tale of mine, the slashed and gaping ruins of which appeared recently in the *Illustrated London News*, a perfect synod of appalled editors and apologetic friends had sat and wrangled over the thing in private with astonishing results. The flower of their cuts was this: Two little native children were described as wriggling out of their clothes and running away mother-naked. The celestial idiots cut it out. I wish we could afford to do without serial publication altogether. It is odd that Hardy's adventure with the barrow and mine of the little children should happen in the same year with the publication and success of *Tess*. Surely these editor people are wrong.[2]

Why did Stevenson resort to complaints in his private correspondence as opposed to declarations to the publishers? In part this was due to his habit of personalizing his relations with editors and publishers rather than maintaining them on a business level. On the one hand he would apologize to Burlingame for his complaints in a seriocomic fashion; then he would turn around and aggressively assert his artistic authority. The two

1. RLS to Sidney Colvin, "Friday night, the (I believe) 18th or 20th August or September" 1892. The "little copra story" was set in type for the galley proofs, but pulled before it could appear in the *Illustrated London News* version. It has not heretofore appeared in print. All the previous printed versions go from "There was no smarter trader, and none dodgier, in the islands," directly on to "I thought Falesá seemed to be the right kind of a place; and the more I drank the lighter my heart." For the block of material that was deleted, see this edition of *Falesá*, p. 118, lines 4–27.

2. "Stevenson's 'Celestial Idiots,' " *Colby Library Quarterly*, No. 9 (January 1945), pp. 145–46.

attitudes are of course incompatible, and the results were disastrous. Burlingame and Scribner became accustomed to Stevenson's manner, and when it suited them they simply disregarded his intentions—as long as those intentions were not more specific than homilies directed against the printers. They would never contravene explicit instructions, but explicit instructions were rare and never concerned the language or substance of the story. In effect Stevenson's silence about his art to the very people who were responsible for producing it made the circumvention of his purposes relatively simple.

It is ironic that the one person to whom Stevenson directed his anger was S. S. McClure, the syndicator instrumental in the novelist's financial success during the last years of his life. Stevenson exhibited a curiously divided attitude toward McClure: on the one hand he expressed a snide contempt for the vulgarity of McClure's mercantile profession, a contempt that had a small note of anti-Semitism to it, although McClure was not Jewish. Yet despite his suspicions that he was being dazzled by McClure's proposals, Stevenson was sober enough to recognize that the man who served as the model for Jim Pinkerton in *The Wrecker* was a golden asset. McClure, on his side, had an almost reverential regard for the novelist; he would never have been so bold as to tamper with his writing. Thus on 4 December 1890 McClure wrote to Stevenson: "Your instructions in regard to the publication of your letters I will follow out as wisely as I can, recollecting what a severe man you are if your wishes are not obeyed." And in a handwritten postscript to a letter dated 31 January 1891: "Accept my love & approve my course. I live in fear & trembling of your anger."[3] Surely it is an irony that McClure, who sold popular fiction to newspapers, should have had a respect for art and for Stevenson that was unmatched by literati like Clement Shorter, Sidney Colvin, and Charles Scribner.

Perhaps Stevenson's attitude toward McClure was not odd after all. For in McClure Stevenson must have seen the commercial side of himself that he pursued with passion and alternately loathed. Stevenson had a divided attitude toward the whole enterprise of art: compared to building lighthouses writing *David Balfour* seemed paltry work, self-indulgent. At the least one ought to be able to do both. In Stevenson the artist had always to contend with the man who had at best a skeptical attitude toward the utility of art, and at worst a despairing one. It is as if Stevenson

3. S. S. McClure to RLS, 4 December 1890 and 31 January 1891; Beinecke Library.

divided his life into artist and man, and assumed that the two could not come to terms. Thus in the process of writing, alone in the breaking hours of the morning, he could live absolutely the life of the imagination. But when the household came alive and the life of the world took over, Stevenson discharged responsibility for his work, sacrificing his imagination's treasure for his imagined needs—the needs of a massive home in the tropics, replete with retainers and crops, a plantation that might return its substantial investment in future years, a hedge against the time when imagination failed, perhaps a hedge against death. The tragic irony, of course, was evident for all to see: Stevenson's imagination was never more glorious; he died in the midst of writing his masterwork, *Weir of Hermiston*.

If Stevenson can be faulted for failing to extricate his commercial interests from his artistic talent, the producers of fiction must still bear the major responsibility for the bowdlerization of his work. As Stevenson said to Barrie, "Surely these editor people are wrong." Stevenson's tentative speculation reflects the dilemma of an artist forced to work within the constraints of a prescriptive system, and who suspected that it was not the public who restrained the distributors but rather the distributors who censored the artists. Stevenson never developed this suspicion because of a fundamental misperception of the role of his editors and publishers. As mercenary as he appears in his correspondence with McClure, Scribner's, and Cassell, he nonetheless retained an integrity, almost an innocence, about the process of artistic creation: he could never imagine the battles over his texts involving anything other than artistic disagreements. The belief that he and his publishers were engaged in a common pursuit contributed to his wavering and inconsistent relations with them. By birth and education Stevenson had class ties with the people he dealt with in publishing. But as an artist he was separated from them by an unbridgeable gulf—artists were, as Henry James saw clearly, a classless group. Stevenson sensed this, but never quite appreciated it. Money moved Stevenson, to be sure, but it was never the primary cause of his creativity. It was, however, the essential factor for those who published him, as well as for those who lived off him.

Stevenson's enormous popularity made him a strong commercial figure in his publishers' offices. If he was an artist as well, all the better. But success in publishing had little to do with art, and art was never an issue when it was a matter of the text's acceptability. Of course the publishers were mindful of the proprieties and anxious to avoid religious and political controversy. But it is equally true that they engaged in a form of self-censorship that was habitual and, perhaps, thoughtless and cynical. Stevenson took it on faith that his text would be treated as a given, and not subject to alteration. Yet clearly this faith was misplaced: in fact the text was merely raw material for editors and publishers who thought they could exploit it more effectively. The real bond between creator and producer was nothing more than a commitment to a marketable item that would be distributed under an author's name and a publisher's imprint. But the process by which the final product emerged was far more flexible than any author could have imagined. The text was polished and refined to reach the market in the most advantageous position for the publisher. And anything that even hinted at controversy was editorially deplored and usually expunged. Censorship was possible because the habit of interference with the text was there from the start.

Stevenson's writing was not given the slightest bit of pro forma acceptance. It was scrutinized and reviewed on every conceivable level, and the alterations were decided upon on an ad hoc basis, page by page. The detail was important, and if it seemed objectionable, it was deleted or altered. Large-scale excisions and bowdlerizations are merely symptoms of a disease whose roots lie deep within the entire production process. It is through small cuts, through trimmings, that large ones are made possible. If accidentals can be changed, then why not substantives? Indeed, what distinguishes an accidental from a substantive? We have seen how Stevenson's accidentals, despite his pleas, had no integrity for the compositor. Altering a writer's text must be understood within a context where changes are accepted as a dynamic part of the process, desirable and perhaps even inevitable. For books are viewed as collaborations, the emerging text a consequence of individual decisions arrived at rationally and deliberatively. In reality these decisions—financial, accidental, substantive, promotional—are largely technocratic and managerial reactions, instinctively made by people for whom books are a business and printing a technology. It is hardly surprising, therefore, that Stevenson, omnipotent in his artistic vision, was essentially powerless before this system. The production of *Falesá* might well have been a juggernaut, subject to little control and less reason. And the implications of such a juggernaut are sobering. Books, after all, are the last redoubt of private deliberation, of a single mind confronting and creating the world through the imagination. We would not like to believe that such a potent idea was merely a delusion.

Island Nights' Entertainments was published in London and New York in early April 1893. A note in a Glasgow newspaper reported that the English edition "was exhausted before publication, and a second, which has already been almost entirely subscribed, is issued this week."[4] Nothing less could have been expected. Despite his exile in Samoa, or perhaps because of it, and spurred by the serialization of *David Balfour*, Stevenson's popularity was nearly unsurpassed. We see this in the reviews of his new volume, which began appearing in the daily press almost immediately. Most reviewers had the quickness to separate *The Beach of Falesá* from its companions, "The Bottle Imp" and "The Isle of Voices," and to recognize its innovative technical achievement. The criticism divided itself into three general categories: the nature of the characterization, the veracity of the story, and, as always, the question of style.

Without exception the reviewers were smitten by Uma—"a new possibility in the way of falling in love"—and had nothing but praise for her "grace and tenderness." That Stevenson was notorious for never drawing women only added to the delight of finally discovering one whom readers might want to possess, an attitude only half hidden in the references to her as a "native" or "natural savage girl." The attitude toward Wiltshire was more ambiguous. On the one hand he was a "penetrating study" of the "character of a South Sea trader," or a "wonderful example" of a "common untutored Englishman," a figure whose "manliness" and "innate honesty" were revealed in his treatment of his Polynesian wife. But he was also "disagreeable," neither "an attractive hero" nor an "interesting person," a man so "offensively coarse" that one reviewer went so far as to call him the "Yankee" narrator—presumably on the grounds that only an American could be so rough. Yet when the reviewers turned to the larger impression made upon them by the book, there was unanimous agreement that *Falesá* was a startling piece of realism. *Lifelike, verisimilitude, facts, true, vivid, graphic*—these are the terms consistently applied, with a kind of wonder and astonishment. It will be recalled that *The Wrecker* had appeared in the previous year, so readers knew that Stevenson was locating his work in the Pacific. The subject, however, was still recent enough for them to remark on the milieu and on Stevenson's treat-

4. Stevenson's mother collected notices and reviews of his publications as they appeared in the English-language press—compiling a substantial set of scrapbooks. Occasionally she wrote the title of the newspaper and the date over the clipping, but these may not be altogether accurate and in any case they are not always legible. The scrapbooks are located in the Stevenson House, in Monterey, California. Unless otherwise noted, all cited reviews are drawn from these scrapbooks.

ment of it. From the *San Francisco Chronicle*: "It is probable that this tale was told to Stevenson by the hero, but how wonderfully has the genius of the novelist illuminated the prosaic facts. The story is redolent of the South Sea and the illusion is so strong that we follow the adventures of the trader as though he were a real person before our eyes."[5] And from the *New York Times*: "You catch the true conditions of the natives, the difficulties of the missionaries, and the wild, reckless lives led by some of the white men."[6]

The veracity of the story inevitably led to the question of style, which brought a mixed or ambivalent response. Many reviewers saw that Stevenson had created a unique and to some extent radical style in *Falesá*. The reviewer for *Black and White* said it well: "Bating an occasional lapse into Stevensonian English, John Wiltshire . . . has his own language, the straightforward language of an unlettered Englishman mingled with sailor slang and South Pacific lingo." But this language presented a fundamental problem for the reviewers. There was no question but that Stevenson was an unexcelled master of prose, which in *Falesá* assumed a dramatic power that reinforced the realism and heightened the simplicity of the style. "Stevenson uses words," said one reviewer, "as Velasquez used pigments." Yet it was difficult to reconcile the "glowing prose" with the "dialect" and profanity. In a way the dilemma was best reflected by one reviewer who admired the dramatic appropriateness of Stevenson's diction in *Falesá* but felt relief at returning to Stevenson's "own language" in the companion stories.

Stevenson was certainly not treated badly by the press. And the qualities he worked so hard to secure in *Falesá* were perceived by some very acute readers. However, the response to those qualities was ambiguous. It was fine to aim for dramatic fitness, but it was uncomfortable to see "roaring vulgarities" or "modern vulgarisms" in print.[7] It was fine to create a vivid picture of South Sea life, but it was unclear that an "outcast" trader was appropriate as a model. It was fine, in short, to be an artist who could excel in his craft; but as one writer suggested, *Falesá* does not make for "domestic reading." In effect there was a split between what the reviewer liked and admired, and what he thought the general public ought to read. Yet no reviewer even hinted that the book should not have been written or published. It is clear that the producers of *Falesá* were

5. *San Francisco Chronicle*, 16 April 1893, p. 9.
6. *New York Times*, 9 April 1893, p. 19.
7. W. F. Barry, *Quarterly Review*, 180 (April 1895), 342, 350.

more cautious about decorum and propriety than was warranted by the facts. We can only conclude that the guardians of the text had it in their interests, or saw it as their role, to preempt the reviewers and decide in advance that the bowdlerization of the text was a necessity in order to forestall an adverse reaction.

If the reviewers were not as offended by *Falesá* as they might have been, we have still to remember that what they read was a maimed version of Stevenson's story. That such a ruin was nonetheless received so well—indeed, in 1896 George Lyman Kittredge called it "almost as good a story as ever was written"[8]—says a good deal for Stevenson's art. Either the integrity of the text is less significant than we would like to believe, or the beauty of the tale overrode the handicaps imposed on it. But on a deeper level what happened to *Falesá* was in some fundamental way inevitable. One reviewer, in a prescient aside, remarked that the story might be an allegory: "We may see in it the Devil in Eden—the Devil typified by Captain John Randall, or almost any of the other white men, and Eden by this Paradise of the South Seas." Stevenson had already written in his South Sea *Letters* about the "depopulation" of the Pacific islands. He knew that the responsibility for the destruction of the brown cultures rested with a white civilization whose presumed racial and cultural superiority was nothing more than a cover for European expansionism. This is part of the story he tells in *The Beach of Falesá*. In a way he knew that he could not tell this story explicitly, that he would have to resort to a method and a style that would conceal his theme. And his success, ironically, might be measured by the fact that only one reviewer mentioned prejudice toward blacks as an aspect of the book, and that only as a feature of Wiltshire's character. Nobody could or dared extend the meaning to modern England itself. Perhaps the exotic element of *Falesá* protected Stevenson, kept readers from seeing just how profoundly radical was his study of late-nineteenth-century England.

8. *The Nation*, 9 January 1896, p. 37.

1. "An appreciation of self—drawn by me from a mirror's reflection. Robert Louis Stevenson." Pen-and-ink sketch.

The Beach of Falesá

Chapter I. A South Sea Bridal.

I saw that island first when it was neither night nor morning. The moon was to the west, setting but still high and bright. To the east, and right amidships of the dawn, which was all pink, the daystar sparkled like a diamond. The land breeze blew in our faces and smelt strong of wild lime and vanilla: other things besides, but these were the most plain; and the chill of it set me sneezing. — — — — — —

— . . I should say I had been fifteen years or so in and near the line, living for the most part solitary among natives. Here was a fresh experience; even the tongue would be quite strange to me; and the look of these woods and mountains, and the rare smell of them, renewed my blood.

The captain blew out the binnacle lamp.

"There! said he, "there goes a bit of smoke, Mr Wiltshire, behind the breach of the reef. That's Falesá where your station is, the last village to the east; nobody lives to windward, I don't know why. Take my glass, and you can make the houses out."

I took the glass; and the shores leaped nearer, and I saw the tangle of the woods and the breach of the surf, and the brown roofs and the black insides of houses peeped among the trees.

"Do you catch a bit of white there to the east'ard?" the captain continued. "That's your house. Coral built, stands high, verandahs you could walk on three abreast; best station in the South Pacific. When old Adams saw it, he took and shook me by the hand. — 'I've dropped into a soft thing here,' says he. — 'So you have,' says I, 'and time too!' — Poor Johnny! I never saw him again but this once, and then he had changed his tune — couldn't get on with the natives, or the whites, or something; and the next time we came round, there he was dead and buried. I took and put up a bit of a stick to him: 'John Adams, obit eighteen and sixty eight. Go thou and do likewise.' I missed that man; I never could see much harm in Johnny."

"What did he die of?" I inquired.

"Some kind of sickness," says the captain. "It appears it took him sudden. Seems he got up in the night, and filled up on Pain-Killer and Kennedy's Discovery: no go — he was booked beyond Kennedy. Then he had tried to open a case of gin; no go again — not strong enough. Then he must have turned to and run out on the verandah, and capsized over the rail. When they found him the next day, he was clean crazy — carried on all the time about somebody watering his copra. Poor John!"

2. *The Beach of Falesá.* Holograph, p. 1.

convenient river. Though it's true I was committed to Case; and besides a man ~~with a bad conscience~~ I could never have held my head up in that island, if I had run from a girl upon my wedding night.

The sun was down, the sky all on fire, and the lamp had been some time lighted, when Case came back with Uma and the negro. She was dressed and scented; her kilt was of fine tapa, looking richer in the folds than any silk; her bust, which was of the colour of dark honey, she WORE bare only for some half a dozen necklaces of seeds and flowers; and behind her ears and in her hair, she had the scarlet flowers of the hibiscus. She showed the best bearing for a bride conceivable, serious and still; and I thought shame to stand up with her in that mean house and before that grinning negro. I thought shame, I say; for the mountebank was dressed with a big paper collar, the book he made believe to read from was an odd volume of a novel, and the words of his service not fit to be set down. My conscience smote me when we joined hands; and when she got her certificate I was tempted to throw up the bargain and confess. Here is the document, it was Case that wrote it, signatures and all, in a leaf out of the ledger:

This is to certify that Uma daughter of Faavao of Falesá island of ———, is illegally married to Mr John Wiltshire for one night, and Mr John Wiltshire is at liberty to send her to hell next morning.

                             John Blackamoor
                             Chaplain to the Hulks.

      *Extracted from the register
         by William
           T. Randall
           Master Mariner.

That was a nice paper to put in a girl's hand and see her hide away like gold. A man might easily feel cheap for less. But it was the practice in these parts, and (as I told myself) not the least the fault of us White Men but of the missionaries. If they had let the natives be, I had never needed this deception, but taken all the wives I wished, and left them when I pleased, with a clean conscience.

The more ashamed I was, the more hurry I was in to be gone; and our desires thus jumping together, I made the less remark of a change in the traders. Case had been all eagerness to keep me; now, as though he had attained a purpose, he seemed all eagerness to have me go. Uma, he said, could show me to my house, and the three bade us farewell indoors.

The night was pretty nearly come; the village smelt of trees, and flowers and the sea, and breadfruit cooking; there came a fine roll of sea from the reef and from a

3. Marriage certificate in *The Beach of Falesá*. Holograph, p. 8.

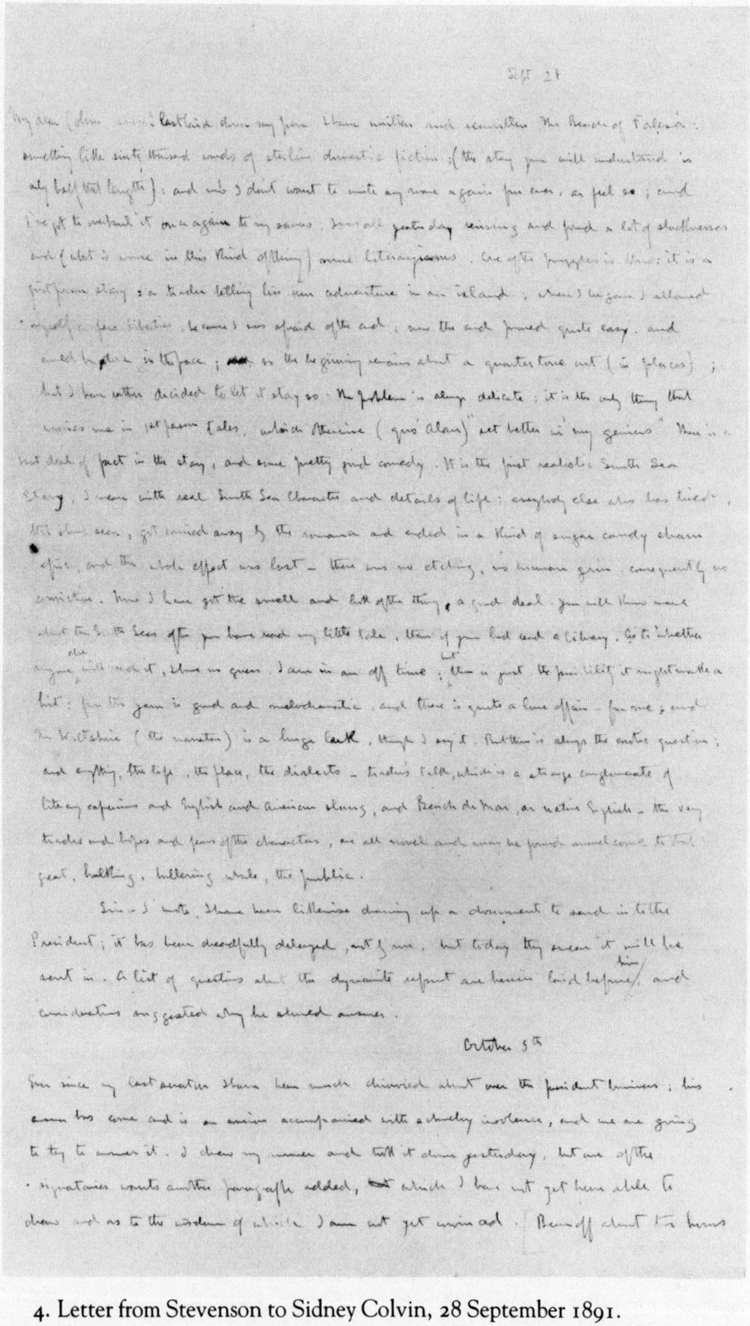

Sept 28

My dear Colvin, Since I last laid down my pen I have written and rewritten The Beach of Falesá: something like sixty thousand words of sterling domestic fiction; (the story you will understand is only half that length); and now I don't want to write any more again for ever, or feel so; and I've got to overhaul it once again to my sorrow. I was all yesterday revising and found a lot of slacknesses and (what is worse in this kind of thing) some literaryisms. One of the puzzles is this: it is a first person story: a trader telling his own adventure in an island; when I began I allowed myself a few liberties, because I was afraid of the end; now the end proved quite easy, and could be done in the pace; so the beginning remains about a quarter tone out (in places); but I have rather decided to let it stay so. The problem is always delicate; it is the only thing that worries me in 1st person tales, which otherwise (quo' Alan) "set better wi' my genius." There is a vast deal of fact in the story, and some pretty good comedy. It is the first realistic South Sea Story; I mean with real South Sea character and details of life: everybody else who has tried, that I have seen, got carried away by the romance and ended in a kind of sugar candy sham epic, and the whole effect was lost — there was no etching, no human grin, consequently no conviction. Now I have got the smell and look of the thing a good deal. You will know more about the South Seas after you have read my little tale, than if you had read a library. As to whether anyone else will read it, I have no guess. I am in an off time; but there is just the possibility it might make a hit: for the yarn is good and melodramatic, and there is quite a love affair — for me; and Mr Wiltshire (the narrator) is a huge lark, though I say it. But there is always the exotic question; and everything, the life, the place, the dialects — trader's talk, which is a strange conglomerate of literary expressions and English and American slang, and Beach de Mar, or native English — the very trades and hopes and fears of the characters, are all novel and may be found unwelcome to that great, hulking, bullering whale, the public.

Since I wrote, I have been likewise drawing up a document to send in to the President; it has been dreadfully delayed, not by me, but today they swear it will be sent in. A list of questions about the dynamite report are herein laid before him, and considerations suggested why he should answer.

October 5th

Ever since my last we have been much exercised about the President business; his answer has come and is an answer accompanied with a studied insolence, and we are going to try to answer it. I drew my answer and took it down yesterday, but one of the signatories wants another paragraph added, which I have not yet been able to draw and as to the wisdom of which I am not yet convinced. Be off about this business

4. Letter from Stevenson to Sidney Colvin, 28 September 1891.

5. Letter from Stevenson to Sidney Colvin, 17 May 1892, with brackets enclosing material excised from the printed edition.

6. Fanua (*above left*),
Mafolu (*above right*),
and Mele (*right*),
three islanders at
Vailima, Stevenson's
home in Samoa.

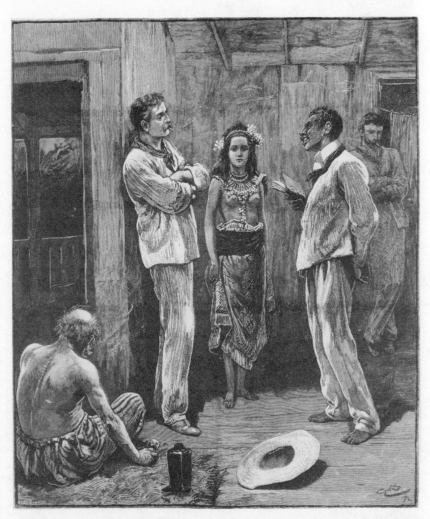

7. Marriage scene from "A South Sea Bridal." *Illustrated London News*, 2 July 1892.

UMA;
OR
THE BEACH OF FALESÁ.
(BEING THE NARRATIVE OF A SOUTH-SEA TRADER)
BY
ROBERT LOUIS STEVENSON

8. *Above*, Title and design for serial publication; *below*, Wiltshire and Case. Both illustrations are from the *Illustrated London News*, 9 July and 16 July, 1892.

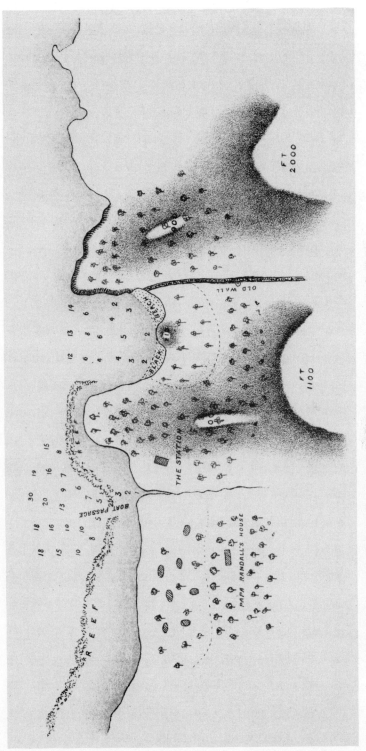

9. Map for *The Beach of Falesá*. *Island Nights' Entertainments* (London, 1893), facing p. 1.

10. Binding for the American edition (New York, 1893).

PART TWO

 The Beach of Falesá

NOTE ON THE TEXT

The text of *Falesá* is that of the holograph fair-copy manuscript. My intention has been to preserve the accidentals as faithfully as possible. However, a number of emendations have been made. The spelling of *niether*, *nieghbour*, *wieghed*, and *siezed* has been regularized, and *Christmass*, *breach*, *sorceror*, *obeissance*, *parasytes*, and *Blavattsky* are printed *Christmas*, *breech*, *sorcerer*, *obeisance*, *parasites*, and *Blavatsky*. Further, the compounds *underway*, *backroom*, *anyman*, and *ill-will* have been separated, and *rëassured* is printed without the diacritical mark. Where Stevenson alternated *Johnny* and *Johnnie* for the same character, the first form has been adopted. Apostrophes have been added to *it's* (three times), *hour's*, *that's*, and *wives'*; *mechanic's* and *mens'* are corrected to *mechanics'* and *men's*; and *aitu's* and *kanaka's* are changed to *aitus* and *kanakas*. Stevenson alternated between *aint* and *ain't*, and the latter form has been adopted. *Monday* has the initial letter capitalized; *Randall* has the second *l* added on two occasions; double quotation marks are added in two cases, and single quotation marks are substituted for double quotation marks in four cases; and terminal periods have been supplied for sixteen sentences. The words *Case*, *part*, and *to* have been added to the text, along with the alteration of *I'* to *I've* and *We'll* to *Well*. These emendations, with the exceptions of making consistent the spelling of *Johnny* and the deletion of the hyphen from ill-will, appear in all the printed texts from the galley proofs to the American edition published by Scribner's.

Stevenson's few lapses from consistency are noted: *Papa-Mālūlū*, emended only in the *Illustrated London News* text to *Papa-mālūlū*, is printed here with the lowercase *m*, in conformity with Stevenson's practice throughout *Falesá*; *lord* is raised to *Lord* in one case, and *Papa* reduced to *papa* in another. *Fale-alii* and *mummy-apples*, again in accordance with Stevenson's practice, have hyphens added. Stevenson's inconsistent hyphenation of *Hard shell* and *hard-shell* has been retained, as well as his alternate writing of *Faavao* and *Fa'avao*. Additionally, in one place *to*, deleted from all previous texts, is emended here to *too*, and an *a* has been supplied where it does not appear in the manuscript.

The more critical question of Stevenson's corrections for the "Bottle Imp" edition proved less difficult than one might have expected. The great majority of his revisions simply restored the punctuation and language of the manuscript. In eleven instances, however, he made changes from the manuscript punctuation. But in these cases he was working with repunctuated or corrupted sentences, so the holograph punctuation has been retained. Stevenson also made three changes where the punctuation was printed correctly: two semicolons were altered to dashes, and an exclamation mark was substituted for a comma. These have been incorporated in this edition. Finally, Stevenson made three changes in wording: *spun* became *span*, *talo pepelo* was corrected to *tala pepelo*, and *since* was changed to *even if*. These revisions have also been incorporated. In cases where the manuscript is illegible or unclear, I have followed the Cassell edition.

A Glossary explaining a number of Stevenson's less obvious slang and nautical terms follows the text.

The Beach of Falesá

To Three Old Shipmates among the Islands

Harry Henderson
Ben Hird
Jack Buckland

Their Friend
R.L.S.

Chapter I

 A South Sea Bridal

I saw that island first when it was neither night nor morning. The moon was to the west, setting but still broad and bright. To the east, and right amidships of the dawn, which was all pink, the daystar sparkled like a diamond. The land breeze blew in our faces and smellt strong of wild lime and vanilla: other things besides, but these were the most plain; and the chill of it set me sneezing. I should say I had been for years on a low island near the line, living for the most part solitary among natives. Here was a fresh experience; even the tongue would be quite strange to me; and the look of these woods and mountains, and the rare smell of them, renewed my blood.

The captain blew out the binnacle lamp.

"There," said he, "there goes a bit of smoke, Mr Wiltshire, behind the break of the reef. That's Falesá where your station is, the last village to the east; nobody lives to windward, I don't know why. Take my glass, and you can make the houses out."

I took the glass; and the shores leaped nearer, and I saw the tangle of the woods and the breach of the surf, and the brown roofs and the black insides of houses peeped among the trees.

"Do you catch a bit of white there to the east'ard?" the captain continued. "That's your house. Coral built, stands high, verandah you could walk on three abreast: best station in the South Pacific. When old Adams saw it, he took and shook me by the hand.— 'I've dropped into a soft thing here,' says he.—'So you have,' says I, 'and time too!' Poor Johnny! I never saw him again but the once, and then he had changed his tune—couldn't get on with the natives, or the whites, or something; and the next time we came round, there he was dead and buried. I took and put up a bit of a stick to him: 'John Adams, *obit* eighteen and sixty eight. Go thou and do likewise.' I missed that man; I never could see much harm in Johnny."

"What did he die of?" I inquired.

"Some kind of a sickness," says the captain. "It appears it took him sudden. Seems he got up in the night, and filled up on Pain-Killer and Kennedy's Discovery: no go—he was booked beyond Kennedy. Then he had tried to open a case of gin; no go again—not strong enough. Then he must have turned to and run out on the verandah, and capsized over the rail. When they found him the next day, he was clean crazy—carried on all the time about somebody watering his copra. Poor John!"

"Was it thought to be the island?" I asked.

"Well, it was thought to be the island, or the trouble, or something," he replied. "I never could hear but what it was a healthy place. Our last man, Vigours, never turned a hair. He left because of the beach; said he was afraid of Black Jack and Case and Whistling Jimmie, who was still alive at the time but got drowned soon afterward when drunk. As for old Captain Randall, he's been here any time since eighteen forty, forty five. I never could see much harm in Billy, nor much change. Seems as if he might live to be old Kafoozleum. No, I guess its healthy."

"There's a boat coming now," said I. "She's right in the pass; looks to be a sixteen foot whale; two white men in the stern sheets."

"That's the boat that drowned Whistling Jimmie!" cried the captain. "Let's see the glass. Yes: that's Case, sure enough, and the darkie. They've got a gallows bad reputation, but you know what a place the beach is for talking. My belief, that Whistling Jimmie was the worst of the trouble; and he's gone to glory, you see. What'll you bet they ain't after gin? Lay you five to two they take six cases."

When these two traders came aboard I was pleased with the

looks of them at once; or rather, with the looks of both, and the speech of one. I was sick for white neighbours after my four years at the line, which I always counted years of prison; getting tabooed, and going down to the Speak House to see and get it taken off; buying gin, and going on a break, and then repenting; sitting in my house at night with the lamp for company; or walking on the beach and wondering what kind of a fool to call myself for being where I was. There were no other whites upon my island; and when I sailed to the next, rough customers made the most of the society. Now to see these two when they came aboard, was a pleasure. One was a negro to be sure; but they were both rigged out smart in striped pyjamas and straw hats, and Case would have passed muster in a city. He was yellow and smallish; had a hawk's nose to his face, pale eyes, and his beard trimmed with scissors. No man knew his country, beyond he was of English speech; and it was clear he came of a good family and was splendidly educated. He was accomplished too; played the accordion first rate; and give him a piece of string or a cork or a pack of cards, and he could show you tricks equal to any professional. He could speak when he chose fit for a drawing room; and when he chose he could blaspheme worse than a Yankee boatswain and talk smut to sicken a kanaka. The way he thought would pay best at the moment, that was Case's way; and it always seemed to come natural and like as if he was born to it. He had the courage of a lion and the cunning of a rat; and if he's not in Hell today, there's no such place. I know but one good point to the man; that he was fond of his wife and kind to her. She was a Sāmoa woman, and dyed her hair red, Sāmoa style; and when he came to die (as I have to tell of) they found one strange thing, that he had made a will like a christian and the widow got the lot. All his, they said, and all Black Jack's, and the most of Billy Randall's in the bargain; for it was Case that kept the books. So she went off home in the schooner Manu'a, and does the lady to this day in her own place.

But of all this, on that first morning, I knew no more than a fly. Case used me like a gentleman and like a friend, made me welcome to Falesá, and put his services at my disposal, which was the more helpful from my ignorance of the native. All the early part of the day, we sat drinking better acquaintance in the cabin, and I never heard a man talk more to the point. There was no smarter trader, and none dodgier, in the islands. I remember one bit of advice he gave that morning, and one yarn he told. The bit of advice was this. "Whenever you get hold of any money," says he—"any christian money, I mean—the first thing to do is to fire it up to Sydney to the bank. It's only a temptation to a copra merchant; some day, he'll be in a row with the other traders, and he'll get his shirt out and buy copra with it. And the name of the man that buys copra with gold is Damfool," says he. That was the advice; and this was the yarn, which might have opened my eyes to the danger of that man for a neighbour, if I had been anyway suspicious. It seems Case was trading somewhere in the Ellices. There was a man Miller a Dutchman there, who had a strong hold with the natives and handled the bulk of what there was. Well one fine day a schooner got wrecked in the lagoon, and Miller bought her (the way these things are usually managed) for an old song, which was the ruin of him. For having a lot of trade on hand that had cost him practically nothing, what does he do but begin cutting rates? Case went round to the other traders. "Wants to lower prices?" says Case. "All right, then. He has five times the turn-over of any one of us; if buying at a loss is the game, he stands to lose five times more. Let's give him the bed rock; let's bilge the ———!" And so they did, and five months after, Miller had to sell out his boat and station, and begin again somewhere in the Carolines.

All this talk suited me, and my new companion suited me, and I thought Falesá seemed to be the right kind of a place; and the more I drank, the lighter my heart. Our last trader had fled the place at half an hour's notice, taking a chance passage in a labour ship from up west; the captain, when he came, had found the station closed, the keys left with the native pastor, and a letter from the runaway confessing he was fairly frightened of his life. Since then the firm had not been represented and of course there was no cargo; the wind besides was fair, the captain hoped he could make his next island by dawn, with a good tide; and the business of landing my trade was gone about lively. There was no call for me to fool with it, Case said; nobody would touch my things, everyone was honest in Falesá, only about chickens or an odd knife or an odd stick of tobacco; and the best I could do was to sit quiet till the vessel left, then come straight to his house, see old Captain Randall, the father of the Beach, take pot luck, and go home to sleep when it got dark. So it was high noon, and the schooner was under way, before I set my foot on shore at Falesá.

I had a glass or two on board, I was just off a long cruise and the ground heaved under me like a ship's deck. The world was like all new painted; my foot went along to music; Falesá might have been Fiddler's Green, if there is such a place, and more's the pity if there isn't! It was good to foot the grass, to look aloft at the green mountains, to see the men with their green wreaths and the women in their bright dresses, red and blue. On we went, in the strong sun and the cool shadow, liking both; and all the children in the town came trotting after with their shaven heads and their brown bodies, and raising a thin kind of a cheer in our wake, like crowing poultry.

"By the by," says Case, "we must get you a wife."

"That's so," said I, "I had forgotten."

There was a crowd of girls about us, and I pulled myself up and looked among them like a Bashaw. They were all dressed out for the sake of the ship being in; and the women of Falesá are a handsome lot to see. If they have a fault, they are a trifle broad in the beam; and I was just thinking so when Case touched me.

"That's pretty," says he.

I saw one coming on the other side alone. She had been fishing; all she wore was a chemise, and it was wetted through, and a cutty sark at that. She was young and very slender for an island maid, with a long face, a high forehead, and a sly, strange, blindish look between a cat's and a baby's.

"Who's she?" said I. "She'll do."

"That's Uma," said Case, and he called her up and spoke to her in the native. I didn't know what he said; but when he was in the midst, she looked up at me quick and timid like a child dodging a blow; then down again; and presently smiled. She had a wide mouth, the lips and the chin cut like any statue's; and the smile came out for a moment and was gone. There she stood with her head bent and heard Case to an end; spoke back in the pretty Polynesian voice, looking him full in the face; heard him again in answer; and then with an obeisance started off. I had just a share of the bow, but never another shot of her eye; and there was no more word of smiling.

"I guess it's all right," said Case. "I guess you can have her. I'll make it square with the old lady. You can have your pick of the lot for a plug of tobacco," he added, sneering.

I suppose it was the smile stuck in my memory, for I spoke back sharp. "She doesn't look that sort," I cried.

"I don't know that she is," said Case. "I believe she's as right as the mail. Keeps to herself, don't go round with the gang, and that. O, no, don't you misunderstand me—Uma's on the square." He spoke eager I thought, and that surprised and pleased me. "Indeed," he went on, "I shouldn't make so sure of getting her, only she cottoned to the cut of your jib. All you have to do is to keep dark and let me work the mother my own way; and I'll bring the girl round to the captain's for the marriage."

I didn't care for the word marriage, and I said so.

"O, there's nothing to hurt in the marriage," says he. "Black Jack's the chaplain."

By this time we had come in view of the house of these three white men; for a negro is counted a white man—and so is a Chinese! a strange idea, but common in the islands. It was a board house with a strip of ricketty verandah. The store was to the front, with a counter, scales and the poorest possible display of trade: a case or two of tinned meats; a barrel of hard bread; a few bolts of cotton stuff, not to be compared with mine; the only thing well represented being the contraband—fire arms and liquor. "If these are my only rivals," thinks I, "I should do well in Falesá." Indeed there was only the one way they could touch me, and that was with the guns and drink.

In the back room was old Captain Randall, squatting on the

floor native fashion, fat and pale, naked to the waist, gray as a
badger and his eyes set with drink. His body was covered with gray
hair and crawled over by flies; one was in the corner of his eye—
he never heeded; and the mosquitoes hummed about the man like
bees. Any clean-minded man would have had the creature out at
once and buried him; and to see him, and think he was seventy,
and remember he had once commanded a ship, and come ashore
in his smart togs, and talked big in bars and consulates, and sat in
club verandahs, turned me sick and sober.

He tried to get up when I came in, but that was hopeless; so he
reached me a hand instead and stumbled out some salutation.

"Papa's pretty full this morning," observed Case. "We've had an
epidemic here; and Captain Randall takes gin for a prophylactic—
don't you, papa?"

"Never took such thing my life!" cried the captain, indignantly.
"Take gin for my health's sake, Mr Wha's-ever-your-name. 'S a
precaution'ry measure."

"That's all right, papa," said Case. "But you'll have to brace up.
There's going to be a marriage, Mr Wiltshire here is going to get
spliced."

The old man asked to whom.

"To Uma," said Case.

"Uma?" cried the captain. "Wha's he want Uma for? 'S he come
here for his health, anyway? Wha' 'n hell's he want Uma for?"

"Dry up papa," said Case. " 'Tain't you that's to marry her. I guess
you're not her godfather and godmother; I guess Mr Wiltshire's
going to please himself."

With that he made an excuse to me that he must move about
the marriage, and left me alone with the poor wretch that was his
partner and (to speak truth) his gull. Trade and station belonged
both to Randall; Case and the negro were parasites; they crawled
and fed upon him like the flies, he none the wiser. Indeed I have
no harm to say of Billy Randall, beyond the fact that my gorge rose
at him, and the time I now passed in his company was like a
nightmare.

The room was stifling hot and full of flies; for the house was dirty and low and small, and stood in a bad place, behind the village, in the borders of the bush, and sheltered from the trade. The three men's beds were on the floor, and a litter of pans and dishes. There was no standing furniture, Randall, when he was violent, tearing it to laths. There I sat, and had a meal which was served us by Case's wife; and there I was entertained all day by that remains of man, his tongue stumbling among low old jokes and long old stories, and his own wheezy laughter always ready, so that he had no sense of my depression. He was nipping gin all the while; sometimes he fell asleep and awoke again whimpering and shivering; and every now and again he would ask me why in Hell I wanted to marry Uma. "My friend," I was telling myself all day, "you must not be an old gentleman like this."

It might be four in the afternoon perhaps, when the backdoor was thrust slowly open, and a strange old native woman crawled into the house almost on her belly. She was swathed in black stuff to her heels; her hair was gray in swatches; her face was tattooed, which was not the practise in that island; her eyes big and bright and crazy. These she fixed upon me with a wrapt expression that I saw to be part acting; she said no plain word, but smacked and mumbled with her lips, and hummed aloud, like a child over its Christmas pudding. She came straight across the house heading for me, and as soon as she was alongside, caught up my hand and purred and crooned over it like a great cat. From this she slipped into a kind of song.

"Who in the devil's this?" cried I, for the thing startled me.

"It's Faavao," says Randall, and I saw he had hitched along the floor into the farthest corner.

"You ain't afraid of her?" I cried.

"Me 'fraid!" cried the captain. "My dear friend, I defy her! I don't let her put her foot in here. Only I suppose 's diff'ent today for the marriage. 'S Uma's mother."

"Well, suppose it is, what's she carrying on about?" I asked, more irritated, perhaps more frightened than I cared to show; and the captain told me she was making up a quantity of poetry in my praise because I was to marry Uma. "All right, old lady," says I, with rather a failure of a laugh. "Anything to oblige. But when you're done with my hand, you might let me know."

She did as though she understood; the song rose into a cry and stopped; the woman crouched out of the house the same way that she came in, and must have plunged straight into the bush, for when I followed her to the door she had already vanished.

"These are rum manners," said I.

" 'S a rum crowd," said the captain, and to my surprise he made the sign of the cross on his bare bosom.

"Hillo!" says I, "are you a papist?"

He repudiated the idea with contempt. "Hard-shell Baptis'," said he. "But, my dear friend, the papists got some good ideas too; and tha' 's one of 'em. You take my advice, and whenever you come across Uma or Faavao or Vigours or any of that crowd, you take a leaf out o' the priests, and do what I do: savvy?" says he, repeated the sign, and winked his dim eye at me. "No, sir!" he broke out again, "no papists here!" and for a long time entertained me with his religious opinions.

I must have been taken with Uma from the first, or I should certainly have fled from that house and got into the clean air, and the clean sea or some convenient river. Though it's true I was committed to Case; and besides I could never have held my head up in that island, if I had run from a girl upon my wedding night.

The sun was down, the sky all on fire and the lamp had been sometime lighted, when Case came back with Uma and the negro. She was dressed and scented; her kilt was of fine tapa, looking richer in the folds than any silk; her bust, which was of the colour of dark honey, she wore bare only for some half a dozen necklaces of seeds and flowers; and behind her ears and in her hair, she had the scarlet flowers of the hybiscus. She showed the best bearing for a bride conceivable, serious and still; and I thought shame to stand up with her in that mean house and before that grinning negro. I thought shame I say; for the mountebank was dressed with a big paper collar, the book he made believe to read from was an odd volume of a novel, and the words of his service not fit to be set down. My conscience smote me when we joined hands; and when she got her certificate, I was tempted to throw up the bargain and confess. Here is the document: it was Case that wrote it, signatures and all, in a leaf out of the ledger.

This is to certify that _Uma_ daughter of _Faavao_ of Falesá island of ————, is illegally married to _Mr John Wiltshire_ for one night, and Mr John Wiltshire is at liberty to send her to hell next morning.

> John Blackamoor
> Chaplain to the Hulks.

Extracted from the register
   by William T. Randall
    Master Mariner.

That was a nice paper to put in a girl's hand and see her hide away like gold. A man might easily feel cheap for less. But it was the practise in these parts, and (as I told myself) not the least the fault of us White Men but of the missionaries. If they had let the natives be, I had never needed this deception, but taken all the wives I wished, and left them when I pleased, with a clear conscience.

The more ashamed I was, the more hurry I was in to be gone; and our desires thus jumping together, I made the less remark of a change in the traders. Case had been all eagerness to keep me; now, as though he had attained a purpose, he seemed all eagerness to have me go. Uma, he said, could show me to my house, and the three bade us farewell indoors.

The night was nearly come; the village smellt of trees, and flowers and the sea, and breadfruit cooking; there came a fine roll of sea from the reef, and from a distance, among the woods and houses, many pretty sounds of men and children. It did me good to breathe free air; it did me good to be done with the captain and see, instead, the creature at my side. I felt for all the world as though she were some girl at home in the old country, and forgetting myself for the minute, took her hand to walk with. Her fingers nestled into mine; I heard her breathe deep and quick; and all at once she caught my hand to her face and pressed it there. "You good!" she cried, and ran ahead of me, and stopped and looked back and smiled, and ran ahead of me again; thus guiding me through the edge of the bush and by a quiet way to my own house.

The truth is Case had done the courting for me in style; told her I was mad to have her and cared nothing for the consequence; and the poor soul, knowing that which I was still ignorant of, believed it every word, and had her head nigh turned with vanity and gratitude. Now of all this I had no guess; I was one of those most opposed to any nonsense about native women, having seen so many whites eaten up by their wives' relatives and made fools of in the bargain; and I told myself I must make a stand at once and bring her to her bearings. But she looked so quaint and pretty as she ran away and then awaited me, and the thing was done so like a child or a kind dog, that the best I could do was just to follow her whenever she went on, to listen for the fall of her bare feet, and to watch in the dusk for the shining of her body. And there was another thought came in my head. She played kitten with me now when we were alone; but in the house she had carried it the way a countess might, so proud and humble. And what with her dress—for all there was so little of it, and that native enough—what with her fine tapa and fine scents, and her red flowers and seeds that were quite as bright as jewels, only larger—it came over me she was a kind of a countess really, dressed to hear great singers at a concert, and no even mate for a poor trader like myself.

She was the first in the house; and while I was still without, I saw a match flash and the lamplight kindle in the windows. The station was a wonderful fine place, coral built, with quite a wide verandah, and the main room high and wide. My chests and cases had been piled in, and made rather of a mess; and there, in the thick of the confusion, stood Uma by the table, awaiting me. Her shadow went all the way up behind her into the hollow of the iron roof; she stood against it bright, the lamplight shining on her skin. I stopped in the door, and she looked at me, not speaking, with eyes that were eager and yet daunted. Then she touched herself on the bosom. "Me—your wifie," she said. It had never taken me like that before; but the want of her took and shook all through me, like the wind in the luff of a sail.

I could not speak, if I had wanted; and if I could, I would not. I was ashamed to be so much moved about a native; ashamed of the marriage too, and the certificate she had treasured in her kilt; and I turned aside and made believe to rummage among my cases. The first thing I lighted on was a case of gin, the only one that I had brought; and partly for the girl's sake, and partly for horror of the recollection of old Randall, took a sudden resolve. I prized the lid off; one by one, I drew the bottles with a pocket corkscrew, and sent Uma out to pour the stuff from the verandah.

She came back after the last, and looked at me puzzled like.

"Why you do that?" she asked.

"No good," said I, for I was now a little better master of my tongue. "Man he drink, he no good."

She agreed with this but kept considering. "Why you bring him?" she asked presently. "Suppose you no want drink, you no bring him, I think."

"That's all right," said I. "One time I want drink too much; now no want. You see I no savvy I get one little wifie. Suppose I drink gin, my little wifie he 'fraid."

To speak to her kindly was about more than I was fit for; I had made my vow I would never let on to weakness with a native; and I had nothing for it but to stop.

She stood looking gravely down at me where I sat by the open case. "I think you good man," she said. And suddenly she had fallen before me on the floor. "I belong you all-e-same pig!" she cried.

Chapter II

The Ban

I came on the verandah just before the sun rose on the morrow. My house was the last on the east; there was a cape of woods and cliffs behind that hid the sunrise. To the west, a swift cold river ran down, and beyond was the green of the village, dotted with cocoapalms and breadfruits and houses. The shutters were some of them down and some open; I saw the mosquito bars still stretched, with shadows of people new wakened sitting up inside; and all over the green others were stalking silent, wrapped in their many-coloured sleeping clothes like Bedouins in bible pictures. It was mortal still and solemn and chilly; and the light of the dawn on the lagoon was like the shining of a fire.

But the thing that troubled me was nearer hand. Some dozen young men and children made a piece of a half circle, flanking my house; the river divided them, some were on the near side, some on the far, and one on a boulder in the midst; and they all sat silent, wrapped in their sheets, and stared at me and my house as straight as pointer dogs. I thought it strange as I went out. When I had bathed and come back again, and found them all there, and two or three more along with them, I thought it stranger still. What could they see to gaze at in my house? I wondered, and went in.

But the thought of these starers stuck in my mind, and presently I came out again. The sun was now up, but it was still behind the cape of woods: say quarter of an hour had come and gone. The crowd was greatly increased, the far bank of the river was lined for quite a way; perhaps thirty grown folk, and of children twice as many, some standing, some squatted on the ground, and all staring at my house. I have seen a house in a South Sea village thus surrounded, but then a trader was thrashing his wife inside, and she singing out. Here was nothing: the stove was alight, the smoke going up in a Christian manner; all was shipshape and Bristol fashion. To be sure, there was a stranger come; but they had a chance to see that stranger yesterday and took it quiet enough. What ailed them now? I leaned my arms on the rail and stared back. Devil a wink they had in them. Now and then I could see the children chatter, but they spoke so low not even the hum of their speaking came my length. The rest were like graven images; they stared at me, dumb and sorrowful, with their bright eyes; and it came upon me things would look not much different, if I were on the platform of the gallows, and these good folk had come to see me hanged.

I felt I was getting daunted, and began to be afraid I looked it, which would never do. Up I stood, made believe to stretch myself, came down the verandah stair, and strolled towards the river. There went a short buzz from one to the other, like what you hear in theatres when the curtain goes up; and some of the nearest gave back the matter of a pace. I saw a girl lay one hand on a young man and make a gesture upward with the other; at the same time she said something in the native with a gasping voice. Three little boys sat beside my path, where I must pass within three feet of them. Wrapped in their sheets, with their shaved heads and bits of top-knots, and queer faces, they looked like figures on a chimney piece. Awhile they sat their ground, solemn as judges; I came up hand over fist, doing my five knots, like a man that meant business; and I thought I saw a sort of a wink and gulp in the three faces. Then one jumped up (he was the farthest off) and ran for his mammy. The other two, trying to follow suit, got foul, came to ground together bawling, wriggled right out of their sheets—and in a moment there were all three of them, two mother naked, scampering for their lives and singing out like pigs. The natives, who would never let a joke slip even at a burial, laughed and let up, as short as a dog's bark.

They say it scares a man to be alone. No such thing. What scares him in the dark or the high bush, is that he can't make sure, and there might be an army at his elbow. What scares him worst is to be right in the midst of a crowd, and have no guess of what they're driving at. When that laugh stopped, I stopped too. The boys had not yet made their offing; they were still on the full stretch going the one way, when I had already gone about ship and was sheering off the other. Like a fool I had come out, doing my five knots; like a fool I went back again. It must have been the funniest thing to see; and what knocked me silly, this time no one laughed; only one old woman gave a kind of pious moan, the way you have heard dissenters in their chapels at the sermon.

"I never saw such damfool kanakas as your people here," I said once to Uma, glancing out of the window at the starers.

"Savvy nothing," says Uma, with a kind of a disgusted air that she was good at.

And that was all the talk we had upon the matter; for I was put out, and Uma took the thing so much as a matter of course, that I was fairly ashamed.

All day, off and on, now fewer and now more, the fools sat about the west end of my house and across the river, waiting for the show, whatever that was—fire to come down from heaven, I suppose, and consume me bones and baggage. But by evening, like real islanders, they had wearied of the business; and got away and had a dance instead in the big house of the village, where I heard them singing and clapping hands till maybe ten at night; and the next day, it seemed they had forgotten I existed. If fire had come down from heaven or the earth opened and swallowed me, there would have been nobody to see the sport or take the lesson, or whatever you like to call it. But I was to find they hadn't forgot either, and kept an eye lifting for phenomena over my way.

I was hard at it both these days getting my trade in order, and taking stock of what Vigours had left. This was a job that made me pretty sick, and kept me from thinking on much else. Ben had taken stock the trip before, I knew I could trust Ben; but it was plain somebody had been making free in the meantime. I found I was out by what might easy cover six months salary and profit; and

I could have kicked myself all round the village to have been such a blamed ass, sitting boozing with that Case, instead of attending to my own affairs and taking stock. However, there's no use crying over spilt milk. It was done now and couldn't be undone. All I could do was to get what was left of it, and my new stuff (my own choice) in order, to go round and get after the rats and cockroaches, and to fix up that store regular Sydney style. A fine show I made of it; and the third morning, when I had lit my pipe and stood in the doorway and looked in—and turned and looked far up the mountain, and saw the cocoanuts waving, and footed up the tons of copra—and over the village green and saw the island dandies, and reckoned up the yards of print they wanted for their kilts and dresses—I felt as if I was in the right place to make a fortune, and go home again, and start a public house. There was I sitting in that verandah, in as handsome a piece of scenery as you could find, a splendid sun, and a fine, fresh healthy trade that stirred up a man's blood like seabathing; and the whole thing was clean gone from me, and I was dreaming England, which is after all a nasty, cold, muddy hole, with not enough light to see to read by—and dreaming the looks of my public, by a kant of a broad highroad like an avenue and with the sign on a green tree.

So much for the morning, but the day passed and the devil any one looked near me, and from all I knew of natives in other islands, I thought this strange. People laughed a little at our firm, and their fine stations, and at this station of Falesá in particular: all the copra in the district wouldn't pay for it (I had heard them say) in fifty years; which I supposed was an exaggeration. But when the day went and no business came at all, I began to get down-hearted, and about three in the afternoon, I went out for a stroll to cheer me up. On the green I saw a white man coming with a cassock on, by which and by the face of him, I knew he was a priest. He was a good natured old soul to look at, gone a little grizzled, and so dirty you could have written with him on a piece of paper.

"Good day, sir," says I.

He answered me eagerly in native.

"Don't you speak any English?" said I.

"Franch," says he.

"Well," said I, "I'm sorry, but I can't do anything there."

He tried me awhile in the French, and then again in native, which he seemed to think was the best chance. I made out he was after more than passing the time of day with me, but had something to communicate, and I listened the harder. I heard the names of Adams and Case and of Randall—Randall the oftenest; and the word "poison" or something like it; and a native word that he said very often. I went home repeating it to myself.

"What does *fussy-ocky* mean?" I asked of Uma, for that was as near as I could come to it.

"Make dead," said she.

"The devil it does!" says I. "Did ever you hear that Case had poisoned Johnny Adams?"

"Every man he savvy that," says Uma, scornful like. "Give him white sand—bad sand. He got the bottle still. Suppose he give you gin, you no take him."

Now I had heard much the same sort of story in other islands, and the same white powder always to the front, which made me think the less of it. For all that I went over to Randall's place, to see what I could pick up, and found Case on the door step cleaning a gun.

"Good shooting here?" says I.

"A one," says he. "The bush is full of all kinds of birds. I wish copra was as plenty," says he, I thought slyly, "but there don't seem anything doing."

I could see Black Jack in the store serving a customer.

"That looks like business, though," said I.

"That's the first sale we've made in three weeks," said he.

"You don't tell me?" says I. "Three weeks? Well, well."

"If you don't believe me," he cries, a little hot, "you can go and look at the copra house. It's half empty to this blesséd hour."

"I shouldn't be much the better for that, you see," says I. "For all I can tell, it might have been whole empty yesterday."

"That's so," says he, with a bit of a laugh.

"By the by," I said, "what sort of a party is that priest? Seems rather a friendly sort."

At this Case laughed right out loud. "Ah," says he, "I see what ails you now! Galuchet's been at you." *Father Galoshes* was the name he went by mostly, but Case always gave it the French quirk, which was another reason we had for thinking him above the common.

"Yes, I have seen him," I says. "I made out he didn't think much of you or Captain Randall."

"That he don't!" says Case. "It was the trouble about poor Adams. The last day, when he lay dying, there was young Buncombe round. Ever met Buncombe?"

I told him no.

"He's a cure, is Buncombe!" laughs Case. "Well, Buncombe took it in his head that as there was no other clergyman about, bar kanaka pastors, we ought to call in Father Galuchet, and have the old man administered and take the sacrament. It was all the same to me, you may suppose; but I said I thought Adams was the fellow to consult. He was jawing away about watered copra and a sight of foolery. 'Look here,' I said. 'You're pretty sick. Would you like to see Galoshes?' He sat right up on his elbow. 'Get the priest,' says he, 'get the priest, don't let me die here like a dog.' He spoke kind of fierce and eager, but sensible enough; there was nothing to say against that; so we sent and asked Galuchet if he would come. You bet he would! He jumped in his dirty linen at the thought of it. But we had reckoned without Papa. He's a hard-shell Baptist, is Papa; no papists need apply; and he took and locked the door. Buncombe told him he was bigoted, and I thought he would have had a fit. 'Bigoted!' he says. 'Me bigoted? Have I lived to hear it from a jackanapes like you?' And he made for Buncombe, and I had to hold them apart—and there was Adams in the middle, gone luny again and carrying on about copra like a born fool. It was good as the play, and I was about knocked out of time with laughing, when all of a sudden Adams sat up, clapped his hands to his chest, and went into the horrors. He died hard, did John Adams," says Case with a kind of a sudden sternness.

"And what became of the priest?" I asked.

"The priest?" says Case. "O, he was hammering on the door outside, and crying on the natives to come and beat it in, and singing out it was a soul he wished to save, and that. He was in a hell of a taking was the priest. But what would you have? Johnny had slipped his cable; no more Johnny in the market! and the administration racket clean played out. Next thing, word came to Randall the priest was praying upon Johnny's grave. Papa was pretty full, and got a club, and lit out straight for the place; and there was Galoshes on his knees, and a lot of natives looking on. You wouldn't think papa cared that much about anything, unless it was liquor; but he and the priest stuck to it two hours, slanging each other in native; and every time Galoshes tried to kneel down, papa went for him with the club. There never were such larks in Falesá. The end of it was that Captain Randall knocked over with some kind of a fit or stroke, and the priest got in his goods after all. But he was the angriest priest you ever heard of; and complained to the chiefs about the outrage, as he called it. That was no account, for our chiefs are protestant here; and anyway he had been making trouble about the drum for morning school, and they were glad to give him a wipe. Now he swears old Randall gave Adams poison or something, and when the two meet they grin at each other like baboons."

He told this story as natural as could be, and like a man that enjoyed the fun; though now I come to think of it after so long, it seems rather a sickening yarn. However Case never set up to be soft, only to be square and hearty and a man all round; and to tell the truth, he puzzled me entirely.

I went home, and asked Uma if she were a *Popey*, which I had made out to be the native word for catholics.

"*E le ai!*" says she—she always used the native when she meant "no" more than usually strong, and indeed there's more of it. "No good, popey," she added.

Then I asked her about Adams and the priest, and she told me much the same yarn in her own way. So that I was left not much farther on; but inclined upon the whole, to think the bottom of the matter was the row about the sacrament, and the poisoning only talk.

The next day was a Sunday, when there was no business to be looked for. Uma asked me in the morning if I was going to "pray"; I told her she bet not; and she stopped home herself with no more words. I thought this seemed unlike a native, and a native woman, and a woman that had new clothes to show off; however, it suited me to the ground and I made the less of it. The queer thing was that I came next door to going to church after all, a thing I'm little likely to forget. I had turned out for a stroll, and heard the hymn tune up. You know how it is; if you hear folk singing, it seems to draw you; and pretty soon I found myself alongside the church. It was a little long low place, coral built, rounded off at both ends like a whale boat, a big native roof on the top of it, windows without sashes and doorways without doors. I stuck my head into one of the windows, and the sight was so new to me—for things went quite different in the islands I was acquainted with—that I stayed and looked on. The congregation sat on the floor on mats, the women on one side, the men on the other; all rigged out to kill, the women with dresses and trade hats, the men in white jackets and shirts. The hymn was over; the pastor, a big, buck kanaka, was in the pulpit preaching for his life; and by the way he wagged his hand, and worked his voice, and made his points, and seemed to argue with the folk, I made out he was a gun at the business. Well, he looked up suddenly and caught my eye; and I give you my word he staggered in the pulpit. His eyes bulged out of his head, his hand rose and pointed at me like as if against his will, and the sermon stopped right there.

It isn't a fine thing to say for yourself, but I ran away; and if the same kind of a shock was given me, I should run away again to-morrow. To see that palavering kanaka struck all of a heap at the mere sight of me, gave me a feeling as if the bottom had dropped out of the world. I went right home, and stayed there, and said nothing. You might think I would tell Uma, but that was against my system. You might have thought I would have gone over and consulted Case; but the truth was I was ashamed to speak of such a thing, I thought everyone would blurt out laughing in my face. So I held my tongue, and thought all the more, and the more I thought, the less I liked the business.

By Monday night, I got it clearly in my head I must be tabooed. A new store to stand open two days in a village, and not a man or woman come to see the trade, was past believing.

"Uma," said I, "I think I'm tabooed."

"I think so," said she.

I thought awhile whether I should ask her more, but it's a bad idea to set natives up with any notion of consulting them, so I went to Case. It was dark, and he was sitting alone, as he did mostly, smoking on the stairs.

"Case," said I, "here's a queer thing. I'm tabooed."

"O, fudge!" says he. " 'Tain't the practise in these islands."

"That may be, or it mayn't," said I. "It's the practise where I was before; you can bet I know what it's like; and I tell it you for a fact: I'm tabooed."

"Well," said he, "what have you been doing?"

"That's what I want to find out," said I.

"O, you can't be," said he; "it ain't possible. However I'll tell you what I'll do; just to put your mind at rest, I'll go round and find out for sure. Just you waltz in and talk to papa."

"Thank you," I said, "I'd rather stay right out here on the ver-andah: your house is so close."

"I'll call papa out here, then," says he.

"My dear fellow," I says, "I wish you wouldn't. The fact is I don't take to Mr Randall."

Case laughed, took a lantern from the store, and set out into the village. He was gone perhaps quarter of an hour; and he looked mighty serious when he came back.

"Well," said he, clapping down the lantern on the verandah steps, "I would never have believed it. I don't know where the impudence of these kanakas 'll go next, they seem to have lost all idea of respect for whites. What we want is a man of war: a Ger-man, if we could—they know how to manage kanakas."

"I am tabooed then?" I cried.

"Something of the sort," said he. "It's the worst thing of the kind I've heard of yet. But I'll stand by you, Wiltshire, man to man. You come round here tomorrow about nine and we'll have it out with the chiefs. They're afraid of me; or they used to be, but their heads are so big by now I don't know what to think. Understand me, Wiltshire, I don't count this your quarrel," he went on with a great deal of resolution; "I count it all of our quarrel, I count it the White Man's Quarrel, and I'll stand to it through thick and thin, and there's my hand on it."

"Have you found out what's the reason?" I asked.

"Not yet," said Case. "But we'll fix them down tomorrow."

Altogether I was pretty well pleased with his attitude, and almost more the next day when we met to go before the chiefs, to see him so stern and resolved. The chiefs awaited us in one of their big oval houses, which was marked out to us from a long way off by the crowd about the eaves, a hundred strong if there was one, men, women and children. Many of the men were on their way to work and wore green wreaths; and it put me in thoughts of the first of May at home. This crowd opened and buzzed about the pair of us as we went in, with a sudden angry animation. Five chiefs were there, four mighty stately men, the fifth old and puckered. They sat on mats in their white kilts and jackets; they had fans in their hands like fine ladies; and two of the younger ones wore catholic medals, which gave me matter of reflection. Our place was set and the mats laid for us over against these grandees on the near side of the house; the midst was empty; the crowd, close at our backs, murmured and craned and jostled to look on, and the shadows of them tossed in front of us on the clean pebbles of the floor. I was just a hair put out by the excitement of the commons, but the quiet, civil appearance of the chiefs reassured me: all the more when their spokesman began and made a long speech in a low tone of voice, sometimes waving his hand toward Case, sometimes toward me, and sometimes knocking with his knuckles on the mat. One thing was clear: there was no sign of anger in the chiefs.

"What's he been saying?" I asked, when he had done.

"O, just that they're glad to see you, and they understand by me you wish to make some kind of a complaint, and you're to fire away, and they'll do the square thing."

"It took a precious long time to say that," said I.

"O, the rest was sawder and *bonjour* and that," says Case—"you know what kanakas are!"

"Well, they don't get much *bonjour* out of me," said I. "You tell them who I am. I'm a white man, and a British Subject, and no end of a big chief at home; and I've come here to do them good and bring them civilisation; and no sooner have I got my trade sorted out, than they go and taboo me and no one dare come near my place! Tell them I don't mean to fly in the face of anything legal; and if what they want's a present, I'll do what's fair. I don't blame any man looking out for himself, tell them, for that's human nature; but if they think they're going to come any of their native ideas over me, they'll find themselves mistaken. And tell them plain, that I demand the reason of this treatment as a White Man and a British Subject."

That was my speech. I know how to deal with kanakas; give them plain sense and fair dealing, and I'll do them that much justice, they knuckle under every time. They haven't any real government or any real law, that's what you've got to knock into their heads; and even if they had, it would be a good joke if it was to apply to a white man. It would be a strange thing if we came all this way and couldn't do what we pleased. The mere idea has always put my monkey up, and I rapped my speech out pretty big. Then Case translated it, or made believe to, rather; and the first chief replied, and then a second and a third, all in the same style, easy and genteel but solemn underneath. Once a question was put to Case, and he answered it, and all hands (both chiefs and commons) laughed out loud and looked at me. Last of all, the puckered old fellow and the big young chief that spoke first, started in to put Case through a kind of catechism. Sometimes I made out that Case was trying to fence, and they stuck to him like hounds, and the sweat ran down his face, which was no very pleasant sight to me; and at some of his answers, the crowd moaned and murmured, which was a worse hearing. It's a cruel shame I knew no native; for (as I now believe) they were asking Case about my marriage, and he must have had a tough job of it to clear his feet. But leave Case alone: he had the brains to run a parliament.

"Well, is that all?" I asked, when a pause came.

"Come along," says he, mopping his face. "I'll tell you outside."

"Do you mean they won't take the taboo off?" I cried.

"It's something queer," said he. "I'll tell you outside. Better come away."

"I won't take it at their hands," cried I. "I ain't that kind of a man. You don't find me turn my back on a parcel of kanakas."

"You'd better," said Case.

He looked at me with a signal in his eye; and the five chiefs looked at me civilly enough but kind of pointed; and the people looked at me and craned and jostled. I remembered the folks that watched my house, and how the pastor had jumped in his pulpit at the bare sight of me; and the whole business seemed so out of the way that I rose and followed Case. The crowd opened again to let us through, but wider than before, the children on the skirts running and singing out; and as we two white men walked away, they all stood and watched us.

"And now," said I, "what is all this about?"

"The truth is I can't rightly make it out myself. They have a down on you," says Case.

"Taboo a man because they have a down on him!" I cried. "I never heard the like."

"It's worse than that, you see," said Case. "You ain't tabooed, I told you that couldn't be. The people won't go near you, Wiltshire; and there's where it is."

"They won't go near me? What do you mean by that? Why won't they go near me?" I cried.

Case hesitated. "Seems they're frightened," says he, in a low voice.

I stopped dead short. "Frightened?" I repeated. "Are you gone crazy, Case? What are they frightened of?"

"I wish I could make out," Case answered, shaking his head.

"Appears like one of their tomfool superstitions. That's what I don't cotton to," he said; "it's like the business about Vigours."

"I'd like to know what you mean by that, and I'll trouble you to tell me," says I.

"Well, you know, Vigours lit out and left all standing," said he. "It was some superstition business—I never got the hang of it—but it began to look bad before the end."

"I've heard a different story about that," said I, "and I had better tell you so. I heard he ran away because of you."

"O, well, I suppose he was ashamed to tell the truth," says Case; "I guess he thought it silly. And it's a fact that I packed him off. 'What would you do, old man?' says he—'Get,' says I, 'and not think twice about it.' I was the gladdest kind of man to see him clear away. It ain't my notion to turn my back on a mate when he's in a tight place; but there was that much trouble in the village that I couldn't see where it might likely end. I was a fool to be so much about with Vigours. They cast it up to me today; didn't you hear Maea—that's the young chief, the big one—ripping out about 'Vika'? That was him they were after; they don't seem to forget it, somehow."

"This is all very well," said I, "but it don't tell me what's wrong; it don't tell me what they're afraid of—what their idea is."

"Well, I wish I knew," said Case. "I can't say fairer than that."

"You might have asked, I think," says I.

"And so I did," says he; "but you must have seen for yourself, unless you're blind, that the asking got the other way. I'll go as far as I dare for another white man; but when I find I'm in the scrape myself, I think first of my own bacon. The loss of me is I'm too good natured. And I'll take the freedom of telling you, you show a queer kind of gratitude to a man who's got into all this mess along of your affairs."

"There's a thing I'm thinking of," said I. "You were a fool to be so much about with Vigours. One comfort, you haven't been much about with me. I notice you've never been inside my house. Own up, now: you had word of this before?"

"It's a fact I haven't been," said he. "It was an oversight, and I'm sorry for it, Wiltshire. But about coming now, I'll be quite plain."

"You mean you won't?" I asked.

"Awfully sorry, old man, but that's the size of it," says Case.

"In short, you're afraid?" says I.

"In short, I'm afraid," says he.

"And I'm still to be tabooed for nothing?" I asked.

"I tell you you're not tabooed," said he. "The kanakas won't go near you, that's all. And who's to make 'em? We traders have a lot of gall, I must say; we make these poor kanakas take back their laws, and take up their taboos, and that, whenever it happens to suit us. But you don't mean to say you expect a law obliging people to deal in your store whether they want to or not? You don't mean to tell me you've got the gall for that? And if you had, it would be a queer thing to propose to me. I would just like to point out to you, Wiltshire, that I'm a trader myself."

"I don't think I would talk of gall if I was you," said I. "Here's about what it comes to, as well as I can make out. None of the people are to trade with me, and they're all to trade with you. You're to have the copra, and I'm to go to the devil and shake myself. And I don't know any native, and you're the only man here worth mention that speaks English, and you have the gall to up and hint to me my life's in danger, and all you've got to tell me is, you don't know why?"

"Well, it *is* all I have to tell you," said he. "I don't know; I wish I did."

"And so you turn your back and leave me to myself: is that the position?" says I.

"If you like to put it nasty," says he. "I don't put it so. I say merely I'm going to keep clear of you, or if I don't I'll get in danger for myself."

"Well," said I, "you're a nice kind of a white man!"

"O, I understand you're riled," said he. "I would be myself. I can make excuses."

"All right," I said, "go and make excuses somewhere else. Here's my way, there's yours."

With that we parted, and I went straight home, in a holy temper, and found Uma trying on a lot of trade goods like a baby.

"Here," I said, "you quit that foolery. Here's a pretty mess to have made—as if I wasn't bothered enough anyway! And I thought I told you to get dinner?"

And then I believe I gave her a bit of the rough side of my tongue, as she deserved. She stood up at once, like a sentry to his officer; for I must say she was always well brought up and had a great respect for whites.

"And now," says I, "you belong round here, you're bound to understand this. What am I tabooed for anyway? or if I ain't tabooed, what makes the folks afraid of me?"

She stood and looked at me with eyes like saucers.

"You no savvy?" she gasps at last.

"No," said I. "How would you expect me to? We don't have any such craziness where I come from."

"Ese no tell you?" she asked again.

(*Ese* was the name the natives had for Case; it may mean foreign, or extraordinary; or it might mean a mummy apple; but most like it was only his own name misheard and put in the kanaka spelling.)

"Not much!" said I.

"Damn Ese," she cried.

You might think it was funny to hear this kanaka girl come out with a big swear. No such thing. There was no swearing in her; no, nor anger; she was beyond anger, and meant the word simple and serious. She stood there straight as she said it; I cannot justly say that ever I saw a woman look like that before or after, and it struck me mum. Then she made a kind of an obeisance, but it was the proudest kind, and threw her hands out open.

"I 'shamed," she said. "I think you savvy. Ese he tell me you savvy, he tell me you no mind—tell me you love me too much. Taboo belong me," she said, touching herself on the bosom, as she had done upon our wedding night. "Now I go 'way, taboo he go 'way too. Then you get too much copra. You like more better, I think. Tofá, alii," says she in the native—"Farewell, chief!"

"Hold on," I cried. "Don't be in such a blamed hurry."

She looked at me sidelong with a smile. "You see, you get copra," says she, the same as you might offer candies to a child.

"Uma," said I, "hear reason. I didn't know, and that's a fact; and Case seems to have played it pretty mean upon the pair of us. But I do know now, and I don't mind: I love you too much. You no go 'way, you no leave me, I too much sorry."

"You no love me!" she cried, "you talk me bad words!" And she threw herself in a corner on the floor, and began to cry.

Well, I'm no scholar, but I wasn't born yesterday, and I thought the worst of that trouble was over. However, there she lay—her back turned, her face to the wall—and shook with sobbing like a little child, so that her feet jumped with it. It's strange how it hits a man when he's in love; for there's no use mincing things; kanaka and all, I was in love with her, or just as good. I tried to take her hand, but she would none of that. "Uma," I said, "there's no sense in carrying on like this. I want you stop here, I want my little wifie, I tell you true."

"No tell me true!" she sobbed.

"All right," says I, "I'll wait till you're through with this." And I sat right down beside her on the floor, and set to smoothe her hair with my hand. At first she wriggled away when I touched her; then she seemed to notice me no more; then her sobs grew gradually less and presently stopped; and the next thing I knew, she raised her face to mine.

"You tell me true? You like me stop?" she asked.

"Uma," I said, "I would rather have you than all the copra in the South Seas," which was a very big expression, and the strangest thing was that I meant it.

She threw her arms about me, sprang close up, and pressed her face to mine in the island way of kissing, so that I was all wetted with her tears and my heart went out to her wholly. I never had anything so near me as this little brown bit of a girl. Many things went together and all helped to turn my head. She was pretty enough to eat; it seemed she was my only friend in that queer place;

I was ashamed that I had spoken rough to her; and she was a woman, and my wife, and a kind of a baby besides that I was sorry for; and the salt of her tears was in my mouth. And I forgot Case and the natives; and I forgot that I knew nothing of the story, or only remembered it to banish the remembrance; and I forgot that I was to get no copra and so could make no livelihood; and I forgot my employers, and the strange kind of service I was doing them, when I preferred my fancy to their business; and I forgot even that Uma was no true wife of mine, but just a maid beguiled, and that in a pretty shabby style. But that is to look too far on. I will come to that part of it next.

It was late before we thought of getting dinner. The stove was out, and gone stone-cold; but we fired up after awhile, and cooked each a dish, helping and hindering each other, and making a play of it like children. I was so greedy of her nearness that I sat down to dinner with my lass upon my knee, made sure of her with one hand, and ate with the other. Ay, and more than that. She was the worst cook I suppose God made; the things she set her hand to, it would have sickened an entire horse to eat of; yet I made my meal that day on Uma's cookery, and can never call to mind to have been better pleased.

I didn't pretend to myself, and I didn't pretend to her. I saw I was clean gone; and if she was to make a fool of me, she must. And I suppose it was this that set her talking, for now she made sure that we were friends. A lot she told me, sitting in my lap and eating my dish, as I ate hers, from foolery: a lot about herself and her mother and Case, all which would be very tedious and fill sheets if I set it down in Beach de Mar, but which I must give a hint of in plain English—and one thing about myself, which had a very big effect on my concerns, as you are soon to hear.

It seems she was born in one of the Line islands; had been only two or three years in these parts, where she had come with a white man who was married to her mother and then died; and only the one year in Falesá. Before that, they had been a good deal on the move, trekking about after the white man, who was one of these rolling stones that keep going round after a soft job. They talk about looking for gold at the end of a rainbow; but if a man wants an employment that'll last him till he dies, let him start out on the soft-job hunt. There's meat and drink in it too, and beer and skittles; for you never hear of them starving and rarely see them sober; and as for steady sport, cockfighting isn't in the same county with it. Anyway, this beachcomber carried the woman and her daughter all over the shop, but mostly to out of the way islands, where there were no police and he thought perhaps the soft-job hung out. I've my own view of this old party; but I was just as glad he had kept Uma clear of Apia and Papeete and these flash towns. At last he struck Fale-alii on this island, got some trade the Lord knows how! muddled it all away in the usual style, and died worth next to nothing, bar a bit of land at Falesá that he had got for a bad debt, which was what put it in the minds of the mother and daughter to come there and live. It seems Case encouraged them all he could, and helped to get their house built. He was very kind those days, and gave Uma trade, and there is no doubt he had his eye on her from the beginning. However, they had scarce settled, when up turned a young man, a native, and wanted to marry her. He was a small chief, and had some fine mats and old songs in his family, and was "very pretty," Uma said; and altogether it was an extraordinary match for a penniless girl and an out-islander.

At the first word of this, I got downright sick with jealousy.

"And you mean to say you would have married him!" I cried.

"*Ioe*," says she. "I like too much!"

"Well!" I said. "And suppose I had come round after?"

"I like you more better now," said she. "But suppose I marry Ioane, I one good wife. I no common kanaka: good girl!" says she.

Well, I had to be pleased with that; but I promise you I didn't care about the business one little bit, and liked the end of that yarn better than the beginning. For it seems this proposal of marriage was the start of all the trouble. It seems, before that, Uma and her mother had been looked down upon of course for kinless folk and out-islanders, but nothing to hurt; and even when Ioane came forward there was less trouble at first than might have been looked for. And then all of a sudden, about six months before my coming, Ioane backed out and left that part of the island, and from that day to this, Uma and her mother had found themselves alone. None called at their house, none spoke to them on the roads. If they went to church, the other women drew their mats away and left them in a clear place by themselves. It was a regular excommunication, like what you read of in the middle ages; and the cause or sense of it beyond guessing. It was some *tala pepelo*, Uma said, some lie, some calumny; and all she knew of it was that the girls who had been jealous of her luck with Ioane used to twit her with his desertion, and cry out, when they met her alone in the woods, that she would never be married. "They tell me no man he marry me. He too much 'fraid," she said.

The only soul that came about them after this desertion was Master Case; even he was chary of showing himself, and turned up mostly by night; and pretty soon he began to table his cards and make up to Uma. I was still sore about Ioane, and when Case turned up in the same line of business, I cut up downright rough.

"Well," I said sneering, "and I suppose you thought Case 'very pretty' and 'liked too much.' "

"Now you talk silly," said she. "White man he come here, I marry him all-e-same kanaka; very well then, he marry me all-e-same white woman. Suppose he no marry, he go 'way, woman he stop. All-e-same thief; empty hand, Tonga-heart—no can love! Now you come marry me; you big heart—you no 'shamed island girl. That thing I love you for too much. I proud."

I don't know that ever I felt sicker all the days of my life. I laid down my fork and I put away 'the island girl'; I didn't seem somehow to have any use for either; and I went and walked up and down in the house, and Uma followed me with her eyes, for she was troubled, and small wonder! But troubled was no word for it with me; I so wanted, and so feared, to make a clean breast of the sweep that I had been.

And just then there came a sound of singing out of the sea; it sprang up suddenly clear and near, as the boat turned the headland; and Uma, running to the window, cried out it was "Misi" come upon his rounds.

I thought it was a strange thing I should be glad to have a mis-sionary; but if it was strange, it was still true.

"Uma," said I, "you stop here in this room, and don't budge a foot out of it till I come back."

Chapter III

The Missionary

As I came out on the verandah, the mission boat was shooting for the mouth of the river. She was a long whale boat painted white; a bit of an awning astern; a native pastor crouched on the wedge of poop, steering; some four and twenty paddles flashing and dipping, true to the boat-song; and the missionary under the awning, in his white clothes, reading in a book, and set him up! It was pretty to see and hear; there's no smarter sight in the islands than a missionary boat with a good crew and a good pipe to them; and I considered it for half a minute with a bit of envy perhaps, and then strolled towards the river.

From the opposite side there was another man aiming for the same place, but he ran and got there first. It was Case; doubtless his idea was to keep me apart from the missionary who might serve me as interpreter; but my mind was upon other things, I was thinking how he had jockeyed us about the marriage, and tried his hand on Uma before; and at the sight of him, rage flew in my nostrils.

"Get out of that, you low, swindling thief!" I cried.

"What's that you say?" says he.

I gave him the word again, and rammed it down with a good oath. "And if ever I catch you within six fathoms of my house," I cried, "I'll clap a bullet in your measly carcase."

"You must do as you like about your house," said he, "where I told you I have no thought of going. But this is a public place."

"It's a place where I have private business," said I. "I have no idea of a hound like you eavesdropping, and I give you notice to clear out."

"I don't take it though," says Case.

"I'll show you, then," said I.

"We'll have to see about that," said he.

He was quick with his hands, but he had neither the height nor the weight, being a flimsy creature alongside a man like me; and besides I was blazing to that height of wrath that I could have bit into a chisel. I gave him first the one and then the other, so that I could hear his head rattle and crack, and he went down straight.

"Have you had enough?" cries I. But he only looked up white and blank, and the blood spread upon his face like wine upon a napkin. "Have you had enough?" I cried again. "Speak up, and don't lie malingering there, or I'll take my feet to you!"

He sat up at that, and held his head—by the look of him you could see it was spinning—and the blood poured on his pyjamas.

"I've had enough for this time," says he, and he got up staggering and went off by the way that he had come.

The boat was close in; I saw the missionary had laid his book to one side, and I smiled to myself. "He'll know I'm a man, anyway," thinks I.

This was the first time, in all my years in the Pacific, I had ever exchanged two words with any missionary; let alone asked one for a favour. I didn't like the lot, no trader does; they look down upon us and make no concealment; and besides they're partly kanaka-ised, and suck up with natives instead of with other white men like themselves. I had on a rig of clean, striped pyjamas, for of course I had dressed decent to go before the chiefs; but when I saw the missionary step out of his boat in the regular uniform, white duck clothes, pith helmet, white shirt and tie, and yellow boots to his feet, I could have bunged stones at him. As he came nearer, queering me pretty curious (because of the fight I suppose) I saw he looked mortal sick, for the truth was he had a fever on and had just had a chill in the boat.

"Mr Tarleton, I believe?" says I, for I had got his name.

"And you, I suppose, are the new trader?" says he.

"I want to tell you first that I don't hold with missions," I went on, "and that I think you and the likes of you do a sight of harm, filling up the natives with old wives' tales and bumptiousness."

"You are perfectly entitled to your opinions," says he, looking a bit ugly, "but I have no call to hear them."

"It so happens that you've got to hear them," I said. "I'm no missionary nor missionary lover; I'm no kanaka nor favourer of kanakas: I'm just a trader, I'm just a common, low, god-damned white man and British subject, the sort you would like to wipe your boots on. I hope that's plain."

"Yes, my man," said he. "It's more plain than creditable. When you are sober, you'll be sorry for this."

He tried to pass on, but I stopped him with my hand. The kanakas were beginning to growl; guess they didn't like my tone, for I spoke to that man as free as I would to you.

"Now you can't say I've deceived you," said I, "and I can go on. I want a service, I want two services in fact; and if you care to give me them, I'll perhaps take more stock in what you call your christianity."

He was silent for a moment. Then he smiled. "You are rather a strange sort of man," says he.

"I'm the sort of a man God made me," says I. "I don't set up to be a gentleman," I said.

"I am not quite so sure," said he. "And what can I do for you, Mr ———?"

"Wiltshire," I says, "though I'm mostly called Welsher; but Wiltshire is the way it's spellt, if the people on the beach could only get their tongues about it. And what do I want? Well, I'll tell you the first thing. I'm what you call a sinner—what I call a sweep—and I want you to help me make it up to a person I've deceived."

He turned and spoke to his crew in the native. "And now I am at your service," said he, "but only for the time my crew are dining. I must be much farther down the coast before night. I was delayed at Papa-mālūlū till this morning, and I have an engagement in Fale-alii tomorrow night."

I led the way to my house in silence and rather pleased with myself for the way I had managed the talk, for I like a man to keep his self-respect.

"I was sorry to see you fighting," says he.

"O, that's part of a yarn I want to tell you," I said. "That's service number two. After you've heard it, you'll let me know whether you're sorry or not."

We walked right in through the store, and I was surprised to find Uma had cleared away the dinner things. This was so unlike her ways, that I saw she had done it out of gratitude, and liked her the better. She and Mr Tarleton called each other by name, and he was very civil to her seemingly. But I thought little of that; they can always find civility for a kanaka; it's us white men they lord it over. Besides I didn't want much Tarleton just then: I was going to do my pitch.

"Uma," said I, "give us your marriage certificate." She looked put out. "Come," said I. "You can trust me. Hand it up."

She had it about her person as usual; I believe she thought it was a pass to heaven, and if she died without having it handy she would go to hell. I couldn't see where she put it the first time, I couldn't see now where she took it from; it seemed to jump in her hand like that Blavatsky business in the papers. But it's the same way with all island women, and I guess they're taught it when young.

"Now," said I, with the certificate in my hand, "I was married to this girl by Black Jack the negro. The certificate was wrote by Case, and it's a dandy piece of literature, I promise you. Since then I've found that there's a kind of cry in the place against this wife of mine, and so long as I keep her, I cannot trade. Now what would any man do in my place, if he was a man?" I said. "The first thing he would do is this, I guess." And I took and tore up the certificate and bunged the pieces on the floor.

"Aué!" cried Uma, and began to clap her hands, but I caught one of them in mine.

"And the second thing that he would do," said I, "if he was what I would call a man, and you would call a man, Mr Tarleton, is to bring the girl right before you or any other missionary, and to up and say: 'I was wrong married to this wife of mine, but I think a heap of her, and now I want to be married to her right.' Fire away, Mr Tarleton. And I guess you'd better do it in native; it'll please the old lady," I said, giving her the proper name of a man's wife upon the spot.

So we had in two of the crew to witness, and were spliced in our own house; and the parson prayed a good bit, I must say, but not so long as some, and shook hands with the pair of us.

"Mr Wiltshire," he says, when he had made out the lines and packed off the witnesses, "I have to thank you for a very lively pleasure. I have rarely performed the marriage ceremony with more grateful emotions."

That was what you would call talking. He was going on besides with more of it, and I was ready for as much taffy as he had in stock, for I felt good. But Uma had been taken up with something half through the marriage, and cut straight in.

"How your hand he get hurt?" she asked.

"You ask Case's head, old lady," says I.

She jumped with joy, and sang out.

"You haven't made much of a christian of this one," says I to Mr Tarleton.

"We didn't think her one of our worst," says he, "when she was at Fale-alii; and if Uma bears malice, I shall be tempted to fancy she has good cause."

"Well, there we are at service number two," said I. "I want to tell you our yarn, and see if you can let a little daylight in."

"Is it long?" he asked.

"Yes," I said, "it's a goodish bit of a yarn."

"Well, I'll give you all the time I can spare," says he, looking at his watch. "But I must tell you fairly I haven't eaten since five this morning; and unless you can let me have something, I am not likely to eat again before seven or eight tonight."

"By God, we'll give you dinner!" I cried.

I was a little caught up at my swearing, just when all was going straight; and so was the missionary I suppose, but he made believe to look out of the window and thanked us.

So we ran him up a bit of a meal. I was bound to let the old lady have a hand in it, to show off; so I deputised her to brew the tea. I don't think I ever met such tea as she turned out. But that was not the worst, for she got round with the salt-box, which she considered an extra European touch, and turned my stew into sea water. Altogether, Mr Tarleton had a devil of a dinner of it; but he had plenty entertainment by the way, for all the while that we were cooking, and afterwards when he was making believe to eat, I kept posting him up on Master Case and the beach of Falesá, and he putting questions that showed he was following close.

"Well," said he at last, "I am afraid you have a dangerous enemy. This man Case is very clever and seems really wicked. I must tell you I have had my eye on him for nearly a year, and have rather had the worst of our encounters. About the time when the last representative of your firm ran so suddenly away, I had a letter from Namu, the native pastor, begging me to come to Falesá at my earliest convenience, as his flock were all 'adopting catholic practices.' I had great confidence in Namu; I fear it only shows how easily we are deceived. No one could hear him preach and not be persuaded he was a man of extraordinary parts. All our islanders easily acquire a kind of eloquence, and can roll out and illustrate with a great deal of vigour and fancy secondhand sermons; but Namu's sermons are his own, and I cannot deny that I have found them means of grace. Moreover he has a keen curiosity in secular things, does not fear work, is clever at carpentering, and has made himself so much respected among the neighbouring pastors that we call him, in a jest which is half serious, the Bishop of the East. In short I was proud of the man; all the more puzzled by his letter; and took occasion to come this way. The morning before my arrival, Vigours had been set on board the *Lion*, and Namu was perfectly at his ease, apparently ashamed of his letter, and quite unwilling to explain it. This of course I could not allow; and he ended by confessing that he had been much concerned to find his people using the sign of the cross, but since he had learned the explanation his mind was satisfied. For Vigours had the Evil Eye, a common thing in a country of Europe called Italy, where men were often struck dead by that kind of devil; and it appeared the sign of the cross was a charm against its power.

" 'And I explain it, Misi,' said Namu in this way. 'The country in Europe is a Popey country, and the devil of the Evil Eye may be a catholic devil, or at least used to catholic ways. So then I reasoned thus; if this sign of the cross were used in a Popey manner, it would be sinful; but when it is used only to protect men from a devil, which is a thing harmless in itself, the sign too must be harmless. For the sign is neither good nor bad, even as a bottle is neither good nor bad. But if the bottle be full of gin, the gin is bad; and if the sign be made in idolatry, so is the idolatry bad.' And very like a native pastor, he had a text apposite about the casting out of devils.

" 'And who has been telling you about the Evil Eye?' I asked.

"He admitted it was Case. Now I am afraid you will think me very narrow, Mr Wiltshire, but I must tell you I was displeased, and cannot think a trader at all a good man to advise or have an influence upon my pastors. And besides there had been some flying talk in the country of old Adams and his being poisoned, to which I had paid no great heed; but it came back to me at the moment.

" 'And is this Case a man of sanctified life?' I asked.

"He admitted he was not; for though he did not drink, he was profligate with women and had no religion.

" 'Then,' said I, 'I think the less you have to do with him the better.'

"But it is not easy to have the last word with a man like Namu; he was ready in a moment with an illustration. 'Misi,' said he, 'you have told me there were wise men, not pastors, not even holy, who knew many things useful to be taught, about trees for instance, and beasts, and to print books, and about the stones that are burned to make knives of. Such men teach you in your college, and you learn from them, but take care not to learn to be unholy. Misi, Case is my college.'

"I knew not what to say. Mr Vigours had evidently been driven out of Falesá by the machinations of Case and with something not very unlike the collusion of my pastor. I called to mind it was Namu who had reassured me about Adams and traced the rumour to the ill will of the priest. And I saw I must inform myself more thoroughly from an impartial source. There is an old rascal of a chief here, Faiaso, whom I daresay you saw today at the council; he has been all his life turbulent and sly, a great fomenter of rebellions, and a thorn in the side of the mission and the island. For all that he is very shrewd, and except in politics or about his own misdemeanours, a teller of the truth. I went to his house, told him what I had heard, and besought him to be frank. I do not think I had ever a more painful interview. Perhaps you will understand me, Mr Wiltshire, if I tell you that I am perfectly serious in these old-wives' tales with which you reproached me, and as anxious to do well for these islands as you can be to please and to protect your pretty wife. And you are to remember that I thought Namu a paragon, and was proud of the man as one of the first ripe fruits of the mission. And now I was informed that he had fallen in a sort of dependence upon Case. The beginning of it was not corrupt; it began doubtless in fear and respect produced by trickery and pretence; but I was shocked to find that another element had been lately added, that Namu helped himself in the store, and was believed to be deep in Case's debt. Whatever the trader said, that Namu believed with trembling. He was not alone in this; many in the village lived in a similar subjection; but Namu's case was the most influential, it was through Namu Case had wrought most evil; and with a certain following among the chiefs, and the pastor in his pocket, the man was as good as master of the village. You know something of Vigours and Adams; but perhaps you have never heard of old Underhill, Adams's predecessor. He was a quiet, mild old fellow, I remember, and we were told he had died suddenly: white men die very suddenly in Falesá. The truth, as I now heard it, made my blood run cold. It seems he was struck with a general palsy, all of him dead but one eye, which he continually winked. Word was started that the helpless old man was now a devil; and this vile fellow Case worked upon the natives' fears, which he professed to share, and pretended he durst not go into the house alone. At last a grave was dug, and the living body buried at the far end of the village. Namu, my pastor, whom I had helped to educate, offered up prayer at the hateful scene.

"I felt myself in a very difficult position. Perhaps too it was my duty to have denounced Namu and had him deposed; perhaps I think so now; but at the time, it seemed less clear. He had a great influence, it might prove greater than mine. The natives are prone to superstition; perhaps by stirring them up, I might but ingrain and spread these dangerous fancies. And Namu besides, apart from this novel and accursed influence, was a good pastor, an able man and spiritually minded. Where should I look for a better? how was I to find as good? At that moment with Namu's failure fresh in my view, the work of my life appeared a mockery; hope was dead in me; I would rather repair such tools as I had, than go abroad in quest of others that must certainly prove worse; and a scandal is, at the best, a thing to be avoided when humanly possible. Right or wrong then, I determined on a quiet course. All that night I denounced and reasoned with the erring pastor; twitted him with his ignorance and want of faith; twitted him with his wretched attitude, making clean the outside of the cup and platter, callously helping at a murder, childishly flying in excitement about a few childish, unnecessary and inconvenient gestures; and long before day, I had him on his knees and bathed in tears of what seemed a genuine repentance. On Sunday I took the pulpit in the morning and preached from First Kings, nineteenth, on the fire, the earthquake and the voice: distinguishing the true spiritual power, and referring with such plainness as I dared to recent events in Falesá. The effect produced was great; and it was much increased, when Namu rose in his turn, and confessed that he had been wanting in faith and conduct, and was convinced of sin. So far, then, all was well; but there was one unfortunate circumstance. It was nearing the time of our 'May' in the island, when the native contributions to the mission are received; it fell in my duty to make a notification on the subject; and this gave my enemy his chance, by which he was not slow to profit.

"News of the whole proceedings must have been carried to Case as soon as church was over; and the same afternoon he made an occasion to meet me in the midst of the village. He came up with so much intentness and animosity that I felt it would be damaging to avoid him.

" 'So,' says he in native, 'here is the holy man. He has been preaching against me, but that was not in his heart. He has been preaching upon the love of God, but that was not in his heart—it was between his teeth. Will you know what was in his heart?' cries he. 'I will show it you.' And making a snatch at my head, he made believe to pluck out a dollar, and held it in the air.

"There went that rumour through the crowd with which Polynesians receive a prodigy. As for myself, I stood amazed. The thing was a common, conjuring trick, which I have seen performed at home a score of times; but how was I to convince the villagers of that? I wished I had learned legerdemain instead of Hebrew, that I might have paid the fellow out with his own coin. But there I was, I could not stand there silent, and the best that I could find to say was weak.

" 'I will trouble you not to lay hands on me again,' said I.

" 'I have no such thought,' said he, 'nor will I deprive you of your dollar. Here it is,' he said, and flung it at my feet. I am told it lay where it fell three days."

"I must say it was well played," said I.

"O, he is clever," said Mr Tarleton, "and you can now see for yourself how dangerous. He was a party to the horrid death of the paralytic; he is accused of poisoning Adams; he drove Vigours out of the place by lies that might have led to murder; and there is no question but he has now made up his mind to rid himself of you. How he means to try, we have no guess; only be sure it's something new. There is no end to his readiness and invention."

"He gives himself a sight of trouble," says I. "And after all, what for?"

"Why, how many tons of copra may they make in this district?" asked the missionary.

"I daresay as much as sixty tons," says I.

"And what is the profit to the local trader?" he asked.

"You may call it three pounds," said I.

"Then you can reckon for yourself how much he does it for," said Mr Tarleton. "But the more important thing is to defeat him. It is clear he spread some report against Uma, in order to isolate and have his wicked will of her; failing of that, and seeing a new rival come upon the scene, he used her in a different way. Now the first point to find out is about Namu. Uma, when people began to leave you and your mother alone, what did Namu do?"

"Stop away all-e-same," says Uma.

"I fear the dog has returned to his vomit," said Mr Tarleton. "And now what am I to do for you? I will speak to Namu, I will warn him he is observed; it will be strange if he allow anything to go on amiss, when he is put upon his guard. At the same time, this precaution may fail, and then you must turn elsewhere. You have two people at hand to whom you might apply. There is first of all the priest, who might protect you by the catholic interest; they are a wretchedly small body, but they count two chiefs. And then there is old Faiaso. Ah, if it had been some years ago, you would have needed no one else; but his influence is much reduced, it has gone into Maea's hands, and Maea, I fear, is one of Case's jackalls. In fine, if the worst comes to the worst, you must send up or come yourself to Fale-alii, and though I am not due at this end of the island for a month, I will see what can be done."

So Mr Tarleton said farewell; and half an hour later, the crew were singing and the paddles flashing in the missionary boat.

Chapter IV

Devil-Work

Near a month went by without much doing. The same night of our marriage, Galoshes called round, made himself mighty civil, and got into a habit of dropping in about dark and smoking his pipe with the family. He could talk to Uma of course, and started to teach me native and French at the same time. He was a kind old buffer, though the dirtiest you would wish to see, and he muddled me up with foreign languages worse than the tower of Babel.

That was one employment we had, and it made me feel less lonesome; but there was no profit in the thing; for though the priest came and sat and yarned, none of his folks could be enticed into my store; and if it hadn't been for the other occupation I struck out, there wouldn't have been a pound of copra in the house. This was the idea: Fa'avao (Uma's mother) had a score of bearing trees. Of course, we could get no labour, being all as good as tabooed. And the two women and I turned to and made copra with our own hands. It was copra to make your mouth water, when it was done—I never understood how much the natives cheated me till I had made that four hundred pounds of my own hand—and it weighed so light, I felt inclined to take and water it myself.

When we were at the job, a good many kanakas used to put in the best of the day looking on, and once that nigger turned up. He stood back with the natives, and laughed, and did the big don and the funny dog, till I began to get riled.

"Here, you, nigger!" says I.

"I don't address myself to you, sah," says the nigger. "Only speak to gen'le'um."

"I know," says I, "but it happens I was addressing myself to you, Mr Black Jack. And all I want to know is just this: did you see Case's figurehead about a week ago?"

"No, sah," says he.

"That's all right, then," says I; "for I'll show you the own brother to it, only black, in the inside of about two minutes."

And I began to walk towards him, quite slow and my hands down; only there was trouble in my eye, if anybody took the pains to look.

"You're a low, obstropulous fellow, sah," says he.

"You bet!" says I.

By that time he thought I was about as near as was convenient, and lit out so it would have done your heart good to see him travel. And that was all I saw of that precious gang, until what I am about to tell you.

It was one of my chief employments these days to go pot-hunting in the woods, which I found (as Case had told me) very rich in game. I have spoken of the cape, which shut up the village and my station from the east. A path went about the end of it, and led into the next bay. A strong wind blew here daily, and as the line of the barrier reef stopped at the end of the cape, a heavy surf ran on the shores of the bay. A little cliffy hill cut the valley in two parts, and stood close on the beach; and at high water the sea broke right on the face of it, so that all passage was stopped. Woody mountains hemmed the place all round; the barrier to the east was particularly steep and leafy; the lower parts of it, along the sea, falling in sheer black cliffs streaked with cinnabar; the upper part lumpy with the tops of the great trees. Some of the trees were bright green, and some red, and the sand of the beach as black as your shoes. Many birds hovered round the bay, some of them snow white; and the flying-fox (or vampire) flew there in broad daylight, gnashing its teeth.

For a long while I came as far as this shooting and went no farther. There was no sign of any path beyond; and the cocoapalms in the front of the foot of the valley were the last this way. For the whole "eye" of the island, as natives call the windward end, lay desert. From Falesá round about to Papa-mālūlū, there was neither house, nor man, nor planted fruit tree; and the reef being mostly absent and the shores bluff, the sea beat direct among crags, and there was scarce a landing place.

I should tell you that after I began to go in the woods, although no one offered to come near my store, I found people willing enough to pass the time of day with me where nobody could see them. And as I had begun to pick up native, and most of them had a word or two of English, I began to hold little odds and ends of conversation, not to much purpose, to be sure, but they took off the worst of the feeling. For it's a miserable thing to be made a leper of.

It chanced one day, towards the end of the month, that I was sitting in this bay in the edge of the bush, looking east, with a kanaka. I had given him a fill of tobacco, and we were making out to talk as best we could; indeed he had more English than most.

I asked him if there was no road going eastward.

"One time one road," said he. "Now he dead."

"Nobody he go there?" I asked.

"No good," said he. "Too much devil he stop there."

"Oho!" says I, "got-um plenty devil, that bush?"

"Man devil, woman devil: too much devil," said my friend. "Stop there all-e-time. Man he go there, no come back."

I thought, if this fellow was so well posted on devils and spoke of them so free, which is not common, I had better fish for a little information about myself and Uma.

"You think me one devil?" I asked.

"No think devil," said he soothingly. "Think all-e-same fool."

"Uma, she devil?" I asked again.

"No, no; no devil; devil stop bush," said the young man.

I was looking in front of me across the bay, and I saw the hanging front of the woods pushed suddenly open, and Case with a gun in his hand step forth into the sunshine on the black beach. He was got up in light pyjamas, near white, his gun sparkled, he looked mighty conspicuous; and the land crabs scuttled from all round him to their holes.

"Hullo, my friend," says I, "you no talk all-e-same true. Ese he go, he come back."

"Ese no all-e-same; Ese *Tiapolo*," says my friend; and with a good bye, slunk off among the trees.

I watched Case all round the beach, where the tide was low; and let him pass me on the homeward way to Falesá. He was in deep thought; and the birds seemed to know it, trotting quite near him on the sand or wheeling and calling in his ears. Where he passed nearest me, I could see by the working of his lips that he was talking in to himself, and what pleased me mightily, he had still my trade-mark on his brow. I tell you the plain truth, I had a mind to give him a gunfull in his ugly mug, but I thought better of it.

All this time, and all the time I was following home, I kept repeating that native word, which I remembered by "Polly, put the kettle on and make us all some tea": tea-a-pollo.

"Uma," says I, when I got back, "what does Tiapolo mean?"

"Devil," says she.

"I thought *aitu* was the word for that?" I said.

"*Aitu* 'nother kind of devil," said she; "stop bush, eat kanaka. Tiapolo big-chief devil, stop home; all-e-same Christian devil."

"Well then," said I. "I'm no farther forward. How can Case be Tiapolo?"

"No all-e-same," said she. "Ese belong Tiapolo; Tiapolo too much like; Ese all-e-same his son. Suppose Ese he wish something, Tiapolo he make him."

"That's mighty convenient for Ese," says I. "And what kind of things does he make for him?"

Well, out came a rigmarole of all sorts of stories, many of which (like the dollar he took from Mr Tarleton's head) were plain enough to me, but others I could make nothing of; and the thing that most surprised the kanakas was what surprised me least: namely, that he could go in the desert among all the *aitus*. Some of the boldest, however, had accompanied him, and had heard him speak with the dead and give them orders, and safe in his

protection, had returned unscathed. Some said he had a church
there where he worshipped Tiapolo, and Tiapolo appeared to him;
others swore there was no sorcery at all, that he performed his
miracles by the power of prayer, and the church was no church but
a prison in which he had confined a dangerous *aitu*. Namu had
been in the bush with him once, and returned glorifying God for
these wonders. Altogether I began to have a glimmer of the man's
position, and the means by which he had acquired it, and though
I saw he was a tough nut to crack, I was noways cast down.

"Very well," said I, "I'll have a look at Master Case's place of
worship myself, and we'll see about the glorifying."

At this time Uma fell in a terrible taking; if I went in the high
bush, I should never return; none could go there but by the protection of Tiapolo.

"I'll chance it on God's," said I. "I'm a good sort of a fellow,
Uma, as fellows go; and I guess God'll con me through."

She was silent for awhile. "I think," said she, mighty solemn;
and then presently: "Victoreea he big chief?"

"You bet," said I.

"He like you too much?" she asked again.

I told her with a grin I believed the old lady was rather partial
to me.

"All right," said she. "Victoreea he big chief, like you too much;
no can help you here in Falesá; no can do, too far off. Maea he
small chief; stop here; suppose he like you, make you all right. All-
e-same God and Tiapolo. God he big chief, got too much work.
Tiapolo he small chief, he like too much make-see, work very
hard."

"I'll have to hand you over to Mr Tarleton," said I. "Your the-
ology's out of its bearings, Uma."

However we stuck at this business all the evening, and with the
stories she told me of the desert and its dangers, she came near
frightening herself into a fit. I don't remember half a quarter of
them of course, for I paid little heed; but two come back to me
kind of clear.

About six miles up the coast there is a sheltered cove, they call

Fanga-anaana, "the haven full of caves." I've seen it from the sea myself, as near as I could get my boys to venture in; and it's a little strip of yellow sand. Black cliffs overhang it full of the black mouths of caves, great trees overhang the cliffs and dangle down lianas, and in one place, about the middle, a big brook pours over in a cascade. Well, there was a boat going by here with six young men of Falesá, "all very pretty," Uma said, which was the loss of them. It blew strong, there was a heavy head sea; and by the time they opened Fanga-anaana, and saw the white cascade and the shady beach, they were all tired and thirsty, and their water had run out. One proposed to land and get a drink; and being reckless fellows, they were all of the same mind except the youngest. Lotu was his name; he was a very good young gentleman and very wise; and he held out they were crazy, telling them the place was given over to spirits and devils and the dead, and there were no living folk nearer than six miles the one way and maybe twelve the other. But they laughed at his words; and being five to one, pulled in, beached the boat, and landed. It was a wonderful pleasant place, Lotu said, and the water excellent. They walked round the beach, but could see nowhere any way to mount the cliffs, which made them easier in their mind; and at last they sat down to make a meal on the food they had brought with them. They were scarce set, when there came out of the mouth of one of the black caves six of the most beautiful ladies ever seen; they had flowers in their hair, and the most beautiful breasts, and necklaces of scarlet seeds; and began to jest with these young gentlemen, and the young gentlemen to jest back with them, all but Lotu. As for Lotu, he saw there could be no living women in such a place, and ran, and flung himself in the bottom of the boat, and covered his face, and prayed. All the time the business lasted, Lotu made one clean break of prayer; and that was all he knew of it, until his friends came back, and made him sit up, and they put to sea again out of the bay, which was now quite desert, and no word of the six ladies. But what frightened Lotu worst, not one of the five remembered anything of what had passed, but they were all like drunken men, and sang and laughed in the boat, and skylarked. The wind freshened and came squally, the sea rose extraordinary high; it was such weather as any man in the islands would have turned his back to and fled home to Falesá; but these five were like crazy folk, and cracked on all sail, and drove their boat into the seas. Lotu went to the bailing; none of the others thought to help him, but sang and skylarked and carried on, and spoke singular things beyond a man's comprehension, and laughed out loud when they said them. So the rest of that day, Lotu bailed for his life in the bottom of the boat, and was all drenched with sweat and cold sea water; and none heeded him. Against all expectation, they came safe in a dreadful tempest to Papa-mālūlū, where the palms were singing out and the cocoanuts flying like cannon balls about the village green; and the same night the five young gentlemen sickened and spoke never a reasonable word until they died.

"And do you mean to tell me you can swallow a yarn like that?" I asked.

She told me the thing was well known, and with handsome young men alone, it was even common. But this was the only case where five had been slain the same day and in a company by the love of the women devils; and it had made a great stir in the island; and she would be crazy if she doubted.

"Well anyway," says I, "you needn't be frightened about me. I've got no use for the women devils; you're all the women I want, and all the devil too, old lady."

To that she answered there were other sorts, and she had seen one with her own eyes. She had gone one day alone to the next bay, and perhaps got too near the margin of the bad place. The boughs of the high bush overshadowed her from the kant of the hill; but she herself was outside in a flat place, very stony and growing full of young mummy-apples, four and five feet high. It was a dark day in the rainy season; and now there came squalls that tore off the leaves and sent them flying, and now it was all still as in a house. It was in one of these still times, that a whole gang of birds and flying-foxes came pegging out of the bush like creatures frightened. Presently after she heard a rustle nearer hand, and saw coming out of the margin of the trees among the mummy-apples, the appearance of a lean, gray, old boar. It seemed to think as it came, like a person; and all of a sudden, as she looked at it coming, she was aware it was no boar but a thing that was a man with a man's thoughts. At that she ran, and the pig after her, and as the pig ran it hollered aloud, so that the place rang with it.

"I wish I had been there with my gun," said I. "I guess the pig would have hollered so as to surprise himself."

But she told me a gun was of no use with the like of these, which were the spirits of the dead.

Well, this kind of talk put in the evening, which was the best of it; but of course it didn't change my notion; and the next day, with my gun and a good knife, I set off upon a voyage of discovery. I made as near as I could for the place where I had seen Case come out; for if it was true he had some kind of establishment in the bush, I reckoned I should find a path. The beginning of the desert was marked off by a wall—to call it so, for it was more of a long mound of stones; they say it reaches right across the island, but how they know it is another question, for I doubt if anyone has made the journey in a hundred years; the natives sticking chiefly to the sea and their little colonies along the coast, and that part being mortal high and steep and full of cliffs. Up to the west side of the wall, the ground has been cleared, and there are cocoa-palms, and mummy-apples, and guavas, and lots of sensitive. Just across, the bush begins outright; high bush at that: trees going up like the masts of ships, and ropes of liana hanging down like a ship's rigging, and nasty orchids growing in the forks like funguses. The ground, where there was no underwood, looked to be a heap of boulders. I saw many green pigeons which I might have shot, only I was there with a different idea; a number of butterflies flopped up and down along the ground like dead leaves; sometimes I would hear a bird calling, sometimes the wind overhead, and always the sea along the coast.

But the queerness of the place, it's more difficult to tell of; unless to one who has been alone in the high bush himself. The brightest kind of a day, it is always dim down there. A man can see to the end of nothing; whichever way he looks, the wood shuts up, one bough folding with another, like the fingers of your hand; and whenever he listens, he hears always something new—men talking, children laughing, the strokes of an axe a far way ahead of him, and sometimes a sort of quick, stealthy scurry near at hand that makes him jump and look to his weapons. It's all very well for him to tell himself that he's alone, bar trees and birds; he can't make out to believe it: whichever way he turns, the whole place seems to be alive and looking on. Don't think it was Uma's yarns that put me out; I don't value native talk a fourpenny piece: it's a thing that's natural in the bush, and that's the end of it.

As I got near the top of the hill, for the ground of the wood goes up in this place steep as a ladder, the wind began to sound straight on, and the leaves to toss and switch open and let in the sun. This suited me better; it was the same noise all the time and nothing to startle. Well, I had got to a place where there was an underwood of what they call wild cocoanut—mighty pretty with its scarlet fruits—when there came a sound of singing in the wind that I thought I had never heard the like of. It was all very fine to tell myself it was the branches; I knew better. It was all very fine to tell myself it was a bird; I knew never a bird that sang like that. It rose, and swelled, and died away, and swelled again; and now I thought it was like some one weeping, only prettier; and now I thought it was like harps; and there was one thing I made sure of, it was a sight too sweet to be wholesome in a place like that. You may laugh if you like; but I declare I called to mind the six young ladies that came, with their scarlet necklaces, out of the cave at Fanga-anaana, and wondered if they sang like that. We laugh at the natives and their superstitions; but see how many traders take them up, splendidly educated white men, that have been bookkeepers (some of them) and clerks in the old country! It's my belief a superstition grows up in a place like the different kinds of weeds; and as I stood there, and listened to that wailing, I twittered in my shoes.

You may call me a coward to be frightened; I thought myself brave enough to go on ahead. But I went mighty carefully, with my gun cocked, spying all about me like a hunter, fully expecting to see a handsome young woman sitting somewhere in the bush, and fully determined (if I did) to try her with a charge of duckshot. And sure enough I had not gone far, when I met with a queer thing. The wind came on the top of the wood in a strong puff, the leaves in front of me burst open, and I saw for a second something hanging in a tree. It was gone in a wink, the puff blowing by and the leaves closing. I tell you the truth; I had made up my mind to see an *aitu*; and if the thing had looked like a pig or a woman, it wouldn't have given me the same turn. The trouble was that it seemed kind of square; and the idea of a square thing that was alive and sang, knocked me sick and silly. I must have stood quite a while; and I made pretty certain it was right out of the same tree that the singing came. Then I began to come to myself a bit.

"Well," says I, "if this is really so, if this is a place where there are square things that sing, I'm gone up anyway. Let's have my fun for my money."

But I thought I might as well take the off-chance of a prayer being any good; so I plumped on my knees and prayed out loud; and all the time I was praying, the strange sounds came out of the tree, and went up and down, and changed, for all the world like music; only you could see it wasn't human—there was nothing there that you could whistle.

As soon as I had made an end in proper style, I laid down my gun, stuck my knife between my teeth, walked right up to that tree, and began to climb. I tell you my heart was like ice. But presently, as I went up, I caught another glimpse of the thing, and that relieved me, for I thought it seemed woundy like a box; and when I had got right up to it, I near fell out of the tree with laughing. A box it was, sure enough, and a candle box at that, with the brand upon the side of it; and it had banjo strings stretched so as to sound when the wind blew. I believe they call the thing a Tyrolean harp, whatever that may mean.

"Well, Mr Case," said I, "you've frightened me once. But I defy you to frighten me again," I says, and slipped down the tree, and set out again to find my enemy's head office, which I guessed would not be far away.

The undergrowth was thick in this part. I couldn't see before my nose, and must burst my way through by main force and ply the knife as I went, slicing the cords of the lianas and slashing down whole trees at a blow. I call them trees for the bigness, but in truth they were just big weeds and sappy to cut through like a carrot. From all this crowd and kind of vegetation, I was just thinking to myself the place might have once been cleared, when I came on my nose over a pile of stones, and saw in a moment it was some kind of a work of man. The Lord knows when it was made or when deserted; for this part of the island has lain undisturbed since long before the whites came. A few steps beyond, I hit into the path I had been always looking for. It was narrow but well beaten, and I saw that Case had plenty of disciples. It seems indeed it was a piece of fashionable boldness to venture up here with the trader; and a young man scarce reckoned himself grown, till he had got his breech tattooed for one thing, and seen Case's devils for another. This is mighty like kanakas; but if you look at it another way, it's mighty like white folks too.

A bit along the path, I was brought to a clean stand and had to rub my eyes. There was a wall in front of me, the path passing it by a gap; it was tumble down and plainly very old, but built of big stones very well laid; and there is no native alive today upon that island that could dream of such a piece of building. Along all the top of it was a line of queer figures, idols, or scare-crows, or what not. They had carved and painted faces, ugly to view; their eyes and teeth were of shell; their hair and their bright clothes blew in the wind, and some of them worked with the tugging. There are islands up west, where they make these kinds of figures till today; but if ever they were made in this island, the practise and the very recollection of it are now long forgotten. And the singular thing was that all these bogies were as fresh as toys out of a shop.

Then it came in my mind what Case had let out to me the first day, that he was a good forger of island curiosities: a thing by which so many traders turn an honest penny. And with that I saw the whole business, and how this display served the man a double purpose: first of all to season his curiosities, and then to frighten those that came to visit him.

But I should tell you (what made the thing more curious) that all the time the Tyrolean harps were harping round me in the trees, and even while I looked a green and yellow bird (that I suppose was building) began to tear the hair off the head of one of the figures.

A little farther on, I found the last curiosity of the museum. The first I saw of it was a longish mound of earth with a twist to it. Digging off the earth with my hands, I found underneath tarpaulin stretched on boards, so that this was plainly the roof of a cellar. It stood right on the top of the hill, and the entrance was on the far side, between two rocks, like the entrance to a cave. I went in as far as the bend, and looking round the corner, saw a shining face. It was big and ugly like a pantomime mask, and the brightness of it waxed and dwindled, and at times it smoked.

"Oho," says I, "luminous paint!"

And I must say I rather admired the man's ingenuity. With a box of tools and a few mighty simple contrivances, he had made out to have a devil of a temple. Any poor kanaka brought up here in the dark, with the harps whining all round him, and shown that smoking face in the bottom of a hole, would make no kind of doubt but he had seen and heard enough devils for a lifetime. It's easy to find out what kanakas think. Just go back to yourself anyway round from ten to fifteen years old, and there's an average kanaka. There are some pious, just as there are pious boys; and the most of them, like the boys again, are middling honest and yet think it rather larks to steal, and are easy scared and rather like to be so. I remembered a boy I was at school with at home, who played the Case business. He didn't know anything, that boy; he couldn't do anything; he had no luminous paint and no Tyrolean harps; he just boldly said he was a sorcerer, and frightened us out of our boots, and we loved it. And then it came in my mind how the master had once flogged that boy, and the surprise we were all in to see the sorcerer catch it and bum like anybody else. Thinks I to myself: "I must find some way of fixing it so for Master Case." And the next moment I had my idea.

I went back by the path which, when once you had found it, was quite plain and easy walking; and when I stepped out on the black sands, who should I see but Master Case himself? I cocked my gun and held it handy; and we marched up and passed without a word, each keeping the tail of his eye on the other; and no sooner had we passed, than we each wheeled round like fellows drilling and stood face to face. We had each taken the same notion in his head, you see, that the other fellow might give him the load of a gun in the stern.

"You've shot nothing," says Case.

"I'm not on the shoot today," says I.

"Well, the devil go with you for me," says he.

"The same to you," says I.

But we stuck just the way we were; no fear of either of us moving. Case laughed. "We can't stop here all day, though," said he.

"Don't let me detain you," says I.

He laughed again. "Look here, Wiltshire, do you think me a fool?" he asked.

"More of a knave if you want to know," says I.

"Well, do you think it would better me to shoot you here on this open beach?" said he, "because I don't. Folks come fishing every day. There may be a score of them up the valley now, making copra; there may be half a dozen on the hill behind you after pigeons; they might be watching us this minute, and I shouldn't wonder. I give you my word I don't want to shoot you. Why should I? You don't hinder me any; you haven't got one pound of copra but what you made with your own hands like a negro slave. You're vegetating, that's what I call it; and I don't care where you vegetate, nor yet how long. Give me your word you don't mean to shoot me, and I'll give you a lead and walk away."

"Well," said I, "you're frank and pleasant, ain't you? and I'll be the same. I don't mean to shoot you today. Why should I? This business is beginning; it ain't done yet, Mr Case. I've given you one turn already, I can see the marks of my knuckles on your head to this blooming hour; and I've more cooking for you. I'm not a paralee like Underhill; my name ain't Adams and it ain't Vigours; and I mean to show you that you've met your match."

"This is a silly way to talk," said he. "This is not the talk to make me move on with."

"All right," said I. "Stay where you are. I ain't in any hurry, and you know it. I can put in the day on this beach, and never mind. I ain't got any copra to bother with. I ain't got any luminous paint to see to."

I was sorry I said that last, but it whipped out before I knew. I could see it took the wind out of his sails, and he stood and stared at me with his brow drawn up. Then I suppose he made up his mind he must get to the bottom of this.

"I take you at your word," says he, and turned his back, and walked right into the devil's bush.

I let him go of course, for I had passed my word. But I watched him as long as he was in sight, and after he was gone, lit out for cover as lively as you would want to see, and went the rest of the way home under the bush. For I didn't trust him sixpenceworth. One thing I saw: I had been ass enough to give him warning; and that which I meant to do, I must do at once.

You would think I had had about enough excitement for one morning; but there was another turn waiting me. As soon as I got far enough round the cape to see my house, I made out there were strangers there; a little farther, and no doubt about it, there were a couple of armed sentries squatting at my door. I could only suppose the trouble about Uma must have come to a head, and the station been seized. For aught I could think Uma was taken up already, and these armed men were waiting to do the like by me.

However, as I came nearer, which I did at top speed, I saw there was a third native sitting on the verandah like a guest, and Uma was talking with him like a hostess. Nearer still I made out it was the big young chief Maea, and that he was smiling away and smoking; and what was he smoking?—none of your European cigarettes fit for a cat; not even the genuine, big, knock-me-down native article, that a fellow can really put in the time with, if his pipe is broke; but a cigar, and one of my Mexicans at that, that I could swear to. At sight of this, my heart started beating; and I took a wild hope in my head that the trouble was over, and Maea had come round.

Uma pointed me out to him, as I came up, and he met me at the head of my own stairs like a thorough gentleman.

"Vilivili," said he, which was the best they could make of my name, "I pleased."

There is no doubt when an island chief wants to be civil he can do it. I saw the way things were from the word go. There was no call for Uma to say to me: "He no 'fraid Ese now; come bring copra." I tell you I shook hands with that kanaka like as if he was the best white man in Europe.

The fact was Case and he had got after the same girl, or Maea suspected it and concluded to make hay of the trader on the chance. He had dressed himself up, got a couple of his retainers cleaned and armed to kind of make the thing more public, and just waiting till Case was clear of the village, came round to put the whole of his business my way. He was rich as well as powerful, I suppose that man was worth fifty thousand nuts per annum. I gave him the price of the beach and a quarter cent better, and as for credit, I would have advanced him the inside of the store and the fittings besides, I was so pleased to see him. I must say he bought like a gentleman: rice and tins and biscuit enough for a week's feast, and stuffs by the bolt. He was agreeable besides; he had plenty fun to him; and we cracked jests together, mostly through Uma for interpreter, because he had mighty little English, and my native was still off colour. One thing I made out: he could never really have thought much harm of Uma; he could never have been really frightened, and must just have made believe from dodginess and because he thought Case had a strong pull in the village and could help him on.

This set me thinking that both he and I were in a tightish place. What he had done was to fly in the face of the whole village, and the thing might cost him his authority. More than that, after my talk with Case on the beach, I thought it might very well cost me my life. Case had as good as said he would pot me if ever I got copra; he would come home to find the best business in the village had changed hands; and the best thing I thought I could do was to get in first with the potting.

"See here, Uma," says I, "tell him I'm sorry I made him wait, but I was looking at Case's Tiapolo store in the bush."

"He want savvy if you no 'fraid?" translated Uma.

I laughed out. "Not much!" says I. "Tell him the place is a blooming toyshop! Tell him in England we give these things to the kids to play with."

"He want savvy if you hear devil sing?" she asked next.

"Look here," I said, "I can't do it now because I've got no banjo strings in stock; but the next time the ship comes round, I'll have one of these same contraptions right here in my verandah, and he can see for himself how much devil there is to it. Tell him, as soon as I can get the strings, I'll make one for his picaninnies. The name of the concern is a Tyrolean harp; and you can tell him the name means in English, that nobody but damfools give a cent for it."

This time he was so pleased he had to try his English again. "You talk true?" says he.

"Rather!" said I. "Talk all-e-same bible. Bring out a bible here, Uma, if you've got such a thing, and I'll kiss it. Or I'll tell you what's better still," says I, taking a header. "Ask him if he's afraid to go up there himself by day."

It appeared he wasn't; he could venture as far as that by day and in company.

"That's the ticket, then!" said I. "Tell him the man's a fraud and the place foolishness, and if he'll go up there tomorrow, he'll see all that's left of it. But tell him this, Uma, and mind he understands it; if he gets talking, it's bound to come to Case and I'm a dead man. I'm playing his game, tell him, and if he says one word, my blood will be at his door and be the damnation of him here and after."

She told him, and he shook hands with me up to the hilts, and says he: "No talk. Go up tomollow. You my friend?"

"No, sir!" says I. "No such foolishness. I've come here to trade, tell him, and not to make friends. But as to Case, I'll send that man to glory."

So off Maea went, pretty well pleased, as I could see.

Chapter V

 Night in the Bush

Well, I was committed now; Tiapolo had to be smashed up before next day; and my hands were pretty full, not only with preparations, but with argument. My house was like a mechanics' debating society; Uma was so made up that I shouldn't go into the bush by night, or that if I did I was never to come back again. You know her style of arguing, you've had a specimen about Queen Victoria and the devil; and I leave you to fancy if I was tired of it before dark.

At last, I had a good idea; what was the use of casting my pearls before her? I thought: some of her own chopped hay would be likelier to do the business.

"I'll tell you what, then," said I. "You fish out your bible, and I'll take that up along with me. That'll make me right."

She swore a bible was no use.

"That's just your blamed kanaka ignorance," said I. "Bring the bible out."

She brought it, and I turned to the title page where I thought there would likely be some English, and so there was. "There!" said I. "Look at that! 'London: printed for the British and Foreign Bible Society, Blackfriars'; and the date, which I can't read, owing to its being in these X's. There's no devil in hell can look near the Bible Society, Blackfriars. Why, you silly!" I said, "how do you suppose we get along with our own *aitus* at home? All Bible Society!"

"I think you no got any," said she. "White man he tell me you no got."

"Sounds likely, don't it?" I asked. "Why would these islands all be chock full of them, and none in Europe?"

"Well, you no got breadfruit," said she.

I could have tore my hair. "Now, look here, old lady," said I, "you dry up, for I'm tired of you. I'll take the bible, which'll put me as straight as the mail; and that's the last word I've got to say."

The night fell extraordinary dark, clouds coming up with sundown and overspreading all; not a star showed; there was only an end of a moon, and that not due before the small hours. Round the village, what with the lights and the fires in the open houses and the torches of many fishers moving on the reef, it kept as gay as an illumination; but the sea and the mountains and woods were all clean gone. I suppose it might be eight o'clock when I took the road, loaden like a donkey. First there was that bible, a book as big as your head, which I had let myself in for by my own tomfoolery. Then there was my gun and knife and lantern and patent matches, all necessary. And then there was the real plant of the affair in hand, a mortal weight of gunpowder, a pair of dynamite fishing-bombs, and two or three pieces of slow match that I had hauled out of the tin cases and spliced together the best way I could; for the match was only trade stuff, and a man would be crazy that trusted it. Altogether, you see, I had the materials of a pretty good blow up. Expense was nothing to me; I wanted that thing done right.

As long as I was in the open, and had the lamp in my house to steer by, I did well. But when I got to the path, it fell so dark I could make no headway, walking into trees and swearing there, like a man looking for the matches in his bedroom. I knew it was risky to light up; for my lantern would be visible all the way to the point of the cape; and as no one went there after dark, it would be talked about and come to Case's ears. But what was I to do? I had either to give the business over and lose caste with Maea, or light up, take my chance, and get through the thing the smartest I was able.

As long as I was on the path, I walked hard; but when I came to the black beach, I had to run. For the tide was now nearly flowed; and to get through with my powder dry between the surf and the steep hill, took all the quickness I possessed. As it was even, the wash caught me to the knees and I came near falling on a stone. All this time, the hurry I was in, and the free air and smell of the sea, kept my spirits lively; but when I was once in the bush and began to climb the path, I took it easier. The fearsomeness of the wood had been a good bit rubbed off for me by Master Case's banjo strings and graven images; yet I thought it was a dreary walk, and guessed, when the disciples went up there, they must be badly scared. The light of the lantern, striking among all these trunks, and forked branches, and twisted rope's-ends of lianas, made the whole place, or all that you could see it, a kind of a puzzle of turning shadows. They came to meet you, solid and quick like giants, and then span off and vanished; they hove up over your head like clubs, and flew away into the night like birds. The floor of the bush glimmered with dead wood, the way the matchbox used to shine after you had struck a lucifer. Big cold drops fell on me from the branches overhead like sweat. There was no wind to mention, only a little icy breath of a land breeze that stirred nothing; and the harps were silent.

The first landfall I made was when I got through the bush of wild cocoanuts, and came in view of the bogies on the wall. Mighty queer they looked by the shining of the lantern, with their painted faces, and shell eyes, and their clothes and their hair hanging. One after another I pulled them all up and piled them in a bundle on the cellar roof, so as they might go to glory with the rest. Then I chose a place behind one of the big stones at the entrance, buried my powder and the two shells, and arranged my match along the passage. And then I had a look at the smoking head, just for good-bye. It was doing fine.

"Cheer up," says I. "You're booked."

It was my first idea to light up and be getting homeward; for the darkness, and the glimmer of the dead wood, and the shadows of the lantern made me lonely. But I knew where one of the harps hung; it seemed a pity it shouldn't go with the rest; and at the same time I couldn't help letting on to myself that I was mortal tired of my employment and would like best to be at home and have the door shut. I stepped out of the cellar, and argued it fore and back. There was a sound of the sea far down below me on the coast; nearer hand, not a leaf stirred; I might have been the only living creature this side Cape Horn. Well, as I stood there thinking, it seemed the bush woke and became full of little noises. Little noises they were, and nothing to hurt—a bit of a crackle, a bit of a brush—but the breath jumped right out of me and my throat went as dry as a biscuit. It wasn't Case I was afraid of, which would have been common sense; I never thought of Case; what took me, as sharp as the cholic, was the old wives' tales, the devil-women and the man-pigs. It was the toss of a penny whether I should run; but I got a purchase on myself, and stepped out, and held up the lantern (like a fool) and looked all round.

In the direction of the village and the path, there was nothing to be seen; but when I turned inland, it's a wonder to me I didn't drop. There—coming right up out of the desert and the bad bush—there, sure enough, was a devil-woman, just the way I had figured she would look. I saw the light shine on her bare arms and her bright eyes. And there went out of me a yell so big that I thought it was my death.

"Ah! No sing out!" says the devil-woman, in a kind of a high whisper. "Why you talk big voice? Put out light! Ese he come."

"My God Almighty, Uma, is that you?" says I.

"*Ioe*," says she. "I come quick. Ese here soon."

"You come alone?" I asked. "You no 'fraid?"

"Ah, too much 'fraid!" she whispered, clutching me. "I think die."

"Well," says I, with a kind of a weak grin, "I'm not the one to laugh at you, Mrs Wiltshire, for I'm about the worst scared man in the South Pacific myself."

She told me in two words what brought her. I was scarce gone, it seems, when Faavao came in; and the old woman had met Black Jack running as hard as he was fit from our house to Case's. Uma neither spoke nor stopped, but lit right out to come and warn me. She was so close at my heels that the lantern was her guide across the beach, and afterwards, by the glimmer of it in the trees, she got her line up hill. It was only when I had got to the top or was in the cellar, that she wandered—Lord knows where!—and lost a sight of precious time, afraid to call out lest Case was at the heels of her, and falling in the bush so that she was all knocked and bruised. That must have been when she got too far to the southward, and how she came to take me in the flank at last, and frighten me beyond what I've got the words to tell of.

Well, anything was better than a devil-woman; but I thought her yarn serious enough. Black Jack had no call to be about my house, unless he was set there to watch; and it looked to me as if my tomfool word about the paint and perhaps some chatter of Maea's had got us all in a clove hitch. One thing was clear: Uma and I were here for the night; we daren't try to go home before day, and even then it would be safer to strike round up the mountain and come in by the back of the village, or we might walk into an ambuscade. It was plain too that the mine should be sprung immediately, or Case might be in time to stop it.

I marched into the tunnel, Uma keeping tight hold of me, opened my lantern and lit the match. The first length of it burned like a spill of paper; and I stood stupid, watching it burn, and thinking we were going aloft with Tiapolo, which was none of my views. The second took to a better rate, though faster than I cared about; and at that I got my wits again, hauled Uma clear of the passage, blew out and dropped the lantern; and the pair of us groped our way into the bush until I thought it might be safe, and lay down together by a tree.

"Old lady," I said, "I won't forget this night. You're a trump, and that's what's wrong with you."

She humped herself close up to me. She had run out the way she was with nothing on but her kilt; and she was all wet with the dews and the sea on the black beach, and shook straight on with cold and the terror of the dark and the devils.

"Too much 'fraid," was all she said.

The far side of Case's hill goes down near as steep as a precipice into the next valley. We were on the very edge of it, and I could see the dead wood shine and hear the sea sound far below. I didn't care about the position, which left me no retreat, but I was afraid to change. Then I saw I had made a worse mistake about the lantern, which I should have left lighted, so that I could have had a crack at Case when he stepped into the shine of it. And even if I hadn't had the wit to do that, it seemed a senseless thing to leave the good lantern to blow up with the graven images; the thing belonged to me, after all, and was worth money, and might come in handy. If I could have trusted the match, I might have run in still and rescued it. But who was going to trust the match? You know what trade is; the stuff was good enough for kanakas to go fishing with, where they've got to look lively anyway, and the most they risk is only to have their hand blown off; but for any one that wanted to fool around a blow-up like mine, that match was rubbish.

Altogether, the best I could do was to lie still, see my shot gun handy, and wait for the explosion. But it was a solemn kind of a business; the blackness of the night was like solid; the only thing you could see was the nasty, bogy glimmer of the dead wood, and that showed you nothing but itself; and as for sounds, I stretched my ears till I thought I could have heard the match burn in the tunnel, and that bush was as silent as a coffin. Now and then there was a bit of a crack, but whether it was near or far, whether it was Case stubbing his toes within a few yards of me or a tree breaking miles away, I knew no more than the babe unborn.

And then all of a sudden Vesuvius went off. It was a long time coming; but when it came (though I say it that shouldn't) no man could ask to see a better. At first it was just a son of a gun of a row, and a spout of fire, and the wood lighted up so that you could see to read. And then the trouble began. Uma and I were half buried under a waggonful of earth, and glad it was no worse; for one of the rocks at the entrance of the tunnel was fired clean into the air, fell within a couple of fathom of where we lay, and bounded over the edge of the hill, and went pounding down into the next valley.

I saw I had rather under-calculated our distance, or overdone the dynamite and powder, which you please.

And presently I saw I had made another slip. The noise of the thing began to die off, shaking the island; the dazzle was over; and yet the night didn't come back the way that I expected. For the whole wood was scattered with red coals and brands from the explosion; they were all round me on the flat, some had fallen below in the valley, and some stuck and flared in the treetops. I had no fear of fire, for these forests are too wet to kindle. But the trouble was that the place was all lit up, not very bright but good enough to get a shot by; and the way the coals were scattered, it was just as likely Case might have the advantage as myself. I looked all round for his white face, you may be sure; but there was not a sign of him. As for Uma, the life seemed to have been knocked right out of her by the bang and blaze of it.

There was one bad point in my game. One of the blessed graven images had come down all afire, hair and clothes and body, not four yards away from me. I cast a mighty noticing glance all round; there was still no Case; and I made up my mind I must get rid of that burning stick before he came, or I should be shot there like a dog.

It was my first idea to have crawled; and then I thought speed was the main thing, and stood half up to make a rush. The same moment, from somewhere between me and the sea, there came a flash and a report, and a rifle bullet screeched in my ear. I swung straight round, and up with my gun. But the brute had a Winchester; and before I could as much as see him, his second shot knocked me over like a ninepin. I seemed to fly in the air, then came down by the run and lay half a minute silly; and then I found my hands empty and my gun had flown over my head as I fell. It makes a man mighty wide awake to be in the kind of box that I was in. I scarce knew where I was hurt, or whether I was hurt or not, but turned right over on my face to crawl after my weapon. Unless you have tried to get about with a smashed leg, you don't know what pain is, and I let a howl out like a bullock's.

This was the unluckiest noise that ever I made in my life. Up to then, Uma had stuck to her tree like a sensible woman, knowing she would be only in the way. But as soon as she heard me sing out, she ran forward—the Winchester cracked again—and down she went.

I had sat up, leg and all, to stop her; but when I saw her tumble, I clapped down again where I was, lay still, and felt the handle of my knife. I had been scurried and put out before. No more of that for me; he had knocked over my girl, I had got to fix him for it; and I lay there and gritted my teeth, and footed up the chances. My leg was broke, my gun was gone, Case had still ten shots in his Winchester, it looked a kind of hopeless business. But I never despaired nor thought upon despairing: that man had got to go.

For a goodish bit, not one of us let on. Then I heard Case begin to move nearer in the bush, but mighty careful. The image had burned out; there were only a few coals left here and there; and the wood was main dark, but had a kind of a low glow in it like a fire on its last legs. It was by this that I made out Case's head looking at me over a big tuft of ferns; and at the same time the brute saw me and shouldered his Winchester. I lay quite still and as good as looked into the barrel; it was my last chance; but I thought my heart would have come right out of its bearings. Then he fired. Lucky for me it was no shot gun, for the bullet struck within an inch of me and knocked the dirt in my eyes.

Just you try and see if you can lie quiet, and let a man take a sitting shot at you, and miss you by a hair! But I did, and lucky too. Awhile Case stood with the Winchester at the port-arms; then he gave a little laugh to himself, and stepped round the ferns.

"Laugh!" thought I. "If you had the wit of a louse, you would be praying!"

I was all as taut as a ship's hauser or the spring of a watch; and as soon as he came within reach of me, I had him by the ankle, plucked the feet right out from under him, laid him out, and was upon the top of him, broken leg and all, before he breathed. His Winchester had gone the same road as my shot gun; it was nothing to me; I defied him now. I'm a pretty strong man anyway, but I never knew what strength was till I got hold of Case. He was knocked out of time by the rattle he came down with, and threw up his hands together, more like a frightened woman, so that I caught both of them with my left. This wakened him up, and he fixed his teeth in my forearm like a weasel. Much I cared! My leg gave me all the pain I had any use for; and I drew my knife, and got it in the place.

"Now," said I, "I've got you; and you're gone up, and a good job too. Do you feel the point of that? That's for Underhill. And there's for Adams. And now here's for Uma, and that's going to knock your blooming soul right out of you."

With that, I gave him the cold steel for all I was worth. His body kicked under me like a spring sofa; he gave a dreadful kind of a long moan, and lay still.

"I wonder if you're dead. I hope so," I thought, for my head was swimming. But I wasn't going to take chances; I had his own example too close before me for that; and I tried to draw the knife out to give it him again. The blood came over my hands, I remember, hot as tea; and with that I fainted clean away and fell with my head on the man's mouth.

When I came to myself, it was pitch dark; the cinders had burned out, there was nothing to be seen but the shine of the dead wood; and I couldn't remember where I was, nor why I was in such pain, nor what I was all wetted with. Then it came back; and the first thing I attended to was to give him the knife again a half a dozen times up to the handle. I believe he was dead already; but it did him no harm and did me good.

"I bet you're dead now," I said, and then I called to Uma.

Nothing answered; and I made a move to go and grope for her, fouled my broken leg, and fainted again.

When I came to myself the second time, the clouds had all cleared away except a few that sailed there, white as cotton. The moon was up, a tropic moon. The moon at home turns a wood black; but even this old but-end of a one showed up that forest as green as by day. The night birds—or rather they're a kind of early morning bird—sang out with their long, falling notes like nightingales. And I could see the dead man that I was still half resting on, looking right up into the sky with his open eyes, no paler than when he was alive; and a little way off, Uma tumbled on her side. I got over to her the best way I was able; and when I got there, she was broad awake and crying and sobbing to herself with no more noise than an insect. It appears she was afraid to cry out loud, because of the *aitus*. Altogether she was not much hurt, but scared beyond belief; she had come to her senses a long while ago, cried out to me, heard nothing in reply, made out we were both dead, and had lain there ever since, afraid to budge a finger. The ball had ploughed up her shoulder; and she had lost a main quantity of blood; but I soon had that tied up the way it ought to be with the tail of my shirt and a scarf I had on, got her head on my sound knee and my back against a trunk, and settled down to wait for morning. Uma was for neither use nor ornament; and could only clutch hold of me, and shake, and cry; I don't suppose there was ever anybody worse scared, and to do her justice, she had had a lively night of it. As for me, I was in a good bit of pain and fever, but not so bad when I sat still; and every time I looked over to Case, I could have sung and whistled. Talk about meat and drink! to see that man lying there dead as a herring filled me full.

The night birds stopped after a while; and then the light began to change, the east came orange, the whole wood began to whirr with singing like a musical box, and there was the broad day.

I didn't expect Maea for a long while yet; and indeed I thought there was an off chance he might go back on the whole idea and not come at all. I was the better pleased when, about an hour after daylight, I heard sticks smashing and a lot of kanakas laughing and singing out to keep their courage up. Uma sat up quite brisk at the first word of it; and presently we saw a party come stringing out of the path, Maea in front and behind him a white man in a pith helmet. It was Mr Tarleton who had turned up late last night in Falesá, having left his boat and walked the last stage with a lantern.

They buried Case upon the field of glory, right in the hole where he had kept the smoking head. I waited till the thing was done; and Mr Tarleton prayed, which I thought tomfoolery, but I'm bound to say he gave a pretty sick view of the dear departed's prospects, and seemed to have his own ideas of hell. I had it out with him afterwards, told him he had scamped his duty, and what he had ought to have done was to up like a man and tell the kanakas plainly Case was damned, and a good riddance; but I never could get him to see it my way. Then they made me a litter of poles and carried me down to the station. Mr Tarleton set my leg, and made a regular missionary splice of it, so that I limp to this day. That done, he took down my evidence, and Uma's, and Maea's, wrote it all out fair, and had us sign it; and then he got the chiefs and marched over to Papa Randall's to seize Case's papers.

All they found was a bit of a diary, kept for a good many years, and all about the price of copra and chickens being stolen and that; and the books of the business, and the will I told you of in the beginning, by both of which the whole thing (stock lock and barrel) appeared to belong to the Sāmoa woman. It was I that bought her out, at a mighty reasonable figure, for she was in a hurry to get home. As for Randall and the black, they had to tramp; got into some kind of a station on the Papa-mālūlū side; did very bad business, for the truth is neither of the pair was fit for it; and lived mostly on fish, which was the means of Randall's death. It seems there was a nice shoal in one day, and papa went after them with dynamite; either the match burned too fast or papa was full, or both, but the shell went off (in the usual way) before he threw it; and where was papa's hand? Well, there's nothing to hurt in that; the islands up north are all full of one-handed men, like the parties in the Arabian Nights; but either Randall was too old, or he drank too much, and the short and the long of it was that he died. Pretty soon after, the nigger was turned out of the islands for stealing from white men, and went off to the west, where he found men of his own colour, in case he liked that, and the men of his own colour took and ate him at some kind of a corroborree and I'm sure I hope he was to their fancy!

So there was I left alone in my glory at Falesá; and when the schooner came round I filled her up and gave her a deck cargo half as high as the house. I must say Mr Tarleton did the right thing by us; but he took a meanish kind of a revenge.

"Now, Mr Wiltshire," said he, "I've put you all square with everybody here. It wasn't difficult to do, Case being gone; but I have done it, and given my pledge besides that you will deal fairly with the natives. I must ask you to keep my word."

Well, so I did. I used to be bothered about my balances; but I reasoned it out this way. We all have queerish balances, and the natives all know it and water their copra in a proportion; so that it's fair all round. But the truth is, it did use to bother me; and though I did well in Falesá, I was half-glad when the firm moved me on to another station, where I was under no kind of a pledge, and could look my balances in the face.

As for the old lady, you know her as well as I do. She's only the one fault: if you don't keep your eye lifting, she would give away the roof off the station. Well, it seems it's natural in kanakas. She's turned a powerful big woman now, and could throw a London bobby over her shoulder. But that's natural in kanakas too; and there's no manner of doubt that she's an A one wife.

Mr Tarleton's gone home, his trick being over; he was the best missionary I ever struck, and now it seems he's parsonizing down Somerset ways. Well, that's best for him; he'll have no kanakas there to get luny over.

My public house? Not a bit of it, nor ever likely; I'm stuck here, I fancy; I don't like to leave the kids, you see; and there's no use talking—they're better here than what they would be in a white man's country. Though Ben took the eldest up to Auckland, where he's being schooled with the best. But what bothers me is the girls. They're only half castes of course; I know that as well as you do, and there's nobody thinks less of half castes than I do; but they're mine, and about all I've got; I can't reconcile my mind to their taking up with kanakas, and I'd like to know where I'm to find them whites?

GLOSSARY

GLOSSARY

Stevenson's later style was recognized immediately by his contemporaries for its newness. "The slang of the Pacific," remarked a reviewer of *The Wrecker* in 1892, "is used with such freedom that we should now and then be grateful for a concise glossary." What follows is designed to make clear the meaning of words and phrases that might be unintelligible to a modern reader: English and American slang, archaisms, nautical terms. Definitions are largely drawn from nineteenth-century dictionaries of slang and Americanisms. They convey the flavor of the period and frequently enable us to see how Stevenson manipulated the language for his own ends. Unless otherwise noted, the following texts serve as the sources for the definitions:

AF	Alexander Findlay, *A Directory for the Navigation of the South Pacific Ocean* (5th ed., London, 1884).
B&L	Albert Barrère and Charles G. Leland, *A Dictionary of Slang, Jargon & Cant* (2 vols., London, 1897).
BJT	B. J. Totten, *Naval Text-Book . . . and A Marine Dictionary* (Boston, 1841).
F&H	J. S. Farmer and W. E. Henley, *Slang and Its Analogues* (7 vols., London, 1890–1904).
JCH	John Camden Hotten, *The Slang Dictionary: A New Edition* (London, 1874).
JRB	John Russell Bartlett, *Dictionary of Americanisms* (4th ed., Boston, 1884).
JSF	J. S. Farmer, *Americanisms* (London, 1889).
JW	Joseph Wright, *The English Dialect Dictionary* (6 vols., Oxford, 1898–1905).
MS	The manuscript of *The Beach of Falesá*.
NE	*A Naval Encyclopedia* (Philadelphia, 1881).
SdV	M. Schele de Vere, *Americanisms* (New York, 1872).
WCR	W. Clark Russell, *Sailors' Language* (London, 1883).
WHS	William Henry Smyth, *The Sailor's Word-Book* (London, 1867).
W 1890	*An American Dictionary of the English Language* (Springfield, Mass., 1890). [Webster's.]

[The numbers in the following section are page and line numbers.]

115.7 *line*
The equator (WCR).

116.4 *stick*
Familiar phrase for mast (WHS).

116.4 *John Adams, obit eighteen and sixty eight*
One of Stevenson's invaluable sources for Pacific materials was Alexander Findlay's *Directory* (AF). The novelist wrote to Charles Baxter in early April 1890: "Persons with friends in the islands should purchase Findlay's *Pacific Directories*: they're the best of reading anyway, and may almost count as fiction" (DeLancey Ferguson and Marshall Waingrow, eds., *R. L. S.: Stevenson's Letters to Charles Baxter* [New Haven, Conn., 1956], p. 267). Stevenson's copy, probably purchased for him by S. S. McClure in New York City, had "Stevenson" written in ink across the top of the more than 1,250 pages. Stevenson drew on details from the Samoan section (pp. 653–69) for *Falesá*: "Between the years 1868 and 1873, and again in 1879–80, these islands were devastated by a civil war, but in 1882 the country appeared to be much more settled, under the rule of King Malietoa Laupepa.... *The Pilot* for Pago-Pago lives on the island of Anuu.... His name is John Adams, a native of the Sandwich Islands. He has been here about ten years, and speaks English sufficiently well to make himself understood (1876)."

116.9 *Pain-Killer and Kennedy's Discovery*
Pain-Killer was a nostrum made at Providence, R.I., by Perry Davis & Son; it was as popular in India, China, Japan, and Europe, as it was in the United States (JRB). "Dr. Donald Kennedy advanced a bloodhound theory of medicine. 'My Medical Discovery,' he advertised, 'seldom takes hold of two people alike! Why? Because no two people have the same weak spot. Beginning at the stomach, it goes searching through the body for any hidden humor.... Perhaps it's only a little sediment left on a nerve or in a gland; the Medical Discovery slides it right along, and you find quick happiness from the first bottle. Perhaps it's a big sediment or open sore, well settled somewhere, ready to fight. The Medical Discovery begins this fight, and you think it pretty hard; but soon you thank me for making something that has reached your weak spot.'" (James Young, *The Toadstool Millionaires* [Princeton, N.J., 1961], p. 170.) Dr. Ashbel P. Grinnell, a New York physician who made a statistical study of patent medicines, asserted that more alcohol was consumed in the United States in patent medicines than was dispensed legally by licensed liquor vendors, barring the sale of ales and beer (Samuel Hopkins Adams, "Peruna and the Bracers," reprinted from *Collier's Weekly*, October 28, 1905, in his *The Great American Fraud* [New York, 1905], p. 12).

116.20 *Black Jack*
A black-jack was a piratical-looking individual or the ensign of a pirate (NE). The term could also refer to a capacious tin can for beer (WHS).

116.20 *Whistling Jimmy*
A whistling-shop was a place where spirits were sold without a license (JCH).

116.26 *pass*
A geographical term abbreviated from passage; also, any difficult strait that commands the entrance into a country (WHS). "While the trade wind is blowing vessels may anchor off the village of *Feleasau*, in a small bay just East of the N.W. point of the island [of Manua]. . . . The landing place is a very narrow passage through the reef, only wide enough for a whale boat, and is dangerous if there is much swell on." (AF.)

116.27 *stern sheets*
The after part of an open boat (WCR), often furnished with seats to accommodate passengers (BJT).

116.31 *gallows*
An intensifier signifying very or exceedingly (JCH).

117.21 *kanaka*
Hawaiian term for man; also used pejoratively to signify a native (Lorrin Andrews, A *Dictionary of the Hawaiian Language* [Honolulu, 1865], p. 256).

117.32 *Manu'a*
Manua is the easternmost group of islands of the principal range of Samoan islands (AF).

117.32 *does*
To get on, grow, thrive, flourish (JW).

118.9 *get his shirt out*
Get angry (F&H).

118.14 *Miller a Dutchman*
Sailors often called all northern Europeans "Dutchmen" (WCR).

118.30 *a labour ship*
"The labor traffic, or blackbirding, as it was called by its apologists and its enemies respectively, rivalled the cruelties of the Middle Passage of the African slave trade. . . . The labor is recruited from the unsettled islands of the Western Pacific, from the Solomons and other groups down about New Guinea. Ships are sent recruiting, a formal contract is entered into with each man to labor for three years at a fixed rate, probably a dollar a month and his rations and clothing, payment to be made at the end of his term of service in goods and a box to put them in, the laborer to be returned to the exact place from which he was taken. Only a house with large resources and extensive need for labor can engage profitably in this traffic, therefore all the field labor, the 'black boys,' have been handled in Samoa through one house, which is under direct governmental supervision. These are the men who do the actual work, who cut the copra and dry it, who do not ask more than a dollar a month as wages for an unlimited amount of work, and who never shirk their jobs. The black boy is . . . a dogged worker and the mainspring of whatever industry there is in

Samoa." (Llewella Pierce Churchill, *Samoa 'Uma* [New York, 1902], pp. 233–34.)

119.12 *Fiddler's Green*
A sort of sensual Elysium, the place where sailors expect to go when they die (WHS). It is a place of fiddling, dancing, rum, and tobacco (JCH).

119.29 *cutty sark*
A short or scanty chemise (JCH).

120.19 *the cut of your jib*
The expression on one's face (WHS).

120.23 *to hurt*
To matter, signify (JW).

121.12 *full*
Drunk (F&H).

121.21 *old man*
The term applied to the captain by a crew (WCR).

121.25 *Dry up*
Hush; be quiet (JSF).

122.13 *old gentleman*
The devil (JCH).

123.11 *Hard-shell Baptis'*
"Originally sects of the Baptist denomination were termed *Hard-shells* and *Soft-shells*, by their unregenerate critics" (JSF). "*Hard Shell Baptists*, who call themselves *Primitive* Baptists, set their faces like flint—to use their own term—against an educated ministry, and especially against all foreign evangelical missions" (SdV).

127.9 *mortal*
An intensifier signifying extremely or great (JW).

128.5 *shipshape and Bristol fashion*
A reference to Bristol in its palmy commercial days, before it was superseded by Liverpool as the chief port on the western side of England (WHS).

128.8 *Devil a wink*
An indefinite intensifier: e.g., devil of a mess, devil of a woman, devil of a row (F&H).

129.33 *Ben*
In the spring of 1890 Stevenson left Sydney for a roundabout voyage to Samoa in "the steamship *Janet Nicoll,* an iron screw-steamer of about six hundred tons, chartered by Messrs. Henderson and Macfarlane, a well-known South Sea firm. There was a dock strike in Sydney at the time, but with a 'blackboy' crew on board, the *Janet* got away, carrying a full complement of officers and engineers, and the trio to whom *Island Nights' Entertainments* was afterwards dedicated—Mr. Henderson, one of the partners; Ben Hird, the supercargo;

and 'Jack' Buckland, the living original of Tommy Haddon in *The Wrecker*."
(Graham Balfour, *The Life of Robert Louis Stevenson* [London, 1901], II, 90.)

131.11 *fussy-ocky*
Fasioti is a verb meaning to kill someone (George Pratt, *A Grammar and Dictionary of the Samoan Language* [2d ed., ed. S. J. Whitmee, London, 1878], p. 191).

132.11 *Buncombe*
Bunkum, or talking merely for talk's sake. The original use of the word in this sense is ascribed to Felix Walker, a congressman from Buncombe County, North Carolina, who explained that he was merely talking "Buncombe" when his fellow members could not understand why he was making a speech. "That's all *buncombe*" is equivalent to "that's all nonsense, or an absurdity" (JSF).

132.14 *cure*
A contemptuous term for an odd person; abridged from "curiosity" (JCH). More generally, a humorous, comical person (B&L).

132.35 *horrors*
Delirium tremens (B&L).

133.5 *taking*
Agitation; excitement; distress of mind (W 1890). A fit of petulance or temper (JW).

133.5 *Johnny had slipped his cable*
To "slip the cable" means to let go of the inboard end and allow the entire cable to run out (NE).

133.12 *slanging*
Abusing in foul language (JCH).

133.16 *goods*
"Among the Molly Maguires . . . the signs and pass-words constituted the *goods* of the society. The same usage applies in the case of other secret organizations." (JSF.)

134.21 *buck*
A term often vulgarly applied to a Negro man (JRB).

134.31 *struck all of a heap*
Suddenly astonished (JCH).

137.4 *sawder*
"Soft sawder" is obvious flattery (JSF).

137.14 *to come any of their native ideas over me*
"To come over" or "come it over one" is a vulgar expression for getting the advantage of someone (JRB).

137.25 *put my monkey up*
Rouse one's passion or ill temper (JCH).

138.23 *down*
Suspicion; alarm (F&H).

139.28 *bacon*
Body (JCH).

141.19 *mummy apple*
"The Mammee Apple, which grows well in Hawaii, is a native of the West Indies, and is a fruit much esteemed in tropical countries. . . . The fruit may be eaten raw, and is very delicious when preserved." (Gerrit P. Wilder, *Fruits of the Hawaiian Islands* [Honolulu, 1911], p. 60.)

143.27 *Beach de Mar*
The jargon or "pidgin" of the Western Pacific. According to William Churchill, the term "Beach-la-mar" derived from a common sailor mispronunciation of *bêche-de-mer*, a name given to the edible trepang, or sea cucumber (*Beach-la-Mar: The Jargon or Trade Speech of the Western Pacific* [Washington, D.C., 1911], p. 4).

144.2 *meat and drink*
Strong drink; also liquor thickened with egg yolks (F&H).

144.5 *beachcomber*
A long wave rolling in from the ocean (W 1890). Also, a contemptuous term for someone who hangs about the shore on the lookout for jobs; chiefly applied to runaway seamen and deserters from whalers who lived along the beaches in South America and in the South Sea islands (WCR).

144.9 *Apia and Papeete*
"The other port centres of the Pacific Islands exerted a similar [demoralizing] influence. The beachcombers of Tahiti concentrated in Papeete. It became one of the favourite provisioning centres for whalers. Of course when rowdy ships came in, it was difficult to preserve order. The place got, however, a worse name than it ever deserved. Apia in Samoa was known as the Hell of the Pacific until the 1870's." (Aarne A. Koskinen, *Missionary Influence as a Political Factor in the Pacific Islands* [Helsinki, 1953], p. 130.)

144.9 *flash*
Low and vulgar (W 1890); pertaining to thieves and criminals (F&H).

144.10 *Fale-alii*
"At 8 miles beyond Safatu is *Falealili Harbour*, very small, and obstructed by outlying reefs; there is a large native town here" (AF).

144.24 *Ioe*
"Yes" (MS).

145.17 *cut up downright rough*
Become obstreperous and dangerous (JCH).

145.31 *sweep*
A contemptuous term for a low or shabby man (JCH).

148.31 *bunged*
Threw with force (JW).

150.32 *Aué*
"Alas!" (MS).

153.18 *flying*
Circulating as a tale or rumor, without definite authority (NED).

158.6 *buffer*
A term for a good-humored or liberal old man (JCH).

158.22 *big don and the funny dog*
" 'Don' ... An adept; a swell. 'Dog' ... A man; sometimes used contemptuously." (F&H.)

159.12 *Obstropulous*
A New England corruption of "obstreperous" (JRB).

159.18 *pot-hunting*
"Pot-hunter, a sportsman who shoots anything he comes across, having more regard to filling his bag than to the rules which regulate the sport" (JCH).

163.36 *skylarked*
Originally, to mount the mast and slide down the stays for amusement (WHS); to engage in horseplay or act the fool (WCR).

164.4 *cracked on*
Added sail in a strong wind (WCR).

165.23 *lots of sensitive*
"Right in the wild lime hedge which cuts athwart us just homeward of the garden, I found a great bed of kuikui—sensitive plant—our deadliest enemy. A fool brought it to this island in a pot, and used to lecture and sentimentalise over the tender thing. The tender thing has now taken charge of this island, and men fight it, with torn hands, for bread and life. A singular, insidious thing, shrinking and biting like a weasel; clutching by its roots as a limpet clutches to a rock." (Robert Louis Stevenson, *Vailima Letters* [London, 1895], pp. 13–14.)

167.15 *gone up*
Gone to heaven (SdV); dead (JSF).

167.27 *woundy*
An intensifier signifying "extremely" or "excessively," this word never appeared in any edition of *Falesá*. Branded "a low bad word" by Johnson, and clearly a term that had no common usage in Stevenson's day, it still appeared in Webster's as late as 1890. N. E. Osselton states that "woundy" derives "from the expletive (*Christ's*) *Wounds* ... [and belongs] to the slangy colloquialism of the post-Restoration writers" (*Branded Words in English Dictionaries before Johnson* [Groningen, 1958], p. 88).

167.31 *Tyrolean*
"Query: Aeolian?" (MS).

169.35 *bum*
Cry; have a habit of weeping (JW).

173.24 *header*
"A plunge head foremost into water ... a theatrical expression for any supposedly daring jump of hero or heroine in sensational dramas" (JCH).

176.19 *plant*
  A hidden store of money or valuables (JCH).

182.6 *clapped down*
  Sat down suddenly; crouched; squatted as a hare (JW).

185.1 *sick*
  A vulgar expression meaning very indifferent, contemptible (JRB).

186.20 *trick*
  Intercourse, dealings; trade, business, traffic (JW).

INDEX